Calvin Miller
The Unchained Soul

CALVIN MILLER is a poet, a pastor, a theologian, a painter, and one of Christianity's best loved writers with over thirty published books. His writing spans a wide spectrum of genres, from the best-selling SINGER TRILOGY to *The Book of Jesus* to *When the Aardvark Parked the Ark*.

Miller presently serves as professor of communication and ministry studies and as writer-in-residence at the Southwestern Baptist Theological Seminary. He and his wife, Barbara, make their home in Texas.

Calvin Miller
The Unchained Soul

BETHANY HOUSE PUBLISHERS
MINNEAPOLIS, MINNESOTA 55438

Published by Bethany House Publishers
A Ministry of Bethany Fellowship International
11400 Hampshire Avenue South
Minneapolis, Minnesota 55438
www.bethanyhouse.com

Printed in the United States of America by
Bethany Press International, Minneapolis, Minnesota 55438

ISBN 0-7642-2169-8

*My unending
gratitude as
always
belongs to Barbara,
my friend, my love,
my partner,
and my inspiration in
every venture of
consequence.
My thanks also to the fine
men of my prayer
group:
Chad Harris, David Richardson,
James Shiroma, Deron Spoo,
and Charles Whitmire,
who walked with me through
the writing of this book.*

CONTENTS

FOREWORD

THIS BOOK IS an appeal to all Christians to get God involved in their attempt to swim the river of life. That river rises from the wellsprings of ten thousand experiences that form our lives. The current of that river is demanding, and swimming it requires all the strength we have.

We have been made by God and he longs to see us fashioned in the likeness of his Son. Jesus, the incarnate God, locked himself in flesh with us for thirty-three years. He came to assure us that God was not some Grand Observer living comfortably above that arena where we must meet the gladiators of despair. God came in Christ to live among us, struggling with us through our struggles. To all who have received him, Christ is born in us to be the *Overcomer.* Through the new birth, he indwells us to teach us the overcoming life. For us, becoming more Christlike is the demanding work of reaching upward for his identity and for meaning. But for God, the painful work was reaching downward in Incarnation. Jesus said that to accomplish the work of becoming like him, we need to take up our cross (Luke 9:23), and cross-bearing makes the hellish, driven ascent of Good Friday the time clock of every day's communion. Paul said that becoming man required Christ to pour himself out (Phil. 2:6–7).

The first step of our becoming like him lies in our being born. Out of the womb and into the world; that's how life happens. Physically Jesus, like ourselves, knew first the pain of being born and later dying.

Walter Wangerin describes the birth of his own son in these words:

"The baby," I say, "with a shock is born. . . . My son flew out of his mother." . . .

"Here it comes!" . . .

"A boy!" . . .

All at once his body is assaulted. He discovers his nostrils by the jabbing in them. He feels chill wind on his skin. The light crashes his eyes. The sounds are hard and foreign—and *he's falling!* . . .

Some deep part of the infant begins dimly to know that he is here, he is a discrete being, he is alive, he *is*.

Oh, but this becoming is such hard work.[1]

Birth is of the instant, but becoming Christlike demands years. It requires all the strength we have. Where are we to get this strength?

Our strength should come from God. "I will lift up mine eyes to the hills / from whence comes my help," said David in Psalm 121:1. He further counsels, "God is our refuge and strength, / a very present help in trouble" (46:1). Life in Christ is not one which shields us from trouble. It is one in which Christ is present in our troubles. None of our hard times are pointless. God allows us our struggles to conform us to the image of Christ. The old spiritual has it right: "Nobody knows the trouble I've seen; Nobody knows but Jesus." All of us carry life's lessons imbedded deeply within our hearts. We talk about them, praise them, maybe even deny them. Their pain, however, conforms us to the image of Christ. It deepens our lives from shallow surface vessels to roomy reservoirs of godly wisdom and joy.

The sources of this strength are easily identified: the indwelling Christ, the Bible, counselors, friends, and the voices of those devoted Christians who, across the ages, have fought battles similar to our own. Their voices come to us in the great classics of Christian devotion. It will be the aim of this book to show you how these specific friends of the faith, whom we shall not meet until eternity, have given us bread for the journey. Their counsel, coupled with that of the Bible, can make us strong. With their wisdom we will be set, not just to survive life, but to feel the triumph over life which God meant for us to enjoy. There are many of these friends of the faith, but my focus shall fall on ten. This book, I hope, will be a counselor to you on your journey into Christlikeness. I pray that these ten friends who have so helped me will strengthen you as well.

Calvin Miller
Ft. Worth, Texas

THE
CONFESSIONAL
WALK
OF FAITH

I N THE NEVER-ENDING interchanges that compose our lives we are constantly being asked for our names and two or three pieces of identification. "Are you who you say you are?" is the underlying question behind these probings. But there are lots of other questions that accompany these probes. "Is your check good?" "Can you be trusted?" In the process of becoming accountable we are always being asked to affirm both our identity and our integrity.

Nothing is so glorious as the reception of Christ into our lives. There, deep in the center of our true identity, he is Lord. We bow to him, leaving self and self-interest behind us. At that moment, it is no longer enough to explain ourselves by owning up to our own names. We must own up to his. We must confess him before others (Matt. 10:32–33) and unashamedly say that our own identity is of such small importance we have replaced it with his. When the Jewish leaders come to ask John the Baptist who he is, he refuses to give them his name. He replies simply, "I am the voice" (John 1:23). He is not refusing to confess his identity. He is saying,

"Once you really know Jesus, the importance of your own identity will lose its stranglehold on your soul."

The excellence of his lordship is often learned when we are locked in the jaws of need and failure. As long as we are winning in life, we bask in a glory that celebrates only ourselves. But when we begin to fail, our celebration of ourselves will not sustain us. Then we call out to Christ, confessing his name. How true are the words of David: "The LORD is near to those who have a broken heart" (Ps. 34:18).

At these moments of utter brokenness, our strength comes not in the cry of our own weak name—the poor identity of our own shabby arrogance. When our souls are *in extremis,* we breathe the name of Jesus. We sigh like Bartimaeus groping in his blindness, "Jesus, Son of David, have mercy on me!" (Luke 18:38). But he summons us to bless the dark times of our lives. It is these which summon the light.

Those trials which do not break us make us stronger. Scottish patriarchs, looking for walking sticks, always passed over the untried wood of the lower slopes. They climbed to the wuthered heights to search for rods made strong by storm and wind. These iron-strong canes were once young trees that fought the icy Northers. With each storm they bent and twisted and broke a bit inside. But gradually each inner scar became the steely fiber they bought with every storm that they endured. Only such woody steel will serve as the rod of God. Ask Moses! Such rods can speak to threaten Pharaoh or order Suez into water-walls that let God's children pass. Such rods make cobras and skatter frightened kings. Such rods spit lightning from their knobby heads, ordering angels to attention.

But do not let their majesty delude you. These mighty rods were once just spindling trees. Therefore, never bless the rods; rather, bless the gales that broke their sinews, lacing them with stone, until the storms they so despised had changed them into scepters. Such storms change Midianites and shepherds into kings.

So all real saints are fashioned in the crucible of God. To be all they became, they were broken, crushed between mortar and pestle. Gradually their soft nothingness was changed to that granite from which God fashions monuments to his own glory. Thus, a Jew of Tarsus—beaten, stoned, shipwrecked, imprisoned (2 Cor. 11:23ff.)—speaks to praise the brokenness that forged him. Paul does not brag of being strong. He boasts only of his weakness and praises the storms (2 Cor. 12:10), for in his heart he knows that human ego finds little volume in its own soft authority. But when such spindling egos are battered by the storms, the gales do their transforming work. Thus, grace and brokenness together can take a frightened Asian Jew and rename him as Jehovah's thunder.

As a watercolorist, I understand the principle of contrast in art. Setting dark objects against light backgrounds makes art possible. This simple technique creates form as it moves objects around in the painting. As images blend in color, they retreat to the rear of a canvas. As they contrast in color, they move forward in the painting. During one of those nameless, small crises out of which my life—and every life—is shaped, God reminded me of his own artistry in my life. He has long been at work to produce art from the mucky palette of my discipleship. But on this one occasion, my usually talkative spirituality sat in silence before him. I listened to his accounting of the greatest moments of my life. There were not many that came quickly to my mind. Still, they stood like monuments of joy in the level and uninteresting deserts of my journey.

Next, he played across the cinema of my mind the darker events of pain and disappointment I have known. As I examined these two very different lists of joy and pain, I was surprised to find both lists identical. God is a wonderful artist whose contrast of bright joy and dark needs creates life. These contrasts remain in full view from year to year as reminders that joy and pain are but opposite ends of the same great lessons of God.

These lessons are never hard to identify. Like oysters, we believers all react the same way when a hunk of sharp silica enters our shells. We cry and complain; we even rail against God. But the pearl is born in the pain, built by coating our adversity with maturity. As each lesson of life passes, we move on to others. We glory in knowing that at the core of our best pearls there exists a ragged hurt that once stabbed us with ripping pain. Then God came. His grace pearlized our pain with dependency. Our deep moans gave way to glad Hosannas! He transformed our hurt into a beautiful, usable ministry.

"I will turn their mourning to joy" (Jer. 31:13), says the Lord at these times of great loss. Then such times become for us occasions of great gain. No wonder our finest picture of heaven has to do with God establishing his eternal adequacy over our broken circumstances: God shall indeed wipe away all tears from our lives (Rev. 21:4). Joy will inhabit heaven because, in that great land, the confessing church will have lost all interest in confessing its own identity. Then, having escaped old self-concern, we will join in the grand anthem, "Worthy is the Lamb" (5:12). How grand will this singing be? It will be made grand by all those who have "come out of the great tribulation" (7:14), those whose martyred lives taught them that there was no other worthy name to be confessed but that of Jesus.

In that once-needy time, while I quietly waited for God's accounting, I asked one other question about these joy-pain events. How did my heavenly Father want me to react to them? They all evoke a single response: confession. Examining every pearl made from the pain of life, I found the martyr's truth. When my pain was covered up in joy I spoke his name. I confessed. Confession was his gift to me by which I remained in touch with him. His name alone destroyed all my self-absorption. At times, it unlocked my silent anger toward him. At other times it broke apart the thin shell of my callous ingratitude. Always it started me talking to God. I came to realize that confession is the way we say, "I'm saved, I'm healed, I'm well, I'm forgiven, I surrender." So the pattern of my journey is the Grand Cycle of Relationship: I hurt, I rejoice, I confess. In this joyous, ever-circling pattern, I ever so slowly become more like the Master.

Is this joy-pain continuum tedious? Hardly. It is our inescapable autobiography written in our confessions, and our confessions can never be tedious, at least to us. In our most glorious needs we exalt the name. But what follows his name when we confess? We always say the same thing: "Lord, I believe; help my unbelief!" (Mark 9:24). Even so, staying alive, really alive, in Christ is hard work. Sometimes faith is hazardous work. In transforming our heartaches to joy, we face doubts that nudge us uncomfortably close to unbelief. In the painful act of pearl-making, we are often prone to rail at God and point out as Martha did at the tomb of Lazarus, "Lord, if you had been here, this never would have happened" (John 11:21, author's paraphrase). Are our accusations of God wasted? Never! Are they not foolish and immature? Of course they are, but in most every life there are temper tantrums. Like precocious children we even say, "Father, I'll never speak to you again!" Then our hostility subsides. God comes and the pearl begins to grow smooth within our injured systems. When enough time has passed, we can see that this is no ordinary pearl with which we purchase joy. It is a pearl of great price. Its beauty lies in the all-sufficiency of Christ. We cry out our confession and honor his name. We fall down before our Father crying, "The pain is too desperate and I am too weak for irrelevant issues. Jesus is Lord! I believe." The name suffices. The Christ of Galilee rebukes the storms of our denial. The thunder sheepishly apologizes and slinks away. The gales are ashamed. All is peace.

But the dogs of doubt never sleep long. Our peace is forever stalked by two predators. The first is our culture of convenience. We are the well-fed, the secure. We are lovers of the large plate and the broad sofa. Material abundance keeps us from seeking any other kind. But could it be that our wonderful, abundant culture is really the jackal that preys on our peace? Yes, because our love of convenience trains us to believe that we can have as much as we want, of whatever we want, whenever we want it. We are deceived into believing that material abundance grants us peace, not that it steals it. But steal it does. For no matter what life gives us, we always want more. Our craving for things never sleeps long enough to allow us peace. We are the walking wanton.

The second predator that stalks our peace is narcissism. Narcissists worship themselves. This self-love produces only those inner values that we ourselves can create. In the Andrew Lloyd Webber musical *Starlight Express,* one of the characters sings what was meant to be inspirational, "Only You Have the Power Within You." Alas, this is not the hymn of the settled soul. We do not have such power within us. When our self-contrived image begins to crumble, we always crave a more solid foundation; for "the solid foundation of God stands, having this seal: 'The Lord knows those who are His'" (2 Tim. 2:19). Our peace is born in God's knowledge of us—who we are and where we are going.

Oh, but we *are* fickle.

From the sweetness of each *yes-Lord-I-believe* we draw back again from his adequacy to our foolish self-sufficiency. His blessings themselves spoil us. He forever wakes us on some glorious Sinai morning to gather manna and bless his loving providence. But when we have eaten of his blessings and are full, we wander off in barren complaints, longing for the onions of Egypt (Num. 11:5). Soon we are completely out of touch with God. Once again comes arid living. We seldom see that it is our wandering, not his faithlessness, which is at fault. And so again the pain comes. The rituals of doubt and trust begin anew.

Are we doomed to this endless, cyclical marathon? I think not. The escape from this "no-exit" cycle is to see confession not as a step in our pain-joy cycle but as a substitute for it. Is there a way out of the cycle? To be sure! The key to freedom is confessional living. It is learning to say, "Lord, I believe" as a continuing focus of life and not just as an intermittent end to our cyclical desperation.

Paul pays the greatest tribute to confessional living when he cries, "I have learned to be content whatever the circumstances. I know what it is to be in need, and I know what it is to have plenty. I have learned the secret of being content in any and every situation, whether well fed or hungry, whether living in plenty or in want. I can do everything through him who gives me strength" (Phil. 4:11–13 NIV). This contentment came because Paul held no confidence in his own ability to find power over his circumstances. Circumstances are as fickle as the wind. When they change we feel the pain of abandonment. Do we not suspect, deep down, that when we say, "Lord, I believe," that those three short words are but the preface to "Let the good times roll!"? Paul obviously found confession not as a part of some despairing cycle, but a displacement of that ugly routine. Is there a steady confessional life that eliminates those spiritual "upsies and downsies"?

"I can do everything through Christ." Did Paul mean it? Could he really do it? In the book of Acts (16:22ff.), with his back cut to pieces, he sang hymns at midnight from a Philippian jail. God's timpani kept seismic time with his singing. God answered Paul's music with a seven-point Richter reply, and an earthquake opened the steel door. Once outside the cell Paul heard the Philippian jailer cry, "What must I do to be saved?" Paul answered, in loose translation, "Pretty much what you will have to do after you're saved, confess Christ."

Instead of confessing Christ only when we experience pain, we should learn to confess Christ even before the pain arrives. When attacked, stripped, and left naked, St. Francis of Assisi was found singing (not crying) in the snow. Confessing Christ while you're being robbed and beaten guarantees that you will be able to confess Christ after the trial is over. Paul also counsels us: "In everything give thanks; for this is the will of God in Christ Jesus for you" (1 Thess. 5:18). Continual communion results in meaningful living. If we can bless our pain in never-ceasing confession, then we will "rejoice always" (v. 16).

What then of life's pearl-making? Does confession destroy the possibilities of that deep understanding that can only be learned by hurt? Is the art lost? If our confession allows us to bypass the pain of those sharp, injuring circumstances, can we ever make pearls again? Can our confession become so all-encompassing that we forbid suffering and thus have *no pain, no gain?* Judging from the writings of the saints, I think Paul makes it clear in 2 Timothy, the last book he ever wrote, that even in his final moments, pain still dogged his life. Jesus, utterly holy and completely God, was still the Man of Sorrows. There were still riddles to be confronted. Still, grace can make even the lesser lessons of our lives a single offering of wealth—a sacrifice for our Father in heaven. Our trivial complaints are usable to God and our great hurts are the sources of great joy. We become a living sacrifice of praise (Gal. 2:20). Our continual confession can circumvent some of the "ups and downs" of life, but remember, Paul told the Philippians his whole life was in the process of being poured out as a sacrifice (Phil. 2:17).

It is in this pouring out that we learn the hard work of becoming like Christ. How hard is that task? Well, Jesus himself was not exempt from pain. "He poured out His soul unto death" (Isa. 53:12). No, not even our Lord could escape the nasty business of pearl-making, for "though He was a Son, yet He learned obedience by the things which He suffered" (Heb. 5:8).

This "pouring out" is always the work of pain. Remember Walt Wangerin's conclusion of the matter, cited in the preface,

> Oh, but this becoming is such hard work.[1]

Becoming is indeed hard work—it is the work of being poured out.

Julian of Norwich cried in the ardor of all that is required of us:

> During our lifetime here we have in us a marvelous mixture of both well-being and woe. We have in us our risen Lord Jesus Christ, and we have in us the wretchedness and the harm of Adam's falling. Dying, we are constantly protected by Christ, and by the touching of his grace we are raised to true trust in salvation. And we are so afflicted in our feelings by Adam's falling in various ways, by sin and by different pains, and in this we are made dark and so blind that we can scarcely accept any comfort. But in our intention we wait for God, and trust faithfully to have mercy and grace; and this is his own working in us, and in his goodness he opens the eye of our understanding, by which we have sight, sometimes more and sometimes less, according to the ability God gives us to receive.[2]

This pain is the pouring out of self. Once empty we are then ready to be filled with something more than ourselves. But the emptying is continual. As the emptying is unending, so our confession is continual. When the mind of Christ (1 Cor. 2:16) fills our own mind, our tongues can't help but invoke a never-ending litany to his lordship. No wonder the author of *The Cloud of Unknowing* wrote, "Be on your guard lest you think of anything but God, Himself."[3] "If he is in your heart he will be in your gestures, in your eyes, in your mouth . . . so that you may say with St. Paul, 'It is no longer I who live, but Christ lives in me' " (Gal. 2:20), said Francis de Sales.[4]

But such conformity to Christ eludes most of us. How close do we actually come to this step of total identity? How much do we remain captive to this present world? Our busy lives are always there to ensnare us in trivia. "The world is too much with us!" exclaimed Wordsworth on Westminster Bridge. The ultimate step of total Christ identity is somewhere further along on our pilgrimage. Our Christ confession must serve until our Christ-conformity is in place.

The Sufficiency of Christ

This book is intended to be a walk with saints of old through our contemporary lives. But who are the saints? Where did they come from? Of this we may be sure: Saints do not spring holy or whole from the forehead of God. They are made, crisis by crisis, need by need. Those who wish to be conformed to his image only make real progress after they discover their own insufficiency. We are converted the very moment we admit that our own management of life is inadequate. We need to be forgiven and filled with Christ. Does not our greatest need teach us we are altogether incapable?

But to gain the great supply of God in any area, we must first face our poverty. In our sin we are indeed poor, yet Christ said, "Blessed are the poor in spirit" (Matt. 5:3). For it is the poor who most hunger after riches. I have often seen very poor people buying lottery tickets with the fragile earnings of their souls. Why do they throw their living away? Because they think this sacrifice, which they can ill afford, may shortly make them rich.

In facing our poverty of spirit, we turn to him who is able to make us rich in all good things: in hope, in confidence, in the management of life. We are not only poor, we are fragile. How wisely Isaac of Syria counsels us, "Blessed is the man who knows his weakness, because awareness of this becomes for him the foundation and beginning of all that is good and beautiful. For whenever someone realizes and perceives that he is truly and indeed weak . . . will he realize how great is the assistance which comes from God."[5]

Isn't it negative to dwell on our poverty? Why should we rehearse our constant need? Because the admission of our poor fragility rolls out the carpet for his glorious strength. Our insufficiency is the soil of his all-sufficiency. Paul gained power from his struggle with that debilitating weakness he saw as a terrible thorn in the flesh. He confessed his need openly and his confession supplied the power.

> To keep me from becoming conceited because of these surpassingly great revelations, there was given me a thorn in my flesh, a messenger of Satan, to torment me. Three times I pleaded with the Lord to take it away from me. But he said to me, "My grace is sufficient for you, for my power is made perfect in weakness." Therefore I will boast all the more gladly about my weaknesses, so that Christ's power may rest on me. That is why, for Christ's sake, I delight in weaknesses, in insults, in hardships, in persecutions, in difficulties. For when I am weak, then I am strong.
>
> (2 Cor. 12:7–10 NIV)

Fragile trust is stronger than swaggering self-reliance. I have a friend, a beautiful woman, whose childhood bout with polio left her terribly crippled. As a child, before the polio came, she was quite good at playing the piano. As the disease ravaged her body, she promised God that if she escaped the disease with one good foot (to work the pedal) and two good hands (for the key-board), she would never cease to praise him with the best music she could offer. When her struggle was over, she did indeed have one leg that was free of the heavy, steel brace which the other required. And her hands seemed as strong as those of the carpenter Christ when he swung the mallet and wielded the saw. Thus she played. She is but another whose slight and fragile soul met the all-sufficiency of Christ.

Her life, like every great life, is one that confesses Christ continually. Her talent and music rise from the glory of her confession. But Jesus warned us of the long stretch between our confession and our deeds. "Why do you call Me 'Lord, Lord,' and not do the things which I say?" (Luke 6:46). What is the error that causes us to confess without surrendering to him? It has to do totally with our view of his sufficiency. If we say his name with no sense of need, our confession is meaningless.

The victorious believer has but one confession: Jesus Christ, Son of God, Savior. The Greek acronym that begins each of these words forms a creed—*ichthus,* fish—the simplest drawing of this suggesting the church's earliest confession. Jesus gloried in his oneness with his Father. "No one," he said, "knows the Father except the Son, and those to whom the Son chooses to reveal Him" (Matt. 11:27). Jesus everywhere spoke of his intimate relationship with his Father (John 5:20). He even said that he was so close to his Father that to see him was to see God (John 14:9) and to hear him was to hear the Father. Jesus even said that to become one with him was to be one with the Father and to be united with all who confessed him and the Father (John 17:21). All of these great promises suggest that to confess the name of Jesus is to ready the soul for oneness with God. Confessing is the exercise that creates and sustains the kingdom of God (Matt. 10:32–33).

The confessing life must say the word *Lord* as a strong word to be laid alongside our needy lives. I remember Alice, a poor dying woman in our congregation. She begged God daily to save her from the cancer that was destroying her. Even as she prayed for strength, her fragile body weakened; it did not grow stronger.

Was her confession powerless? No! In her weakness she became the lesson that life is a war not always physically winnable. She continued to call Christ Lord until at last she entered into his presence. Then alone was her weak confession housed in God's unbreakable strength.

Is weakness the best place to search out the power of confession? Are not our justifications of unanswered prayers just a saccharine way of sugar-coating our questions about God? Who has not known a strong contempt for what appears to be God's weakness? Are we not ashamed to confess, "I prayed but my need went unmet"? Still, in comforting the dying woman, I brought her only my confession of Christ as Lord. She brought me only her confession of Christ. She confessed and died and I confessed and lived, but I knew in my heart that her trip to the bosom of the Father would in time be my own journey. Someday I might pray to live, confess God's adequacy, and die also. Yet the glory of either of us entering into his presence is in the undying sufficiency of the word *Lord*. Confessing Christ is the antidote both to our living weaknesses and our dying weaknesses. We so often cry, "Christ, please come, my life is on the ropes again." Come he does, striding through the iron gates of our locked lives, opened only by our confession of his name.

But does God ever answer the plea for extending our earthly lives by giving us death? No, if we beg to live and he calls us home to heaven, it is life. If we beg to live and do so, it is also life. Alice does not get death as she begs for life. She gets life with a better definition. It only appears to be death to earth's smaller way of defining life. So life of every kind is always the companion of confession.

Two sentences must remain forever linked: *God, I am not able;* and *Christ is Lord.* How often I have seen these sentences of our insufficiency and his all-sufficiency follow hard upon the other. Not long before I left the pastorate, I led an older couple to confess Christ for the first time and be converted. Their new life in Christ was wondrously alive with light. She was to go into the hospital for routine bypass surgery. For some reason that baffled the doctors, she died suddenly on the operating table. Her husband was crushed. Still, Christ remained his joyous, new confession. Yet his life seemed stripped of hope. His wife of thirty-five years was gone. In his prayers I could hear him struggling to form the word *Lord*. But it came slowly. His own grief was so overwhelming that it became a barrier to the coming of Christ to meet his needs. In his utter need, only his confession could free him to live again.

Confessing Christians are armed with the only power that can successfully counter the circumstances of their needy world. The world is a poor place, filled with poor people. Carl Sandburg wrote of the true picture of humanity:

> One day I got a true look at the Poor,
> millions of the poor, patient and toiling;
> more patient than crags, tides, and stars;
> innumerable, patient as the darkness of night—
> and all broken, humble ruins of nations.[6]

Sandburg saw the poor as the broken ruins of nations, but Jesus said, "Blessed are the poor in spirit" (Matt. 5:3).

Why would Jesus bless the poor? Because the poor turn from their own pitiful inadequate understanding to embrace that true wealth which lies beyond themselves. The poor quickly learn that to confess their own name in their own strength is but a confession of weakness. But to confess his name gives them a sudden and marvelous significance. Sandburg saw people as the ruins of nations, but Jesus sees them as confessing citizens of the kingdom of God. Sandburg, like we often do, saw the poor as ruined, but Jesus sees all people only as potential kings and queens, guardians of a liberating, saving name.

Throughout my thirty-five years of ministry, God has repeatedly taught me that the confessing life can only issue from the resigned life. Resignation to Christ is all that can set the word *Lord* singing in our lives. John Wesley wrote of it this way:

We ought to suffer whatever befalls us, to bear the defects of others and our own, to confess them to God in secret prayer, or with groans which cannot be uttered. . . . We ought to bear with those we cannot amend and to be content with offering them to God. This is true resignation. To abandon all, to strip oneself of all, in order to seek and follow Jesus Christ naked to Bethlehem, where he was born: naked to the hall where he was scourged: and naked to Calvary where he died on the cross, is so great a mercy that neither the thing nor the knowledge of it is given to any but through faith in the Son of God.[7]

It is in the pain that resignation comes hardest. Pain brings all the tough questions about the goodness of God. We cannot help but ask: "Why should I resign myself to this pain when it tears my body and screaming nervous system to shreds?" Because while we fight against our circumstances we often fight against God. We cannot fight and confess his Lordship at the same time. When we do not confess his Lordship we do not appropriate his sufficiency. I always admire the sweetness that sits quietly with me when I at last abandon my hostility with God, but it is a hard-fought peace. C. S. Lewis said in *God in the Dock* that sometimes God has to say, speaking to our hostility, "If you'll put down your guns we'll talk." How true! But more important than talking with God is our confession, for it is confession that begins the talk. Only when we have quit gunning for God can we take up the confessing life.

His Sovereignty
But what is prior in our walk of faith?

Is the main goal of our discipleship his sufficiency or his sovereignty? Should we love him just because he provides things or because he rules over our lives? To crave his sovereignty is to understand his kingdom. Kings may or may not provide for their subjects; but to be kings, they must rule. And is not their rule, good or bad, the end of chaos? Our current lives are often disordered. Just as God once spoke over chaos, we have but to speak his name once again and our own private chaos will subside. Thus in his strong name we confess a word that organizes and simplifies. In short, it brings order to our private world.

It is probably for this reason that Augustine wrote, "We must flee to God in our many tribulations whatever they may be—domestic worries, ill health, danger to those dear to us. The Christian can have no other refuge but his Saviour, his God. He will have no strength in himself, but in Him in whom he has taken refuge."[8] Do we not seek our refuge in him because he alone can manage our uncontrollable lives? Is not our hunger for refuge a heart cry for his sovereignty?

Lord is the one-word definition of his sovereignty. The "saints" whose lives will bear us audience in the ensuing pages will teach us this: To invoke his stable presidency over our spastic chaos is a saving act. This book will see "saving" in a new way. Saved is a state (Eph. 2:8) but saved is also a process (1 Cor. 2:1ff.). Our initial confession of Christ saves us once for all time. But this initial confession is but the start of the process by which his glorious work of saving us goes on. We err in the matter when we see confession as that single event which only begins the Christ life. Confession is the daily ordering of chaos from our lives by calling out his name over every tempest. Then daily we will marvel at how even the winds and waves of our stormy lives continue to obey him (Matt. 8:27).

Dame Julian knew well the power of the name to call the storms of life to peace. She exalted Christ in her confession: "So I saw that God is our true peace. He watches over us when we can find no rest and he works continually to bring us to peace that shall never end. . . . And our Lord takes our strivings and sends them up to Heaven where they are made more sweet and delectable than the heart can think, or tongue can tell."[9] His peace always issues from our confession of Christ and his sovereignty over any issue of our lives.

Recently a man who was diagnosed with malignant melanoma called me and said, "Pastor, do you do laying on of hands?"

"If you mean in the cable-television sense of the word, no! But if you mean 'will I touch you in prayer and the name of Christ,' of course, I will. Better yet," I said, "bring a group of your other friends in Christ and we will all lay hands on you and pray. Christ in his mercy will have to heal you if healing is to be yours; but if our hands may serve as symbols of his hands, then we will gladly touch you and pray."

He came to us. We touched him and confessed the name. He left our circle of faith and went off to the finest cancer clinic in America. Doctors and technologists join their science to our faith even as I write. Will this man be healed? Who can say except our heavenly Father who keeps both faith and science in his own hands.

The point remains fixed. Have we any other name to confess? Have we any other sovereignty to honor? His sovereignty over all our cares is fixed in our submission. He who is sovereign cannot mend our broken affairs while we are too much in his way. We are like a child who goes to his father with a broken toy. He wants the toy mended but he also wants to help his father. As long as the child's hands are in the way, his father's work is hampered. Are we not like this overeager child? Doesn't our need to help God mean that we don't quite trust the Father to do it well? Have we really gotten over the notion that our own effort is necessary to the quickening work of God?

His adequacy works best without our interference. His name alone is completely capable. We are best his children when we best submit to him. We watch him quickly solve our worst predicaments when we utterly surrender to his will. This surrender is not an exercise; it is a release. It is a voluntary leaning backward into the armchair of the third and fourth chapters of the book of Hebrews. It is a trusting, a resting. It is submission to a single viewpoint of life. Saint John of the Cross said that the total management of Christ was possible when we learn that Christians are helped by one thing: loving God!

"My soul is occupied" he said,
"And all my substance in his service.

Now I guard no flock,
Nor have I other employment,
My sole occupation is love.

Before the soul succeeded in effecting
This gift and surrender of itself to the beloved,
It was entangled in many useless occupations
    by which it
Sought to please itself and others.

All this is over now—
For all its thoughts, words and actions
Are directed to God.

All my occupation now is the practice
Of the love of God. All I do
Is Done in Love."[10]

And yet the lessons of love and sovereignty come slowly. We
once owned a dog which we were trying to train to jump through
a hoop. We coupled treats—bits of jerky, pieces of biscuit—with
our every command during this time of training. The dog was
quite welcome to the treats we offered, but only if he jumped
through the hoop to get them. A thousand times we held the
goody in one hand and the hoop in the other and called, "Jump!"
He didn't jump. He merely walked around our hoop disobeying
our command. So we laid the goody on a shelf as he watched
disappointedly.

I tried to reason what he must be thinking: *How cruel my master
is. He could do something about my disappointment but he doesn't. I don't
believe in my master anymore. I think I'll just give up on him and try some
less-requiring philosophy.* We played this fruitless game for a long
time, then suddenly he seemed to catch the connection between
my command, the hoop, and the goody. He leapt to our excited
applause, sailing through the hoop, and we—true to our bargain—
gave him the treat. The cruel hoop was now redefined, and beyond
his newfound obedience was a pleasant way of life in which his

obedience supplied him all the good things. It is indeed God's sovereignty that makes life settled and abundant.

His Presence

The best gift of the confessional life is his presence. It is a constant presence (Heb. 13:5). It is a Quaker presence that sits with us without talking. "Christ in you, the hope of glory," said Paul (Col. 1:27). This doctrine is held in place for me by two songs. In our little Baptist church we used to sing "No, Never Alone." The words went:

> I've seen the lightning flashing and heard the thunder roll,
> I've felt sin's breakers dashing, trying to conquer my soul,
> I've heard the voice of Jesus telling me still to fight on,
> He promised never to leave me, Never to leave me alone.

From my earliest days I have treasured his unforsaking presence. It conquers the storms of my life. Like those apostles, I have wakened my Lord with my anxieties and cried, "Lord, save [me]! [I am] perishing!" (Matt. 8:25). Then he stands and rebukes the storms. The metaphor comforts me, for I know that whatever sea I sail, he is on board. His unforsaking presence leaves me unafraid.

It is a rich psalmist-shepherd who said, "Yea, though I walk through the valley of the shadow of death, I will fear no evil; for You are with me; Your rod and Your staff, they comfort me" (Ps. 23:4). He is there in perilous days to walk with me. We even share a meal surrounded by our enemies (v. 5). Isn't eating with our Lord always an occasion of joy? But what of my enemies? Can I sit in the midst of hatred and share with Christ in love? Joy is the proof of how thoroughgoing his presence is. I can have a wonderful meal even while my enemies pray for my indigestion.

This is the greatest aspect of his presence: Joy. "Joy," said one of the martyrs, "is the most infallible proof of the presence of God." What would we be able to say of his presence if it were only a morose presence? Who would want to eat with a sourpuss Savior? No, our lives will be fraught with many trials, but he will sit at meat with us and teach us to laugh in the presence of our trials. The martyrs died singing, not sulking over their woes or rebuking the unfair Christian life.

Joy is inherent in our confession of Christ. Christ is role model to our living. He was severely criticized by the Pharisees as being a kind of social animal: a glutton and winebibber (Matt. 11:19), the sinner's party-goer (Luke 7:34). How are we to reconcile the fact that Christ continually enjoyed good times and yet he came to earth on a mission of the gravest possible consequences? In being at parties he became fully aware that while he had to die, he came to teach us the best lessons of joy. We are not ever to be so serious about our trials that his never-forsaking presence does not waken us to joy. Our table may be menaced but his presence is the defiant laughter that scatters our fears.

Gloom is a separating device of Satan even as joy is a unifying ploy of God. Ray Bradbury's marvelous work *Something Wicked This Way Comes,* shows Will and his father dealing with the near death of Will's young friend, Jim, in grief. In yielding to the pain of Jim's dying, Will's father cries out that "feeling badly is just the kind of gloom the dark force [Satan] has in mind." They need rather to laugh, for laughter itself defeats the forces of darkness. They do laugh and their laughter produces a resurrection. Doesn't Christ always want his presence to waken our grieving world to laughter? Is not earth too often a vale of tears? Beyond doubt, every day of our lives is an invitation to feel badly over the pain of living. But confessional living invokes the bright name of his living presence in the middle of our shadowy valleys. And in the light of eternity, those shadowy valleys are brief.

The church is the place for laughter. Psalm 126 describes the joys of the exiles. They were the gloriously emancipated. Notice the joy of their anthem:

Bring back our captivity, O LORD,
As the streams in the South.
Those who sow in tears
Shall reap in joy.
He who continually goes forth weeping,
Bearing seed for sowing,
Shall doubtless come again with rejoicing,
Bringing his sheaves with him.

(vv. 4–6)

See how these exiles were set free. See how they entered into a broken land of burned-out houses. But the psalmist said they carried little bags of seeds and they planted the seeds in the scorched earth, crying over the desolation of their war-torn farms; then came the rain and the sun and the faithfulness of God. Then Harvest—sheaves of grain, and bread, and laughter.

When barrenness begins to yield to God, there is always laughter. Sarah laughed when she overheard the angels telling Abraham that she would have a child in her old age. The angels rebuked her and, just so she wouldn't forget that God had a sense of humor, they instructed her to name her son "Laughter." When the boy was born, Sarah said, "God has made me laugh, and all who hear will laugh with me" (Gen. 21:6).

The laughter of God is the healing of his church. God does not laugh at our predicaments because they are free from hurt, but simply because in the light of our eternal lives these troubles do seem short.

I remember my daughter struggling with me because I was resolved not to let her date until she was sixteen years old. When she was fifteen years and ten months old, a "dreamy hunk-of-a-guy" asked her to go to the senior prom. She asked me if I wouldn't consider relinquishing law in favor of grace. When I insisted that I would not set aside the rule, she became morose and somewhat angry. "Well," she said, "I hope Jesus comes back before my sixteenth birthday and you have to live with yourself all through eternity, knowing I never had a date!"

She was so sincere about this that she was nearly in tears. On the contrary, I broke into laughter. Why? Did I not want to be an understanding father? Of course, but I knew that in light of all the times she would have to live (and date), this small requirement was of no real consequence.

Getting the God view of our troubles would indeed help us to see that from the overview of eternity much of the concern we spend is counterfeit currency. Paul does not speak of the laughter of God, but he does beg us to get the blessing of real perspective when he says: "For I consider that the sufferings of this present time are not worthy to be compared with the glory which shall be revealed in us" (Rom. 8:18).

Confessional living sees the true nature of things; it is then free to live above the cruelty of negativism. Joy is the stuff of an honest spiritual perspective.

Not long ago I attended the funeral of a marvelous professor. During his long years of teaching he was a ready wit and a joyous Christian. I dreaded the funeral, for I was afraid the preacher would paste a gloomy "eulogy" over a very happy life. To my delight there was not one preacher but five, and all of them told of their own personal encounters of the professor's joyous life. Each of them correctly focused on his jokes, his humor, his happy demeanor. Soon the entire service was rollicking like his classes had always done. It was all so delightful I had to keep looking at the casket to remember that I was at his funeral and not one of his lectures.

Was the levity out of place? Not at all. We were gathered; Christ was present with us. We celebrated the passing of a friend whose life of joy was made possible by the presence of Christ. The Pharisees rebuked Jesus because his disciples refused to fast. They were in effect saying, "Jesus, tell your disciples to get serious." But Jesus replied, "Can the friends of the bridegroom fast while the bridegroom is with them?" (Mark 2:19). The presence of Jesus evokes a sense of joy. We will from time to time trust in the presence of Jesus. We will from time to time weep in the presence of Jesus. But when he is with us, and he always is, laughter will mark our lives. Joy is indeed the most infallible proof that his indwelling Spirit is in us: God is in his heaven and all's right with our lives and our world.

Confessional living celebrates the continual and abiding presence of Christ and that evokes a true joy, which brings to remembrance a second hymn of my childhood. I learned it in a Pentecostal Assembly filled with marimbas and accordions, tambourines and clappy hymns. The song was called "Constantly Abiding":

> Constantly abiding, Jesus is mine;
> Constantly abiding, Rapture divine!
> He never leaves me lonely, whispers, oh so kind:
> "I will never leave thee." Jesus is mine.

Our confession first introduces his presence in our lives and then keeps on working in our lives. St. John of the Cross counsels us to fix our minds on our confession and his presence will make possible his peace: "When anything disagreeable happens to you, remember Christ crucified and keep silent."[11]

His presence enables us, said Dame Julian. "Whenever we feel the need to pray, our good Lord follows us, helping our desire."[12] Paul, in 2 Timothy, laments, "At my first defense no one stood with me . . . but the Lord stood with me" (4:16–17). So should every confession quicken our remembrance of his unforsaking presence.

There is but one word to unlock joy and triumph in our lives. It is the word *Kyrios, Lord. Kyrios* is the grand confession that makes possible our growth in Christ. It is the only word that will suffice in making our darker circumstances an occasion of light. In the pages which follow I hope to show by way of my own experience that the name of Christ is sufficient, sovereign, and present. In these ten circumstances I will walk with the counsel of Christ and two other kinds of counselors: first, those immediate "priests" and friends who have shared life with me and blessed my journey. Second, I will call to witness the power of the confession of Christ as it comes through the classic writings of men and women who lived triumphant lives in days gone by. My own life bears witness to the truth of these holy ones of old. I do not use my own personal pilgrimage because it is so worthy but because I know it best. My prayer is that my story will speak to yours and that the ageless counsel of Christianity's noblest lovers-of-God will bear witness to us both.

Calvin Miller
The Unchained Soul

BEGINNING

THE

JOURNEY

Saint Augustine

The very toys of toys and vanities of vanities, my ancient mistresses, still held me; they plucked at the garment of my flesh and whispered softly, "Will you cast us off for ever? And from that moment shall we no longer be with you—for ever?", and I hesitated, for a strong habit said to me, "Do you think you can live without them?"

But continence said to me, "Why do you rely on yourself and so waver? Cast yourself upon him, fear not, he will not withdraw himself and let you fall; he will receive you and heal you."

So I rose and, throwing myself down under a certain fig tree, wept bitterly in contrition of heart. Suddenly I heard from a neighboring house the voice of a child, singing over and over again, "Take up and read, take up and read."

Checking my weeping I got up and went back to where I had been sitting, and had laid down the volume of the apostle, and read the first passage which met my eyes: "Not in rioting and drunkenness, not in impurity and wantonness, not in strife and envy; but put on the Lord Jesus Christ, and make no provision for the flesh, to fulfill its lusts."

I needed to read no further, for suddenly, as it were by a light infused into my heart, all darkness vanished away.

—From *Confessions*

IN AUGUST OF 1945, my walk with Christ began. I was nine years old and in many ways awed by the impact of the closing years of World War II. The pictures of that war, which appeared in the *Daily Eagle* of Enid, Oklahoma, along with huge black headlines, told of the destruction of war. Those images haunted me and created in me a security–need during my struggling childhood. My father, some years earlier, had set up this need by abandoning our family and leaving us in dire circumstances. Being the seventh child in a family of nine, I had already known one other devastating insecurity. At the age of four, I learned that my eight-year-old brother had died in a drowning accident. At that age, of course, I could not grasp all that his dying meant. Still, at the shadowy front of my memory, the ache of this undefined event remained.

By the end of the war, my older sisters had married servicemen and left home. My mother, to support what remained of her brood, took a job as a laundress to add to the small welfare subsistence she received. I never shall forget those newspaper headlines. Nor shall I forget the darkness I felt at knowing people were killing each other and millions were dying. I can still see my mother, torn by the notion that her four oldest daughters were all married to servicemen. These men sooner or later might go overseas and have to die in the war. When World War II ended, I felt a major sense of relief from knowing that all of my older sisters and their husbands were still unharmed. But more than this, I felt the easing of tension in our small community which was for me "the world."

When the Pentecostals set up a revival tent at the corner of Tenth and Ash, I was curious about the event and, through the influence of a school chum, found myself inside that tent. There, amid the happy, weepy, exuberant Pentecostals, I was born again.

I had gone to that revival as a very needy child. I joyfully laid aside my insecurity to allow God to come into my life. To say we receive Christ rather misleads. The curious term implies that we stalk God until we capture him and then we "receive Christ." The dishonesty of such a notion approaches blasphemy. It is he who receives. We but seek! My desperation was so immense I could only confess and beg his forgiveness. God was the stalker and I was the needy soul who begged him enter.

This was the first time in my life that I realized how the worst and best days of my life could be one. I have had people say to me that in adulthood I have constructed this imaginary melodrama, but it is not so. I remember an awful sense of darkness that marked my childhood. I lived through a child's dark night. But when I went to the revival, I knew the brightness of his coming. Then the worst day of my life became the best day of my life.

It is ludicrous to compare my awakening to that of Augustine's. His classic struggle eludes the childish simplicity of my own discovery. His coming to Christ is couched within the theological and philosophical struggle of his own scholarly surrender. He was a prime mover in the formation of Christian thought. I was a child from near-rural Oklahoma. Still, some similarities are common to everyone's discovery of Christ. Augustine defines that experience in wonderful concepts. There are seven footsteps of Christ's coming into our lives.

Seven Footsteps of Christ's Coming into Our Lives

The First Footstep: The Fountain of Mercies

How indebted each of us is for those who bear our names to God in prayer for our salvation. The names of Christianity's heroes usually begin in the hearts of concerned people whose names we have not heard nor will we ever hear. We each existed as prayer requests before we came to exist as believers. The tears of unknown saints become, in time, the water of life to those they pray for.

Augustine's life in Christ did not issue from his marvelous mind. He was brought to Christ by the concern of others who could not abide his separation from God: namely his mother.

> And Thou sentest Thine hand from above, and drewest my soul out of that profound darkness, my mother, Thy faithful one, weeping to Thee for me, more than mothers weep the bodily deaths of their children. For she, by that faith and spirit which she had from Thee, discerned the death wherein I lay, and Thou heardest her, O Lord; Thou heardest her, and despisedst not her tears, when streaming down, they watered the ground under her eyes in every place where she prayed; yea Thou heardest her.[1]

Augustine's mother, Monica, supplied that refreshing water that can only be drunk from God's "fountain of mercies." Without her prayers for his conversion, would our world have ever known his witness? Augustine's mother reminds us that the way Christ advances into our lives is paved with the prayers of those who are concerned about our lostness. Who knows how much these prayers, offered by those who precede us in commitment, redeem our lostness to the Father who makes all heaven a vast yearning as he eagerly awaits our confession. I remember that wonderful first-grace feeling I had when I came to know the Lord. It seemed as though Christ and I were the only two souls in the universe. Augustine's conversion to Christ came because he had been prayed over, wept over, and claimed in a special agony of concern. We must remember that God is a waiting, longing Father "not willing that any should perish but that all should come to repentance" (2 Peter 3:9). Christ's all-consuming eagerness to save us is somehow quickened by what Augustine called the fountain of mercies—the increasing prayers of those who want for our lives exactly what God wants: our salvation. Augustine's mother anguished so for her son's salvation that Augustine wrote of her:

> My mother had now come to me, resolute through piety, following me over sea and land . . . full of confidence, she replied to me, she believed in Christ, that before she departed this life, she should see me a Catholic believer . . . Fountain of mercies, poured she forth more copious prayers and tears, that Thou wouldest hasten Thy help, and enlighten my darkness.[2]

Monica had followed Augustine from Africa to Milan, Italy, bathing her journey in prayer for his soul. St. Augustine confesses that her fountain of tears created a hunger for God that would not forsake him.

I well remember a missionary mother of seven children. Six of them followed Christ and loved him. But her seventh child, self-willed and determined to make his own way in life, had left home never having received Christ as his Savior. She followed him in her old age all the way to the university he attended. She took an apartment in that city and continued to pray for his salvation. It was while she was living near the university that I met her. I could never cease being touched by this fountain of tears that washed her eyes to make the eyes of her rebel son burn bright with the possibility of Christ.

My own mother did not come knowingly to Christ till after I did. Still, I could not escape the impression that she never ceased to pray for her children. My own childish salvation was imbedded in her prayers long before she ever publicly acknowledged Christ as her own Savior.

R. A. Torrey's confession of Christ is reported to have come when he was desperate and near suicide. He remembered the words of his mother: "Son, in your darkest hour, call on the name of your mother's God." Torrey claims that he could not even name the name of Jesus, but that he called on his mother's God and found salvation. Torrey's mother, like Augustine's, was also a fountain of tears.

Whether it's a mother or someone else, there is often some concerned believer who calls our name. In that calling is his coming.

The Second Footstep: The Ulcer of Our Sin Life

Sin is ever with us, and who among us is so impious he or she will not confess it? But repentance results only when we see the consequence of our sin.[3] We dare not forget that salvation has two components: repentance and faith. Repentance is that overwhelming sense of godly sorrow for the sin of our lives. If there is any fault among modern church folk, it is the dangerous notion that salvation is the accepting of Christ into our lives as they are. So many are "coming to Christ" without any notion that they are sinners. They suppose themselves "born again," but in truth they are only the illegitimate children of an I'm OK–you're OK confession. Psychology has gutted repentance. There is little necessity of being cleansed, since psychological positivism teaches that spiritual cleansing is unnecessary in a world where no one is really dirty.

How our generation is to be pitied for surrendering its greatest treasure: the truth that we are sinners, therefore lost, and therefore in need of salvation. The psalmist gave us the recipe for spiritual joy: "Oh, taste and see that the LORD is good" (Ps. 34:8). Unfortunately, positivistic psychology has all but killed our spiritual taste buds. A starving man, yes even a dieter, finds food wonderful because hunger has created a yearning. But we cannot really taste what we have never been hungry for. But we have become so I'm-OK-you're-OK in our own eyes we do not need to hunger for God. Contemporary secular psychology has taught us how to survey our faulty morality and grade it passing. We look for sin in our lives and find it absent. Once sin is gone, God is less necessary. We still chew on theology but our taste for God is gone. T. H. White said of Gwenevere that while she loved theology, she didn't care much for God.

Notice the passion of the psalmist: "Oh, taste and see that the LORD is good." We who now find godhood in ourselves have run out of the passion of needy souls. We have no significant weaknesses that cause us to need the Savior's strength. We are so wise in our own conceits (Rom. 12:16) that we have no need for seeking the wisdom of God (James 1:5). We are so full of self that we no longer hunger for his fullness (Ps. 34:8).

Consider the tale of the four travelers who, having crossed a wide desert, finally reached an oasis. Each arrived dying of thirst, having consumed all the water in the ordeal of crossing the desert. Each of the wayfarers was stopped by the old leper who was the sole keeper of the well. With an eroded hand the old leper dipped the gourd into the cool clear water and extended it to each of the dying travelers. Each of them was repulsed by the diseased hands and face of their leprous host. The first nomad was a positivist, the second a relativist, the third a psychologist, and the fourth a simple but honest soul. The first three pilgrims in turn refused the water. The positivist refused saying, "Thirst isn't really so bad." The psychologist refused, believing that if he could only get in touch with his childhood, his thirst would take care of itself. The relativist thought that there were others who had been even thirstier than he and that his condition was more or less like others who had doubtless happened by the oasis. The three left the oasis and traveled on, looking for an oasis more to their liking. They all perished in the desert.

The fourth pilgrim was honest. "It is better to drink from a leper's cup than to die of thirst in the desert," he said as he reached for the gourd. As he took it, he looked down to see that his own hands were eroded with the same affliction as that of his host. "Ah," said the keeper of the oasis, "hope is always one dying leper giving the next a drink of life. We are all lepers. Some receive the taste of water in the desert and live. Most do not. Be sure of this, when you find the bodies of your three friends, you will see that in spite of their vain imaginings, they died not of thirst but of our contagion."

The parable defines our culture of denial. Consider how Augustine viewed sin:

> Thou Oh, Lord . . . didst turn me towards myself, taking me from behind my back, where I had placed me, unwilling to observe myself; and setting me before my face, that I might see how foul I was, how crooked and defiled, bespotted and ulcerous. And I beheld and stood aghast; and whither to flee from myself I found not. . . . Thou didst set me over against myself, and thrustedst me before my eyes, that I might find out mine iniquity, and hate it. I had known it, but made as though I saw it not, winked at it, and forgot it.[4]

Did not Isaiah relate with Augustine when he said, "Woe is me, for I am undone!" (6:5)? Did not Paul also say it: "Christ Jesus came into the world to save sinners, of whom I am chief" (1 Tim. 1:15)? Did not our Lord rebuke those who seemed outwardly to have conquered sin when he said, "Woe to you, scribes and Pharisees, hypocrites! For you are like whitewashed tombs which indeed appear beautiful outwardly, but inside are full of dead men's bones and all uncleanness. Even so you also outwardly appear righteous to men, but inside you are full of hypocrisy and lawlessness" (Matt. 23:27–28).

Sin is the great divorce of God and man. It resulted in the

cross, and perhaps the greatest of all sins is not to take sin seriously. Augustine said sin is ulcerous, a sore on the soul without whose cleansing the spirit cannot be well.

The Third Footstep: The New Inebriation

Augustine further called out of his soul's necessity a growing hunger for God. Even when he was quite young his hunger of soul announced itself:

> Oh! That I might repose on Thee! Oh! That Thou wouldest enter into my heart, and inebriate it, that I may forget my ills, and embrace Thee, my sole good! What art Thou to me? In Thy pity, teach me to utter it. Or what am I to Thee that Thou demandest my love, and, if I give it not, art wroth with me, and threatenest me with grievous woes? Is it then a slight woe to love Thee not? Oh! For Thy mercies' sake, tell me, O Lord my God, what Thou art unto me. Say unto my soul, I am thy salvation.[5]

Our affair with Christ, at whatever age we find him, is a matter of appetite. As a child of nine I understood this. Even then I experienced this marvelous, inebriating desire for a taste of new wine. To his cup of grace I was drawn. My heart echoed the words of St. Ignatius when he prayed, "Blood of Christ, inebriate me."[6]

Then I came to know the force of Jesus' words: "And I, if I am lifted up from the earth, will draw all peoples to Myself" (John 12:32). The heady intoxication of the Spirit made me want what I could never have without letting it possess me. I was hungry. I was thirsty. And the Beatitude welcomed such an appetite for grace: "Blessed are those who hunger and thirst for righteousness, / for they shall be filled" (Matt. 5:6).

The Fourth Footstep: The Severe Mercy

The issue of being under conviction is a part of the gentle brutality of God. It is God prompting our suffering so that he can be kind. There is no pain like the pain of knowing how much our sins cost

Christ. Augustine called this the mercy of God for it leads us to repentance, but it is, indeed, a severe mercy.

> Thus soul-sick was I, and tormented, accusing myself much more severely than my wont, rolling and turning me in my chain, till that were wholly broken, whereby I now was but just, but still was, held. And Thou, O Lord, pressedst upon me in my inward parts by a severe mercy, redoubling the lashes of fear and shame, lest I should again give way. . . .

> I cast myself down I know not how, under a certain fig-tree, giving full vent to my tears; and the floods of mine eyes gushed out an acceptable sacrifice to Thee. . . . O Lord, how long? How long, Lord, wilt thou be angry for ever? Remember not our former iniquities.[7]

Did not the writer cry, "Do not remember the sins of my youth" (Ps. 25:7)?

I remember a certain man who came forward at the end of our services and said to our whole congregation, "I need to be forgiven, but I think my sins are too black. My life is too rotten to ever be forgiven." How beautiful it was to see him caught in the joyous web of a severe mercy. Following his confession, many in our church came to know Christ, and the joy of his honesty resulted in a season of revival.

This severe mercy is the footstep of Christ's coming. How much he loves us. Yet his love remains inaccessible while we are smugly self-confident, insisting that our sins are of no consequence. I am told that the Asbury Revival was the result of a student or two who took the pain of their own sin seriously. This severe mercy flowed not only through Kentucky but throughout much of the United States.

The Fifth Footstep: The Abandonment of the Toy Box

I am convinced that very few people want to die without Christ. Even those who are not altogether sure that there is a Christ fix in their minds the importance of not dying without him. The problem with most of us is that dying remains a future event. We rationalize that the way to get the most out of our hedonistic lives is to schedule our confessions as close as possible to our dying time. We all want to be saved . . . but not yet. Augustine prayed even as sexual indulgence consumed his life:

> But I wretched, most wretched, in the very commencement of my early youth, had begged chastity of Thee, and said, "Give me chastity and continency, only not yet."[8]

We want our lives renovated of sin and self-serving. Still, we had rather wait until we've tasted the world's dessert before we begin the feast of God.

In my youth, even at nine years of age, I knew that Pentecostals did not go to movies. After all, they said Jesus could come again at any moment. If he should come again, we must certainly not be found in a theater. Pentecostals and other kinds of churches were severe about this matter. And I must confess that even as I contemplated the church, I wondered if I could ever give up Saturday afternoon movies—mostly westerns—just to be a Christian. Could one or should one trade Hopalong Cassidy for Jesus? One could clearly not have both. How oddly I felt the very night I went forward to be saved. I thought to myself, "So long, Hopalong."

Augustine called these attachments which hold us back from Christ the Toy Box. Augustine's toys were significantly different from those things I considered toys. His carnal, free-sex life begged him not to cast its fleshly pleasures aside.

> The very toys of toys, and vanities of vanities, my ancient mistresses, still held me; they plucked my fleshy garment, and whispered softly, "Dost thou cast us off? And from that moment shall we no more be with thee for ever?" . . . Yet they did retard me, so that I hesitated to burst and shake myself free from them, and to spring over whither I was

called; a violent habit saying to me, "Thinkest thou, thou cans't live without them?"[9]

The trinkets of life keep us from the gold of our spiritual inheritance. How foolish were Augustine's mistresses to hold him in their infernal clutches and keep him from the embrace of God. And how foolish, too, was my own childish infatuation with Hopalong Cassidy that kept me from a baptism of grace.

This is all a bit reminiscent of C. S. Lewis's ghost in *The Great Divorce*. He approaches heaven with a lizard on his lapel. The ghost is informed at the gate that heaven holds no lizards and that while he is quite welcome to come in, the lizard may not. The lizard begins to plead and beg that there be no separation. The poor ghost is hungry to honor his toy, but he is also most desirous of heaven. In a moment of decision he rips the shrieking lizard from his lapel and throws it to the ground. Even as it begs for life, he stomps it to death. No sooner is it dead than it begins to change into a great steed, on which the decisive new saint rides gloriously into heaven.

It is difficult even now for me to separate repentance from union with Christ. To renounce the foolish toys of life is to enter into union. Grasping the trinkets of earth's toy box, the riches of God remain inaccessible.

The Sixth Footstep: The Lordship of Christ

Augustine's coming to Christ is detailed in the epigraph to this chapter. At a child's words *"Tole, Lege,"* "take up and read," he opened his Bible at random, pointing down at a text. At the urging of God, his finger fell on Romans 13:13–14: "Not in rioting and drunkenness, not in chambering and wantonness, not in strife and envying. But put ye on the Lord Jesus Christ, and make not provision for the flesh, to fulfil the lusts thereof" (KJV). He needed read no further; light infused his heart.

It was glorious that Augustine happened on this marvelous passage dealing with sin and lordship. The text was very specific about Augustine's sins. God's Word often speaks to us exactly where we have been living.

The Bible gets specific with our generation just as it did with Augustine's. The problem is that we don't want to believe because believing mandates changes in our lives. We compartmentalize such passages as the one that brought Augustine to Christ. We read God's mandates and assign them to our "church-going self." Then we allow our "more realistic" market place self to live by less strenuous rigors. We are the "double-minded" people that James says are unstable in all their ways (James 1:8).

Augustine let Romans 13:13 convict him of sin, and Romans 13:14 bind his cleansed life to the lordship of Jesus Christ. There were not two Augustines—one who took interest in godly things, and the other who lived in the more practical world. He was made one, possessed by the indwelling Christ who ruled over all of his life.

Scripture drew him to Christ and Christ was all there was of significance in the world. He could exult with the psalmist: "Your testimonies . . . are my delight / and my counselors" (119:24). Thus the schizoid Augustine moves from being many-faceted to being singular in heart and purpose. Romans 13:14 impacts the self-willed Augustine with the word *Lord*. The word integrates all his appetites and taste beneath a singular appetite—the pleasure of Christ. Now all the various demons that confused him are exorcised under one dynamic headship—the sovereignty of Christ.

He is the image of the invisible God, the firstborn over all creation. For by Him all things were created that are in heaven and that are on earth, visible and invisible, whether thrones or dominions or principalities or powers. All things were created through Him and for Him. And He is before all things, and in Him all things consist. And He is the head of the body, the church, who is the beginning, the firstborn from the dead, that in all things He may have the preeminence. For it pleased the Father that in Him all the fullness should dwell. (Col. 1:15–19)

Søren Kierkegaard spoke of the marvelous healing of the mind which occurs when all of our various drives are unleashed under one control. The word *Lord* makes single the eye so that our whole body can be full of light (Luke 11:34). This passage really teaches that a healthy eye makes vision possible. An unhealthy eye creates an unreal world.

Scripture is the lens through which we perceive and measure the true course of things. A single eye correctly filters the light. Only under a single sovereignty do our many struggles surrender themselves to one glorious integration.

It is the coming of our Lord Jesus Christ that possesses us with a single worldview. We spoke earlier of how often we err when we speak of "accepting Christ." It is a kind of statement that puts God's indwelling Son at the mercy of our caprice. Who are we to accept Christ or speak of it as though by accepting him, humanity does divinity a favor? No, to think in such a manner means that we have not sufficiently seen our sin nor felt the severity of God's mercy. One gets the impression in Augustine's confession that he quit bracing himself against God and thus he was claimed. The coming of Christ into our lives is an issue of surrender and opening our lives. Our many quarreling selves become one in salvation.

Without this integration of souls, none of us will ever know who we are. We only find out who we are when we find out who God is and what he expects of us. "I haven't a clue who Peter Sellers is," said Peter Sellers.[10] Only when Christ comes in do we discover our own definition and why we are in the world. We are not merely saved from our own immorality. We are saved from living the undefined life.

The Seventh Footstep: The Sacrifice of Praise
The sacrifice of praise, said Augustine, followed hard upon the coming of Christ. It is not properly one of the steps of his coming, but it is so immediate in its occurrence that it is inseparable from the born again experience. Joy and Jesus enter the life together.

Where brokenness and tears had come from Augustine's life, now joy breaks forth:

> O Lord, I am Thy servant; I am Thy servant, and the son of Thy handmaid: Thou has broken my bonds in sunder. I will offer to Thee the sacrifice of praise. Let my heart and my tongue praise Thee; yea, let all my bones say, O Lord, who is like unto Thee? Let them say, and answer Thou me, and say unto my soul, I am thy salvation. Who am I, and what am I? What evil have not been either my deeds, or if not my deeds, my words, or if not my words, my will? But Thou, O Lord, are good and merciful, and Thy right hand had respect unto the depth of my death, and from the bottom of my heart emptied that abyss of corruption. And this Thy whole gift was, to nil what I willed, and to will what Thou willedst. But where through all those years, and out of what low and deep recess was my free-will called forth in a moment, whereby to submit my neck to Thy easy yoke, and my shoulders unto Thy light burden, O Christ Jesus, my Helper and my Redeemer? . . . Now was my soul free from the biting cares of canvassing and getting, and weltering in filth, and scratching off the itch of lust. And my infant tongue spake freely to Thee, my brightness, and my riches, and my health, the Lord my God.[11]

The wellspring is uncapped by the nail-marked hands of Christ, and praise rings forth.

To read of Augustine's joy makes me look at the contemporary church with doubt. On the Lord's Day, stiff of arm and countenance, we hold the hymnal. We are the cold congregations from whence, as Dickens said of Ebenezer, "No flint has ever struck out generous fire." We are truly God's frozen people. We are often afraid of spontaneity. I'm glad I discovered Christ in Pentecostalism. There, celebration was not a nuance, it was expected. Our praise was childlike; we knew nothing of worship liturgies I would later love. We didn't suspect Bach or Beethoven as ever having been. While I would afterwards learn the elegance of their classical praise, I at first found simple wonder in reedy accordions and the joyous jangling of the tambourines.

It is not possible to receive Christ and not to receive his joy. For *his* joy *is* joy! It is the delirious music of those who have been delivered. Joy is the leveler of all the people of God. It makes of us one age, for children who receive Christ are somehow instantly mature. And the mature who receive him are instantly childlike. Augustine cannot fool us. He may be a grand rhetorician and professor, but we have heard his praise of God with that singular joy children may know.

I was serving at an altar service recently when one of the associate minister's children came forward. He knelt on one side of the communion rail as I knelt on the other. He was quiet, but, in league with the Holy Spirit, he ferreted through his own needs. I, too, was quiet as I tried to think how to help him form the words of that confession he so wanted to form. I could not coax them forth; neither could he. We prayed silently with only the communion rail and fifty years of age between us, but we were both children. Suddenly he reached across the rail and kissed me under the ear. It was a superb passing of the peace, and I found myself reluctant to wash the spot where he kissed me for a whole week. It was not a man praying with a child; we were both children, lost somehow in the sacrifice of praise.

Augustine could not ever again be set free of the sacrifice of praise. For the remainder of his life, his works were an anthem to Romans 13:13–14 and the reign of his Lord. I do not compare my life to his, either by excellence or influence. But I know that my sin cannot prevent my song and for fifty years since that night in 1945, I can scarcely wake up without breathing the name of Jesus into the first light of morning.

Monica, Augustine's mother, died at Ostia, but only five days before her death she extolled the Christ in the life of her son— the goal which had brought her to Milan from Carthage and had brought her son from bondage to freedom. She said to Augustine:

"Son, for mine own part I have no further delight in any thing in this life. What I do here any longer, and to what end I am here, I know not, now that my hopes in this world are accomplished. One thing there was for which I desired to linger for a while in this life, that I might see thee a Catholic Christian before I died. My God hath done this for me more abundantly, that I should now see thee withal, despising earthly happiness, become His servant: what do I here?"[12]

At her funeral service he celebrated that glorious salvation which his mother had sought for him:

Unto the Sacrament of which our ransom, Thy handmaid bound her soul by the bond of faith. Let none sever her from Thy protection: let neither the lion nor the dragon interpose himself by force or fraud. For she will not answer that she owes nothing, lest she be convicted and seized by the crafty accuser: but she will answer that her sins are forgiven her by Him, to Whom none can repay that price which He, Who owed nothing, paid for us.[13]

We are the ransomed. We were bought with a price (1 Cor. 6:20). And the cost of our freedom was Christ's obedience to his Father. It costs to obey, but then it costs to disobey too. Obedience knows the price of our immediate surrender. Never surrendering also knows that cost wherein Christ describes our condition as lost. Lost to God, lost to ourselves, lost to all hope.

But on the day of our conversion, conviction for our sins makes us weep as we encounter the darkness of our lostness. Thus, the same dark day becomes a day of light as well. It is indeed the worst and the best day of our lives.

That first night I knew Christ, I came home from that revival with a "diamond in my pocket." I sensed its value, but I was wrapped in a kind of euphoria that kept me from esteeming the gift. In such an all-engulfing new romance, one never treasures the gift, only the giver. I have often heard free churchmen thanking

God for their salvation and high churchmen thanking God for grace. But real thankfulness bypasses the giver in favor of the gift.

Not so with me. I moved inside a new affection. I loved not what I owned, but I loved who owned me. And in this double love I was set free.

ARRIVING

AT

SECURITY

Madame
Guyon

After the accident which befell me (a fall from a horse) from which I soon wonderfully recovered, the Devil began to declare himself more openly mine enemy, to break loose and become outrageous. One night, when I least thought of it, something very monstrous and frightful presented itself. It seemed a kind face, which was seen by a glimmering bluish light. I don't know whether the flame itself composed that horrible face or appearance; for it was so mixed and passed by so rapidly, that I could not discern it. My soul rested in its calm situation and assurance, and it appeared no more after that manner. As I arose at midnight to pray, I heard frightful noises in my chamber and after I had lain down they were still worse. My bed often shook for a quarter of an hour at a time, and the sashes were all burst. Every morning while this continued, they were found shattered and torn, yet I felt no fear. I arose and lighted my wax candle at a lamp which I kept in my room, because I had taken the office of sacristan and the care of waking the sisters at the hour they were to rise, without having once failed in it for my indispositions, ever being the first in all the observances. I made use of my little light to look all over the room and at the sashes, at the very time the noise was strongest. As he saw that I was afraid of nothing, he left off all on a sudden, and attacked me no more in person.

—From *Autobiography of Madame Guyon*

IN THE LORD'S prayer Jesus taught us to pray for deliverance from the evil one. I never knew of the power of evil until I came to Calvary. There Jesus' cross was the place of the great showdown. He not only conquered death there, he conquered fear, which is the parent of death. He could not conquer fear without vanquishing Satan, the source of fear. The cross was the end of Satan's reign of terror.

Another one of those best-worst days of my life came when I had to deal with the prince of fear. I have been afraid many times in my life, and always I have felt a weakness in my knees and a trembling in my spirit. But most of those times I have experienced fear, it was only because my own well-being was under some kind of threat.

Fear has its origin in Satan and his angels. Henri Nouwen wrote: "God is love and only love, and . . . every time fear, isolation, or despair begin to invade the human soul this is not something that comes from God."[1] Terror slithers up from the abyss and leaves us crying in our insecurity. This worst day, like the others I describe in this book, turned out to be one of the best days of my life.

Some years ago, I was with my wife and children on an outing. We had gone for a picnic on a Labor Day weekend. The day was beautiful. The outing was wonderful. But it shortly became memorable. Our picnic ended abruptly. Two men intruded on our sunny experience and began terrorizing us. Brandishing heavy pieces of pipe, they threatened to kill me. We ran from them and got into our little car and locked the doors. They pursued us and stood in front of the car, preventing our escape. They soon began to beat upon our car with the pipes. They tried to pry the doors off our automobile, shouting that they intended to beat me to death. I feared any moment that the fragile locks on our Volkswagen sedan would give way, and they would make good their threats. To deny that I was frightened would be a lie; I was terrified. But as they continued beating on the car, I looked into the back seat where my children quailed in fright. All of a sudden I no longer feared for my own life. Now I was hostile over the panic in the faces of my children. I saw there the satanic nature of all fear.

Their tiny bodies were rigid with terror. Wide-eyed and frozen in stone, they emitted no sound. Tears streaming from their eyes were the only evidence that they were even alive. Forgetting all about my life, I found myself all but unable to forgive those who had frightened my children into paralysis. Suddenly the noise of those pipes stopped. For joyous reasons known only to God, a stream of cars began to approach our picnic area. This queue of welcome witnesses sent our assailants scurrying away. The crisis was past. Our children reentered the world of movement, pulse, and breath. Still, I came to understand the meaning of that familiar billboard: "Never Hurt a Child . . . Never, Never, Never!"

How could such a day of terror ever become a day of blessing? I found that in a time of utter fear, my adrenalin poured out faster than my trust. To my shame, I confess, it was only later I recalled that trust is rooted in the closeness of our walk with God. The psalmist said, "The LORD is my light and my salvation; / whom shall I fear? The LORD is the strength of my life; / of whom shall I be afraid?" (27:1). He also said, "You shall not be afraid of the terror by night, / nor of the arrow that flies by day" (91:5). I learned that day that the devil is indeed a destroyer. Fear is the weapon of the tempter. It is a venom that poisons. It is the paralyzing ploy of the grand enemy of God. Madame Guyon tells of her fears when she was but a child of four years:

> I loved to hear God spoken of, to be at church and to be dressed in a religious garb. I was told of the terrors of Hell which I imagined was to intimidate me as I was exceedingly lively and full of a little petulant vivacity which they called wit. The succeeding night I dreamed of Hell, and though I

was so young, time has never been able to efface the frightful ideas impressed upon my imagination. All appeared horrible darkness, where souls were punished, and my place among them was pointed out. At this I wept bitterly.[2]

In 1 Timothy 3:7, Paul speaks to ministers against falling into the "devil's trap" (NIV). The King James Version of the Bible calls this the "snare of the devil." Like a huntsman stalks rabbits, so the devil lays traps for our lives. In the jaws of his traps we know fear—terrible, portentous fear. James Stephens wrote long ago of our plight:

> I hear a sudden cry of pain
> There is a rabbit in a snare.
> Now I hear the cry again
> And I cannot tell from where.
>
> But I cannot tell from where
> He is calling out for aid.
> Crying in the frightened air
> Making everything afraid.
>
> Making everything afraid
> Wrinkling up his little face
> As he cries again for aide
> And I cannot find the place.
>
> And I cannot find the place
> Where his pain is in the snare
> Little one, Oh little one
> I am searching everywhere.[3]

Peter compared this savage trickster to a "roaring lion" walking about "seeking whom he may devour" (1 Peter 5:8). In her autobiography, Madame Guyon tells us how we may set ourselves free from such fear. I draw from her writing these six defenses.

Six Defenses for Triumphing Over Fear

The First Defense: Prayer

Not only is prayer the first defense, it is quite naturally a child's best defense. So I must return to my early years as a Christian—my childhood years—when I first began to learn about the nature of evil.

Madame Guyon knew that there is power in prayer to exorcise the demons of fear. I came gradually to this view of prayer after conversion. After my childhood confession there slowly awakened in me a sense of the immensity of evil. I have mentioned that I was raised in a family of nine children. When I was only four, my father left home. My mother's struggle with divorce was soon compounded by her attempts to make enough money to keep our large family together. Financial need stalked our confidence and made us shudder that insolvency might send us all packing into the courts and such foster care as they might provide. We wanted to be protected. We longed for someone bigger than ourselves to shield us from those fears that threatened to undo us. Insecurity was written into our earnest need to survive.

In my youth necessity taught me to work. Following my conversion I learned to pray also. I was too young to articulate Brother Lawrence's wisdom, but I understood his phrase, *Labore et Orare,* work and pray. Naturally, coming from a single-parent home, I loved my mother, whose presence for me was the very symbol of security. I was at peace when she was near. Life was stable when I could see her. When I could not see her, the darkness terrified me and my fears were unmanageable. The little house where we were reared had never been properly finished. My father's drinking habits gave him neither the funds nor the inclination to complete the house inside. So along with my eight other siblings, we lived in that small house as World War II began.

By the age of ten or twelve I had a firmly fixed phobia for darkness that in many ways still survives. I have already confessed in an earlier chapter that I often "cheated church law" and went to movies. My sins were greater than merely liking cowboy movies. I was intrigued by darker things. While they were not good soul-fodder for one afraid of the dark, in my teens I particularly liked horror movies. I was intrigued by Frankenstein, Dracula, and the Werewolf—played by actors like Lon Chaney and Bela Lugosi. Somehow Lon Chaney, facing the full moon and changing into a wolf, fascinated me with a compelling horror. I could not, or at least would not, avoid these films. Mine was a movie-made phobia, yet compelling. I looked with dread on the coming of a full moon. I'm embarrassed now when I think about the emotional currency I spent at such films, but then my fears seemed real.

There was a grove of locust trees in our semirural section of the city. To be coming home from a wolf-man movie and to pass through that grove of trees when the moon was full was a fearsome passage of life. It was always an occasion for loud whistling—that kind of breathy whistling that drives away the night-stalkers. In the woods I listened for footfalls in the dry grass. Fear grew! Things too horrible to define stalked my insecurity. Imaginary felt-footed creatures followed me home from many a movie. But whenever I no longer found the "spit" to whistle, I traded my childish fears on the one thing children do best—prayer! I know now what Ray Stedman wrote: "Prayer is the cry of a beloved child to his father, and frequently it is the cry of a child who is lost in dark woods, with noises in the brush—strange frightening noises."[4] Prayer for children is light in darkness.

Prayer delivers us from evil, or as Jesus said, from "the evil one" (Matt. 6:13). Prayer is the best defense against the devil and his demons of fear. Samuel Chadwick wrote, "The one concern of the Devil is to keep the Saints from praying. He fears nothing from prayerless study, prayerless work, prayerless religion . . . but he trembles when we pray."⁵ J. Edwin Hartill remarked, "Prayer is the slender sinew that moves the muscle of omnipotence."⁶ But the hymnist Samuel Cowper sang it better than anyone ever said it:

> Restraining prayer we cease to fight;
> Prayer makes the Christian's armor bright,
> And Satan trembles when he sees,
> The weakest Saint upon his knees.

One of the great fears that prayer destroys is future fear. Satan easily makes us quail before the "not yet." His ability to make us afraid means we leave unclaimed Jesus' promise, "Do not worry about your life" (Matt. 6:25). Anxiety is the way we demonstrate our future fear.

Demons are not the same thing as fear, but all fear is demonic. First John 4:18 reminds us that "perfect love casts out fear." Every exorcism is a rebuke of Satan. In such times the strong voice of God indwells our own weakness to order Satan from our souls.

Satan wears many masks to thwart God's being among us. He often masks himself with discouragement, a powerful mask indeed. He likewise disguises himself with grief, shame, and self-importance. By each of these masquerades we may be deceived. But fear is the most outrageous mask of the tempter. We live in the valley of Elah, and daily, Goliath stomps into our terrified lives, shouting, "I defy you!" (1 Sam. 17:10). In God's powerful name we must come to take our stand. Like David, we must say, "You come against me with sword and spear and javelin, but I come against you in the name of the LORD Almighty, the God of the armies of Israel, whom you have defied" (v. 45 NIV). If we tremble in the face of Satan, it is never because Satan has grown large, but because our God has grown small.

The strength of our rebuke must come from an inward trust based on our own personal relationship with Christ. It is never possible to exorcise a demon with secondhand faith. The sons of

Sceva tried to cast out a demon, saying, "We exorcise you by the Jesus whom Paul preaches" (Acts 19:13). These ministerial mimics, claiming a power they had never known, were suddenly set upon by hell. The evil spirit answered, "Jesus I know, and Paul I know; but who are you?" (v. 15). Satan is no match for those who order him out of their lives in the mighty name of Jesus. But a second-hand faith holds no power over his reign of terror. Christians are often defeated because they face Goliath with *only* slingshots. Remember, it requires both a slingshot and his mighty name. To rebuke Satan is to tell him bluntly that God forbids him to chain his fear to our courage. Prayer confines Satan to his realm and forbids him to operate in ours. Madame Guyon wrote:

> The Devil is outrageous only against prayer, and those who exercise it; because he knows it is the true means of taking his prey from him. . . . No sooner does one enter into a spiritual life, a life of prayer, but they must prepare for strange crosses. All manner of persecutions and contempts are prepared for that life.[7]

Prayer is the believer's weapon given to deliver us from Satan and all possibility of his victory in our lives.

The Second Defense: Attachment to God

It is Madame Guyon's second suggestion that Satan and the entire realm of fear can be defeated by attachment to God. Attachment to God suggests a further step than prayer. "The Lord was pleased to make me pass wholly into Him by an entire internal transformation. He became more and more the absolute master of my heart, to such a degree as not to leave me a movement of my own."[8] Madame Guyon moved from that kind of prayer which occupies us with God to the sort of prayer which welds us to him. Attachment to God is a kind of spiritual security we cannot otherwise know.

Henri Nouwen says that all of our lives may be freed of fear if we are content to glory in his presence:

Three fathers used to go and visit blessed Anthony [St. Anthony: the "father of monks"] every year and two of them used to discuss their thoughts and the salvation of their souls with him, but the third always remained silent and did not ask him anything.

After a long time Abba Anthony said to him: "You often come here to see me, but you never ask me anything," and the other replied, "It is enough to see you, Father."[9]

Our attachment to God is made secure by knowing God close up. The God who reveals himself by his awesome attributes may, at close hand, frighten us. Yet our attachment to him in prayer must welcome him in all of his three-fold sovereignty.

Omnipotence. Fixed to our omnipotent Savior, the three "omnis" teach us his nature. The first "omni" is *omnipotent,* which teaches us that his strength is available for all our needs. We need only attach ourselves to God, to make him our fortress (Ps. 91:2). His almighty power is the shield of our security (18:35). Our attachment is like this: It's as if an empty conch, washed upon the shore, has become a house for a sand crab. The crab in seeing the old organism, long dead, attaches himself to the inside of the shell. There, in that strong calcium house, his new attachment makes him secure.

Our security derives from the strength and capability of our Guardian. Like Annie with Punjab, we trust the strength of our great Ally. Madame Guyon was one who knew that all real security is directly derived from attachment to God.

This protection is not only self-defensive, it has an element of offensive power in it as well. Remember David, the shepherd, went against a titan unafraid because of his attachment to God. He said to Goliath:

"This day the LORD will deliver you into my hand, and . . . I will give the carcasses of the camp of the Philistines to the birds of the air and the wild beasts of the earth, that all the earth may know that there is a God in Israel."

(1 Sam. 17:46)

The passage illustrates that even our giantesque fears are small in proportion to the size of our God.

The hero of *Quo Vadis* found herself martyred when she was strapped across the horns of a taurus. She would have died except for the strength of the giant Ursus, who, massive as Hercules, grasped the godlike head of the bull and saved her life. In a struggle of some length, Ursus turned the bull's head inch by inch until the huge animal stumbled to his knees. The eyes of the bull rolled back in pain. The bronze arms of this Christian Hercules twisted the animal's head until the neck snapped with a crack like summer thunder. Soon all those meant to be martyred had turned their fears to triumph.

There is a lesson for us in the legend of Christopher, who sees the flood but does not fear. He bears our Lord, as a weak human child, across the flood. While Christopher's story may be untrue, I do know that I have often ridden on the shoulders of my own great Savior through the threatening passages of life.

Omniscience. The second kind of strength that derives from our attachment to God is omniscience. As we gain physical strength from our attachment to God, so we also gain strength from his wisdom. James counsels us: "If any of you lacks wisdom, let him ask of God, who gives to all liberally" (1:5).

Just as physical strength can comfort us and free us from fear, so can the power of wisdom. Madame Guyon knew this power and she wrote: "Divine wisdom is unknown, even to those who pass in the world for persons of extraordinary illumination and knowledge. To whom then is she known, and who can tell us any tidings concerning her? Destruction and death assure us, that they have heard with their ears of her fame and renown. It is, then, in dying to all things, and in being truly lost to them, passing forward into God, and existing only in Him, that we attain to some knowledge of the true wisdom." But divine wisdom is often gained by exorcising our fears and ordering the tempter from our path.

A few months ago, I accompanied a friend of mine who ministers in Cleveland. Because it is an inner-city world filled with fear and gang-led wars, I must admit I was unnerved. Before going out he asked me to take off my watch and leave it in my hotel room. I also left my wallet. I took off my coat and tie, for he said even the coat and tie would make me look "prosperous" enough to be robbed. Finally, when I was sufficiently undressed and voluntarily made poor, we "went out to minister." I must confess that the half-lit streets and marijuana-smoking youths made me nervous. I confessed my fear to him. "Stick close," he said, "you're going to be all right." And so I did, and so I was.

I did not find my security in his physical size; I was bigger than he. I found my security in his wisdom; he was "streetwise" as they say in this drive-by-shooting world where he ministers. That night James 1 came true for me. If I need wisdom—even courage—I must find it in my attachment. James 1 wisely orders our lives and leaves no chaos for evil to inhabit.

Omnipresence. But perhaps the real glory of my attachment is in Christ's omnipresence. I cannot go where he is not. My future cannot be Christless. I have him with me even as I move into the future. As my attachment deepens he gives me courage equal to my fears. Joshua 1:9 is my counselor: "Have I not commanded you? Be strong and of good courage; do not be afraid, nor be dismayed, for the LORD your God is with you wherever you go." Everywhere present! He is present in the valley of death (Ps. 23:4) and in hell itself (139:8).

This attachment lives at the heart of Brother Lawrence's thirty years in a kitchen. It made Africa a cathedral to Dr. Livingston. It made Hudson Taylor's China, pagan and lost, radiate with his inwardness. Dr. Helen Roseveare enumerated the "joyous woes" she experienced in her book, *He Gave Us a Valley.* Her imprisonment and personal violation seemed at first eclipsed by what she perceived as an abandonment by God, but later she came alive in the certain knowledge of his presence.

But all of his gifts for fear management seem to say love only the Giver, never his gifts. His gifts are so wondrous and mighty they may take our affections from God. The more he gives us, the more we turn to his gifts as our security and not to God himself. Why is it so important that we honor God and not the gifts he has given us? Because Satan is well able to counterfeit most of the things we are prone to treasure. In commenting on the ghost that has stalked his grief, Hamlet says:

> The spirit that I have seen
> May be the devil: and the devil hath power
> To assume a pleasing shape; yea, and perhaps
> Out of my weakness and my melancholy,
> As he is very potent with such spirits,
> Abuses me to damn me.[10]

It is wise to remember that Satan rarely wears the same face twice. He is, as Madam Guyon points out, the master of masquerade. The revelations of things to come are also very dangerous. The Devil can counterfeit them, as he did formerly in the heathen temples, where he uttered oracles. Frequently they raise false ideas, vain hopes, and frivolous expectations. They take up the mind with future events, hinder it from dying to self, and prevent it from following Jesus Christ in His poverty, abnegation, and death.

Widely different is the revelation of Jesus Christ, made to the soul when the eternal Word is communicated (Gal. 1:16). It makes us new creatures, created anew in him. This revelation is what the Devil cannot counterfeit. From hence proceeds the only safe transport of ecstasy, which is operated by naked faith alone, and dying even to the gifts of God. As long as the soul continues resting in gifts, it does not fully renounce itself. Never passing into God the soul loses the real enjoyment of the Giver, by attachments to the gifts. This is truly an unutterable loss.[11]

I have a young friend who counsels, "The only thing Satan

cannot emulate is the presence of God." Our loss will be great as we transfer our affections from God to the source of his abundance.

Years ago I was forced to learn that my financial circumstances were imprisoning me. Christ had delivered me from the near-poverty of my early ministry by furnishing me with some new and more-than-adequate sources of income. But his gifts lured me away from my former, utter dependency on him. I came to cherish too much what he had given me. I had a car, a home, a bank account. These gifts, though not those of a millionaire, still lured me to esteem them more than I honored the Giver. After all, what car is ever shiny enough that we do not desire a later model? What bank account ever had enough money in it that we wanted no more? Greed is always hungry, ever yearning, and it always rises up to challenge grace in our lives. I struggle yet with the goodness of God, but to love his gifts more than himself chains me to defeat and leaves me subject to old fears.

The Third Defense: Submission in the Midst of Satan's Hostility

Fear in general, and Satan in particular, raises our hackles and dumps adrenalin into our systems. It is not in us to answer Satan's hostility with submission. Everything in us rises against Satan's aggression. Madame Guyon tells of her ongoing struggle with her husband's abusive threats.

She wrote of the end of one of his tirades:

> I saw my husband coming like a lion, he was never in such a rage as this. I thought he was going to strike me; I awaited the blow with tranquillity; he threatened with his up-lifted crutch; I thought he was going to knock me down. Holding myself closely united to God, I beheld it without pain. He did not strike me for he had presence of mind enough to see what indignity it would be. In his rage he threw it at me. It fell near me, but it did not touch me. He then discharged himself in language as if I had been a street beggar, or the

most infamous of creatures. I kept profound silence, being recollected in the Lord.[12]

Our surrender gives God the chance to fight for us. Are we not forever touched by our Lord's submission to his cross? "As a sheep before its shearers is silent, / so He opened not His mouth" (Isa. 53:7). Moses tells Israel, when she is intimidated by the army of Egypt, "Do not be afraid. Stand still, and see the salvation of the LORD. . . . The LORD will fight for you, and you shall hold your peace" (Ex. 14:13–14).

The preeminence of Christ's silence is the strong word of our redemption. While demonic kingdoms raged against him, he greeted them with the weapon of submission and won. But what can Madame Guyon mean when she says she kept a profound silence . . . a deep silence? I believe Madam Guyon is speaking of the silence of attachment. Submission in the onslaught takes our indefensible weaknesses and hands them into the grasp of God. "Keep quiet and let me handle this, son," my mother used to say to me when I was in trouble. She did this not to downplay my importance in a crisis but to assure me of the best outcome. Thus, I could win by submitting and never by insisting I could handle it.

Consider these passages that bid us be silent so that God can do the talking: "Be still, and know that I am God" (Ps. 46:10) really says, "Submit that I may empower your life and triumph over your circumstances!"

"The LORD is in His holy temple. / Let all the earth keep silence before Him" (Hab. 2:20) is an invitation to wait in quietness as the power issues from Zion. Furthermore, it invites us to get in a position to watch God, shut down our own nervous systems, and allow him to act. At the end of our helplessness, it is God who defends us, and the salvation is from God.

The same may be said of that wonderful passage where Jesus is about to empower his church. "Stay in the city until you have been clothed with power from on high," said Jesus (Luke 24:49 NIV).

Do all these passages suggest that submissive waiting is inactivity? Hardly! The most severe discipline is to make ourselves stand when every fiber of our do-it-yourself energy is ordering us to action. Our condescension comes as hard as a semi slowing down to let a motorcycle pass. Only a teaspoon of gasoline is required for the tiny, flighty cycle. But the diesel must cease to flow, and the pistons cease to pound for the truck to submit.

Years ago a friend of mine asked me to help her have her husband committed to a detoxification center for treatment. I agreed to help her. Her husband, who was also my friend, had refused to go to the center voluntarily. He was customarily inebriated, or, as he put it, "skunk-drunk!" When I came in to assist his wife with his involuntary hospitalization, he greeted me with a smile. But when he found I had come to help his wife get him into a "paddy wagon," he became enraged. He drew back his fist and punched me solidly in the jaw. He was surprisingly strong for a drunk! I reeled backward and fell to the floor. I was briefly "down for the count."

"Tommy," said his wife, "why did you do that? You love Calvin. He's your friend."

In the fog and delirium of that punch, I was glad I heard her remind him.

I liked myself later for not punching back. Maybe I was obeying God. Maybe I just don't like "fisticuffs." Maybe I was afraid I would be beaten to a pulp. But for whatever reason, my submission brought a sense of shame to my friend. He apologized to me. After that, he volunteered to go peaceably to the hospital. The power of submission served our friendship and until his death we remained very close. Satan never gains advantage when we are submissive. There is an old Japanese proverb which says, "He who smiles rather than rages is always the stronger."

The Fourth Defense: Celebrating
Our Crosses of Mortification

Satan may be the source of our pain and ultimately our death. Still, we deal with him as we accept our cross as a means of dying to self. Dying to self has been called mortification by many of the saints. Dying to self has about it a renunciation of self-interest.

This self-denial sets us free of the necessity of having always to celebrate our successes.

In the New Testament dying is presented as the end to ambition. Dead people have lost, along with pulse and respiration, all selfishness. Paul said, "I die daily" (1 Cor. 15:31). By this he meant he was daily clearing egotistic living from his life. Jesus said, "Take up [your] cross daily" (Luke 9:23), signifying that Christians are to "mortify," that is, to put to death their need to achieve some good for their own sake.

Stories of the martyrs tell us that they could never be deprived of their lives because they had already given them away. Jesus made it clear that, in the cross, his first prerogative was to please his Father. Of his life he said, "No one takes it from Me, but I lay it down" (John 10:18). In essence he mortified every hint of his own ambition. Then, stripped of all personal agenda, he could live totally in the interest of his Father. See him in his wilderness temptation (Luke 4). Three times he mortified his own desires to slay every possibility of being a selfish servant. Six weeks without food, he mortified his hunger (vv. 3–4). Wanting to build a mighty kingdom, he mortified his desire to rule all the kingdoms of the world in his own name (vv. 6–8). Waiting to display the power of God, he mortified his own need to reign, and ordered Satan "behind him" (v. 8).

In Gethsemane, at thirty-three years of age, he didn't want to die, but even so he mortified his desire to live and received the cup of passion (Matt. 26:39). In this mortification, Christ not only pleased the Father, he dealt directly with Satan. Satan is the fallen saint of unholy self-interest. We sin when we try to picnic in Gethsemane. Every time we refuse the cup of our own crucifixion, we serve the enemy of him whom we say we love. When we seek to blame our sickness on God, we do not serve our loving Father. Pain may draw us to God but it never comes from God. Crosses draw us to him and bind us to Christ in a fellowship of suffering (Phil. 3:10). At Calvary, he mortified his own desire to live, and suffering was the glory of his obedience.

Viktor Frankl pointed out that strong trials demonstrate strong faith:

> To paraphrase what LaRochefoucauld once remarked with regard to love, one might say that just as the small fire is extinguished by the storm whereas a large fire is enhanced by it—likewise a weak faith is weakened by predicaments and catastrophes whereas a strong faith is strengthened by them.[13]

Viktor Frankl understood. No wonder Madame Guyon would say, even of her sickness, that it was a blow to the dark lord.

> To resume my history, the smallpox had so much hurt one of my eyes, that it was feared I would lose it. The gland at the corner of my eye was injured. An imposthume arose from time to time between the nose and the eye, which gave me great pain till it was lanced. It swelled all my head to that degree that I could not bear even a pillow. The least noise was agony to me, though sometimes they made a great commotion in my chamber. Yet this was a precious time to me, for two reasons. First, because I was left in bed alone, where I had a sweet retreat without interruption; the other, because it answered the desire I had for suffering—which desire was so great, that all the austerities of the body would have been but as a drop of water to quench so great a fire. Indeed the severities and rigor, which I then exercised were extreme, but they did not appease this appetite for the cross. It is Thou alone, O Crucified Saviour, who cans't make the cross truly effectual for the death of self. Let others bless themselves in their ease or gaiety, grandeur or pleasures, poor temporary heavens; for me, my desires were all turned another way, even to the silent path of suffering for Christ, and to be united to Him, through the mortification of all that was of nature in me, that my senses, appetites and will, being dead to these, might wholly live in Him.[14]

Suffering brings us to an awareness of spiritual status. It is heavy but it produces a sensitive life. Suffering is the last, best instructor of things eternal. Again it is Frankl who said:

> When a man finds that it is his destiny to suffer, he will have to accept his suffering as his task; his single and unique task. He will have to acknowledge the fact that even in suffering he is unique and alone in the universe. No one can relieve him of his suffering or suffer in his place. His unique opportunity lies in the way in which he bears his burden.[15]

The suffering of the Christian has special meaning. For the Christian it is a "de-clutterer" of the throne room of the heart. It mortifies all pointless appetites. It teaches us that materialism is a flabby pursuit, offering nothing in our time of need. Mortification fastens the heart to things eternal. Still, mortification is so against our nature that few can manage it. It is an ability to celebrate even pain if it will draw us to that attachment which breaks Satan's control of our lives.

The Fifth Defense: Kneeling on Serpents

This fifth defense is a symbolic step. Whether or not Madame Guyon meant to suggest it as a symbol of the Christian's authority is only a guess. Yet in her devotional life comes that strong suggestion that the Christian is to have a real authority over Satan, and this authority is to proceed from our prayer life, our sense of mortification, and above all our union with Christ, which she suggests as our sixth defense.

The Serpent from Eden has been a symbol of personal evil. In the Old Testament the evil one is called Satan, the anti-god angel. In Isaiah 14:12 and in Revelation 12:12, he is pictured as that defeated angel come down to earth, furious in his descent because he knows his time is short.

While the serpent is a symbol of Satan, Satan is no symbol. Satan is real and not only set against God but set against all that

God loves. But Christianity knows no dualism. Satan's evil reality does not suggest that he is a power equal and opposite to God. Satan has great power only in reference to our weak and needy lives. He has no power in reference to God. He has already been defeated by God, judged by God, and cast out of heaven.

There are three ways we triumph over Satan. One is by a direct rebuke of Satan in the powerful name of Christ. In the epigraph at the beginning of this chapter, Madame Guyon wrote of hearing "frightful noises in her chamber" and that "her bed often shook for a quarter of an hour." She goes on to say:

> I made use of my little light to look all over the room and at the sashes, at the very time the noise was strongest. As he saw that I was afraid of nothing, he left off all of a sudden, and attacked me no more in person.[16]

Madame Guyon found there was one more subtle way of defeating the devil. She could worship the holy God in his presence. Once again we find that Satan is driven out not by addressing him directly, but by adoring God in his presence.

The psychologist Dysart says in Peter Shaffer's *Equus:* "Can you think of anything worse one can do to anybody than take away their worship?"[17]

Madame Guyon's metaphor of kneeling on serpents illustrates the second way. We do not need to rebuke the serpent if we kneel on him in worship. As we have already said, Satan fears our prayers. When he becomes our prayer cushion, he is defeated most often without even focusing on our warfare. Our worship authority over Satan always rather surprises us.

It also surprised the disciples who went out on a preaching–healing tour and came back excited over all that they had accomplished in the name of Christ:

> Then the seventy returned with joy, saying, "Lord, even the demons are subject to us in Your name."

And He said to them, "I saw Satan fall like lightning from heaven. Behold, I give you the authority to trample on serpents and scorpions, and over all the power of the enemy, and nothing shall by any means hurt you. Nevertheless, do not rejoice in this, that the spirits are subject to you; but rather rejoice because your names are written in heaven."

(Luke 10:17–20)

Only a few times in our lives will we know this sort of direct rebuke the disciples experienced. However, from time to time, we will know the courage of bending our vulnerable knees in the reptile pit. When we worship we set loose the power of Christ. Soon our worship focus allows no place for evil. Thus, we conquer not by focusing on the foe before us but on the power behind us. With such worship serpents are disenvenomed by the power of love.

So let us hear Madam Guyon's symbol and believe:

When I was at this country house, which was only a little place of retreat before the chapel was built, I retired for prayer to woods and caverns. How many times, here, has God preserved me from dangerous and venomous beasts! Sometimes, unawares, I kneeled upon serpents, which were there in great plenty; they fled away without doing me any harm. Once I happened to be alone in a little wood wherein was a mad bull; but he betook himself to flight. If I could recount all the providences of God in my favor, it would appear wonderful. They were indeed so frequent and continual, that I could not but be astonished at them. God everlastingly gives to such as have nothing to repay Him.[18]

The gift is complete. Triumph is a matter of focus. To focus on what makes us afraid divides our courage and weakens us. But to focus on what makes us strong allows our soul a furious offense.

The third way of "kneeling on serpents" relates to the power of the Word of God. There is a subtle, exorcising power in spoken

Scripture. Though we have observed Jesus rebuking Satan in the wilderness, the point bears repeating here. In the mere quoting of Scripture—three short verses from Deuteronomy—Satan is driven from him: "Man shall not live by bread alone" (8:3); "You shall not tempt the LORD your God" (6:16); "You shall fear the LORD your God" (v. 13). Small wonder John Calvin said, "The Bible is the scepter by which the heavenly King rules his church."[19]

I once felt the oppression of evil spirits while I was speaking to a small college in the eastern part of the United States. I was staying in the campus guest house, a late-nineteenth-century three-story house that looked like a house in Amityville. There was an all-night thunderstorm during my stay on the campus. During that storm I felt the presence of the evil one. I quoted Scripture aloud into that horrible atmosphere of satanic oppression and felt the tension of spiritual warfare begin to ease. As Jesus proved, Scripture has its effect. Satan left my quarters and the resulting peace made it seem, even in my case, that angels had come to minister to me (Matt. 4:11). It was even as Madam Guyon testified, "Sometimes, unawares, I kneeled upon serpents. . . . If I could recount all the providences of God in my favor, it would appear wonderful."[20]

The Sixth Defense: Union with Christ

It is this final defense that wins what we might otherwise lose. Satan can have no lasting work when we are in union with Christ. There may be times when the whole world turns against us, but the power of our union with Christ is ultimately effective against the tempter's every onslaught. How powerfully this union serves us. St. Ignatius wrote of its power:

> . . . we are offered a support, namely, the example of Jesus Christ, than whom there is no guide more skilled, no way more secure, no companion more faithful, no helper more ready or more powerful to render us assistance. For this reason his virtues and the principal mysteries of his life are proposed to us as the subject of our meditation.[21]

Why is there power in this meditation? Because it brings us into union with Christ: There, in union with him, our weakness dissolves in his strength. Madam Guyon describes her trial in this way:

> A poor girl of very great simplicity, who earned her livelihood by her labor, and was inwardly favored of the Lord, came all sorrowful to me, and said, "Oh my mother, what strange things have I seen!" . . . "I have seen you like a lamb in the midst of a vast troop of furious wolves. I have seen a frightful multitude of people of all ranks and robes, of all ages, sexes and conditions, priests, friars, married men, maids and wives, with pikes, halberds and drawn swords, all eager for your instant destruction." Some days after, those, who through envy were raising private batteries against me, broke forth. Libels began to spread. Envious people wrote against me, without knowing me. They said that I was a sorceress, that it was by a magic power I attracted souls, that everything in me was diabolical; that if I did charities, it was because I coined, and put off false money, with many other gross accusations, equally false, groundless and absurd. As the tempest increased every day, some of my friends advised me to withdraw, but before I mention my leaving Grenoble, I must say something farther of my state while here. It seemed to me that all our Lord made me do for souls, would be in union with Jesus Christ. In this divine union my words, had wonderful effect, even the formation of Jesus Christ in the souls of others.[22]

Of course, the bouts with fear I knew in my childhood were defeated in this same way. Then I had not the learning or understanding to speak in terms of my "union with Christ." But even as a child I quickly learned there was but one way out of fear: it was the speaking of his name above my fears. As adults we tend to see the events of our childhood as only melodrama. How wrong this is! Out of our childhood struggles and searches, God equips us to bear our struggles with a sense of overcoming.

Nor is it fair to call our childhood struggles "little trials" and those of our adult years "major trials." In many ways our fears are darker as children than they will ever be again. But children hold Christ to be more powerful over their fear than they will ever see him as adults. It is easy for me to see that when Christ blessed the children, he understood the fullest nature of their trust and doubt. Christ taught that God counts as his best friends those who needed his forgiveness. Children feel this need for his forgiveness and are thrilled by his love for them (Luke 7:47). Satan also knows that his most formidable foes have two qualities, complete trust and holy innocence. Innocence and trust are the virtues of childhood. These qualities combined shake hell. I suspect that the victories Christ gives children will never again come to us with such force during our adult years. And the tempter can stand against neither their trust nor the force of their innocence. So unless we become as little children, we cannot see the kingdom (Matt. 18:3). Unless we trust as little children, we cannot kneel on serpents. In every area of dealing with life or fear, "a little child shall lead [us]" (Isa. 11:6).

FINDING
PURPOSE
IN LIFE

Brother
Lawrence

*I cannot understand how religious people are
able to live satisfied without the practice of the
presence of God. For myself, so far as I am able, I keep
apart, holding Him in my soul, and while I am so with
Him I fear nothing. But the least turning-away is a hell.
This exercise does not wear out the body, and it is well
from time to time, and even often, to deny ourselves
harmless and permissible relaxations. For when a soul
wants to be devoted entirely to Him, God will not suffer it
to have any other delights. That is only what we should
reasonably expect.*

*I do not mean that it is necessary to restrain oneself
immoderately. No. We must serve God in a holy freedom,
going about our business carefully, but without distress or
anxiety, recalling the mind to God quietly and calmly
whenever we find it wandering.*

*It is necessary, however, to put our whole trust in God,
laying aside all other interests and even some of those
particular devotions which, though good in themselves, we
sometimes engage in ill-advisedly. They are only means to
an end, and when, by this exercise of the presence of God,
we are with Him who is our end, it is useless to have
recourse to the means. Rather may we continue our
communion of love with Him, rejoicing in His holy
presence: at one time by an act of worship, of praise, of
desire; at another, by an act of resignation, or of
thanksgiving, or by any other means to which we
may be moved.*

—From *The Practice of the Presence of God*

WHAT DO YOU want to be when you grow up?" This is the number-one question of adolescence. The teenage years for me were long seasons of stalking my unfinished self in the hope of bringing my immaturity to some sort of reasonable conclusion. What teenager does not reach toward the future, hungry for any peg to hang the right career on? Even Christians are possessed of the need to know what we shall be and what God has purposed for us.

Preachers always define it classically from the Westminster confession: "The chief duty of man is to glorify God and enjoy him forever." But this kind of "spiritual talk" makes little money for adolescents. In my childhood, boys especially were seen as future breadwinners. It was their responsibility—once they were men—to make money. After they had a job and could support their families, then they could "glorify God and enjoy him forever." In this struggle between my undiscovered secular career and my innate spiritual calling to glorify God, I was utterly miserable.

It occurred to me in my seventeenth year that God might be calling me to preach. This was a signal revelation to me since it seemed that our pastor, during his longer-than-necessary-sermons, over glorified God. In fact, sometimes it seemed that he was going to enjoy God forever all on a single Sunday morning, whether his congregation did or not. Preaching, having degenerated into the emergency state it was in, mandated that I yield to the call. I, therefore, watching sermons die from lack of interest, announced that I was called to preach.

It must have seemed ludicrous to the congregation as I was quiet and withdrawn—an unlikely candidate. Even my sister said, "If God called you to do *anything,* he must have had a wrong number." So it seemed to me. How could it seem otherwise to the church?

Our congregation was responsible for the preaching services out at the county "old folks' home." Shortly after I announced my calling, I was sent out to preach the Sunday afternoon message to "the old folks." Many were blind, many were deaf, and some were nearly both. It seemed a fitting place to try my new calling with no real money on the game: Those who couldn't see would not make me feel uncomfortable by staring, and those who couldn't hear would have no real objection to my lack of content.

Still, the event was more complex than I had imagined. I had three pages of single-spaced typewritten notes which seemed to me (at ten minutes per page) should occupy the space of half an hour. I actually finished the whole sermon in two and a half minutes. I felt very ashamed that in my arrogance I had assumed I could do what my naïveté prohibited. I stammered through the final prayer and sat down. My pastor, who had ridden along with me to this assignment, rose and finished up with a real thirty-minute sermon.

My sister was right. Anyone could see that. I left the county home and abandoned this first fledgling call to preach. In fact, I couldn't bring myself to speak of it for two or three years. But the end of presumption had come. Now I faced the hard questions of who I was and why I was in the world. God, from that moment on, became the quest. He was no luxury to a two-and-a-half-minute sermonizer. He was all necessity. Indeed my chief calling was no longer to preach to the world or control it. It was to survive the world!

But I now bless this first sermon as my first, best instructor on the nature of true spirituality. I had faced my first sermon as a great gift I was going to give God. It was going to be my surprise to him. I would prepare it on my own, deliver it on my own, and when "thousands came out of their sins" and trusted Christ, I would duck my head and humbly say, "To God be the glory." But it was not a sermon for which God wanted the glory.

I couldn't put it all together the day my face flushed with hot embarrassment. Now, I realize that the way I approached and delivered my first sermon was the way "show-biz" Christians would later approach all kinds of ministry. We all want to do something for God and make him a present of what we do. We want to sing like a popular religious artist so we buy their accompaniment tapes and listen to them do it so we can chimpanzee our way through a similar repertoire. Now that evangelicals have taken to clapping, even mediocre tape-trackers can get thunderous applause, after which there is always time to give God the glory.

Brother Lawrence did not have this kind of preaching and singing in mind. He washed dishes; it was enough for him. He did not need to preach like the superstars of his day (and surely there were some). He had no need to travel about doing some medicine show for Jesus. No, his testimony was simple: "We must serve God in a Holy freedom, going about our business carefully, but without stress or anxiety, recalling the mind to God . . . whenever we find it wandering."[1]

The purpose of God for our lives has to do primarily with fellowship, not entertainment. There is only one basis that we may find this fellowship with God and that is with godliness. First Timothy 4:7 begs us to discipline ourselves for godliness. There are many books out now on discipline. Dietrich Bonhoeffer reminds us that salvation without discipline is merely cheap grace. It is a poor attempt to buy the most of God with the least of our yielding. Dallas Willard, in *The Spirit of the Disciplines* says:

> My central claim is that we can become like Christ by doing one thing—by following him in the overall style of life he chose for himself. If we have faith in Christ, we must believe that he knew how to live. We can, through faith and grace, become like Christ by practicing the types of activities he engaged in, by arranging our whole lives around the activities he himself practiced in order to remain constantly at home in the fellowship of his Father.[2]

In *The Practice of the Presence of God,* Brother Lawrence has this glorious order in mind, that we will practice the discipline of relationship. Charles Spurgeon wrote: "I must take care above all that I cultivate communion with Christ for though that can never be the basis of my peace—mark that—yet it will be the channel of it."³ Our relationship with God and our hunger for that relationship is God's agenda. He does not require our amazing talent to be laid on the altar. He requires our lives to be the altar. We are never to be content with merely doing things for God. We are central in his will only as we hunger for more of him. When we crave his presence, our music will transcend accompaniment tapes, and our preaching will throb with otherworldly power. Seek the kingdom, said Jesus (Matt. 6:33). Then we will be able to dispense with every salute to our weak genius.

This book is a look at ten heroes of the faith. None of them were trying to be better preachers, singers, or heroes of the church. John of the Cross expressed Brother Lawrence's hunger for union in these words:

> On a dark night, kindled in love with yearnings—
> Oh, happy dance, I went forth.
> The light guided me more surely than the light
> of noonday.
> To the place where he (well I knew who!) was
> waiting me.⁴

What is the believer's purpose in the world? To know this thirst for God is to rejoice in this joyous oneness. This thirst is the theme of the wayfaring psalmist: "As the deer pants for streams of water, / so my soul pants for you, O God" (Ps. 42:1 NIV).

God's endless search for thirsty lovers, pursuing his purpose, was another of those bad-days/good-days which comprise the best parts of our lives. I was taught to desire this oneness because of that horrible two-and-a-half-minute sermon. Oh, how I praise him for teaching me that, without his presence, that's all I am capable of. I now understand the early doubts of Moses, Gideon, and Isaiah. The Bible is not the tale of strong men who served God. The Bible is the story of God working through anybody who would treasure his presence. The Bible is the tale of those nobodies who practiced the presence of God. There was not room enough in one slender, holy book to measure the agony of the demand of God over the loud objections of fearful weaklings. Is it fair, as men count fairness, to ask a fugitive shepherd like Moses to storm into the court of Pharaoh, emperor of the most powerful nation on earth, and say, "Let my people go!" No wonder Moses said, "I am not eloquent . . . I am slow of speech" (Ex. 4:10). But Moses does deal with the *"angst"* of soul.

There was also Gideon:

> When the angel of the LORD appeared to Gideon, he said, "The LORD is with you, mighty warrior!"
>
> "But, sir," Gideon replied, "if the LORD is with us, why has all this happened to us?" . . .
>
> "Go in the strength you have and save Israel. . . ."
>
> "But, Lord," Gideon asked, "how can I save Israel? My clan is the weakest in Manasseh, and I am the least in my family." (Judg. 6:12–15 NIV)

We would never have heard of Isaiah except that God filled him with his presence. Only with the incoming God did Isaiah become Isaiah. When God called him, he cried, "Woe is me, for I am undone! / Because I am a man of unclean lips, / and I dwell in the midst of a people of unclean lips" (Isa. 6:6). And how will God answer this? "O yeah, stand back and watch what you will do as you treasure my company and practice my presence!"

The favorite of all my biblical non-heroes was Saul of Israel. When Samuel went to anoint him, he was hiding among the baggage (1 Sam. 10:22). Here on the day of his coronation, the thought of such a call made him a fugitive from God. Saul was the patron saint of my youth. In every fearful instance I fled from the God who would use me. I ran from his light into my own self-imprisonment and strangling darkness. Psychological inferiority creates spiritual fugitives. We flee every role in God's cosmic drama because we suspect the quality of our acting is poor.

The despair of our souls quickens the pace of our running from God. We feel that the God who made us doesn't really know us. So when he comes for us, we run. In my heart I understood Francis Thompson's divine bedevilment. I could not preach, but God insisted that I could. He chased me from my warm relationship into every healing, hiding darkness where I fashioned he could never find me.

> I fled Him, down the nights and down the days;
>   I fled Him, down the arches of the years;
> I fled Him, down the labyrinthine ways
>   Of my own mind; and in the midst of tears
> And under running laughter,
> I hid from Him.[5]

Where does one go to hide from this divine pursuer? But even the depths of our self-imprisoning inferiority are not dark enough to hide us from him:

> Whither shall I go from thy spirit? or whither shall I flee from thy presence?
>
> If I ascend up into heaven, thou art there: if I make my bed in hell, behold, thou art there.
>
> If I take the wings of the morning, and dwell in the uttermost parts of the sea;
>
> Even there shall thy hand lead me, and thy right hand shall hold me.
>
> If I say, Surely the darkness shall cover me; even the night shall be light about me.

Yea, the darkness hideth not from thee; but the night
shineth as the day: the darkness and the light are both alike
to thee.   (Ps. 139:7–12 KJV)

No, it cannot be! We are "unhideable." Our despair but hurries
his pursuit. Our feelings of inadequacy will not conceal us. On
he comes and we are dogged by our *relentless, glorious stalker:* He
gives us no peace till we yield our separating fear of him.

At last I did yield! If I felt inferior and far too small to perform
in the arena God had planned, I would simply have to mature.
The size of my assignment required a new commitment to becoming bigger. I knew that like a reptile splitting and shedding old
skins, I would have to grow. If I were too slow for God's marathon, I would have to strip off the weights and the sins that so
easily dragged me down (Heb. 12:1). I would have to occupy
myself with maturity until I was big enough to fit God's plan.
But I knew the course would be a grueling track.

Brother Lawrence hungered to practice the presence of God.
Because we are so afraid of his demands, we are ever running from
God and miserable in our flight. We find no peace in practicing the
absence of God, but at least we bear none of the burdens of
obedience. Yet this notion is blatantly false. We assume that were
we to practice the presence he would lay on us something ugly
and heavy. Why such foolish logic? Hasn't he promised his yoke
would be easy and his burden would be light (Matt. 11:30)?

Why are we content to live without his presence? We are
self-willed in our determination to live apart from God. As we
read in Psalm 139, such running is fruitless and impossible. I could
flee from my call to preach, but it brought me no victory. I had
to learn that when we seek to be free of God our own inadequacies
smother us with loss. Survival created the necessity of faith for
me. If I was to obey God, I would have to face another preaching
attempt. I would have to stand before a crowd and risk "making
a fool" of myself a second time. Mine was a cross of lunacy and
only a driven soul would attempt it. I understood why Paul said,

"The message of the cross is foolishness to those who are perishing" (1 Cor. 1:18 NIV).

I had taken Paul's Scripture a step further. It was not only lunacy to those who were perishing, it was lunacy to myself who was quite saved but felt incompetent to do all that God asked. Still, to find his purpose in my life meant no going back. I was, therefore, trapped. Self-doubt made it impossible to go forward. I begged God. "Is there a plan? How is that plan to be served?" I understood that seeking to please God might be a kind of crucifixion in itself.

It would be some years before I would discover Brother Lawrence's eleventh letter in which he said:

> I do not pray that you may be delivered from your sufferings, but I ask God earnestly to give you strength and patience to bear them so long as He pleases to afflict you. Fortify yourself with Him who fastens you to the cross: He will deliver you in His own time.[6]

Of course, it was so. But the deliverance is scarcely done in the way we thought it would be. *Deliverance* is a word that has a grand ring about it. If we are to be saved, God must come again and again to our cross. He must "unnail" us, bandage our brokenness, end our search, and exalt us. We want God to show everyone who knows us how gallant our faithful suffering is. Had Calvary been ours to manage, we would have been a bit more showy with it. Asking God for ten thousand angels is *always* our answer to our crosses. We have life simply because it was *not* Christ's solution to his cross. My search for my calling was so barren because I misunderstood God's primary purpose for my life. I assumed his primary calling had to do with my vocation. How very wrong I was! God's central purpose for all of us is our fellowship with him. It is always better to live our affair with Christ than to testify about it. No wonder St. Francis said to preach the good news, using words only if necessary.

The way of the cross is indeed a fellowship but it is a royal fellowship of suffering (Phil. 3:10). This rich fellowship precludes the grandiose notions we so often have of ministry. It amazes me what we have done to this word, *ministry*. Consider the term *concert ministry*. Young, up-and-coming, mike-in-hand artists throw back their heads, stick the microphone close to their mouths, and strut about, rendering something "crossly" and "sacrificial" in song. It may be a way of ministry but it is not the grand way. The way of the cross is only for those willing to bend their egos beneath his demand. Self-crucifixion is beyond the stamina of those who strut their way along the dreamy lanes of self-image. Before "Dove" was ever a gospel song award, it was a metaphor of the descent of the Spirit. The Spirit only descends upon those who, empty of self, long to be filled with God. There are many wonderful and committed artists in gospel music. There may also be many who have mistaken Broadway for the Via Dolorosa!

The Way of God is never a "grand way," it is always a "little way." Brother Lawrence championed not the grand way to God but the "little way!" He was born at Herimesnil, Lorraine in 1611 or so. His real name was Nicholas Herman, and under that name he enlisted in the French Army. He was wounded as a foot soldier. He joined a Christian sect known as the Parisian Carmelites and was christened "Lawrence of the Resurrection." He then began washing pots and pans in the monastery kitchen. There he worked for the last thirty years of his life. With his hands oft immersed in dishwater, he learned the discipline of prayer. But the prayer of the "little way" is never grand. Prayer itself is the link between all of life and him who is the life. And the "little way" is the way of those whose career is but an occupation and whose calling is knowing God. This glorious dishwasher would write of life's priorities in February of 1691, near the time of his death:

> We must concentrate on knowing God: the more we know Him the more we want to know Him. And as knowledge is commonly the measure of love, the deeper and wider our knowledge, the greater will be our love. And if our love of God is great, we shall love Him equally in joy or in sorrow.[7]

Frère Laurenz, the Carmelite dishwasher, defines what I pain-stakingly discovered for myself. Challenges that make us ready for the work of God are not plateaus we reach in single leaps. They are rather the steps of our climb toward the blessedness of his approval.

Further, to hear God say, "Well done!" is the terminal trophy of the Christian life. The intermediate necessity is to have him say, "You're doing well." But Christians are so tied to this world they have little interest in the next. Delayed gratification has no part in our discipleship. We want all our godly goodies now. God's final compliment means less than his momentary affirmations. If we are peaceless in our struggle, it may be because we are more interested in hearing God say, "You're doing well" than "Well done." The glory of life in Christ lies not in the quality of our present performance but in his nearness as we move ever more certainly toward his great "Well done!"

The horror of my first preaching experience appeared more terrible than it was. The reason I felt such pain was that I was trying to do something for God rather than merely enjoying my walk with God. Brother Lawrence warns us about losing this priority:

> Indeed, we can give God no more convincing evidence of
> our faithfulness than often to put aside and avoid the
> creature, that we may rejoice for one moment in the
> Creator. I am not proposing to you to give up material
> things entirely; that is impossible. Prudence, the queen of
> virtues, must be your guide. Nevertheless, I maintain that it
> is a common mistake among religious people to neglect this
> periodical recollection in which they may worship God
> inwardly and enjoy for a few moments the peace of His Holy
> Presence. The digression has been long, but no longer than I
> believe the matter to require; let us then return to our subject.[8]

I failed in my sermon that long-ago day, not because I didn't know Christ, but because, for one brief moment, that was not enough for me. Ego is the grand barrier that separates us from him. It gives only small private dreams and ruins our to-getherness with God. *God* is that glorious word that welds our divided souls into a single piece. He sets us free from the slavery of our own centrality. For make no mistake, it is usually our centrality in our own lives that is the reason for our dark times. Christians are not called to be spotlight people. Even theatrically, spotlights are really "spot-darks" whose intense brightness keep us from seeing the audience at all. God, too, disappears when we insist on the spotlight. Then are we truly alone. None are sent away empty from Christ except those who come to him full of themselves. For us to be present at all he must be present with us, and his presence, said Brother Lawrence, is attained by a simple five-fold means.

Five Means of Attaining Purity of Life

The First Means: Purity of Life

The first means of attaining his presence is purity of life.[9] Brother Lawrence did not comment on this step. Perhaps he thought it adequate to mention and move on. *Holiness* is the word that defines purity of heart. It is the first step of coming into his presence. Brother Lawrence is known to have said:

> That in order to give ourselves to God in the measure that
> He wishes of us, we must carefully watch over the impulses
> of our heart, which affect the actions of the soul, as well as

the actions of the body; and that God would give help to this end to those who had a real desire to be united to Him.[10]

Brother Lawrence has an austere word that makes us feel afraid because it is so exalted. Who can be *holy?* Because it is such an otherworldly word, who would want to be? It is a word which exists opposite the word *fun* for most of us.

We know that saints are holy, but saints never seem to have any fun. You rarely see saints at pizza parties. They never go to Disneyland or the beach. They don't play "Trivial Pursuit" because they never do anything trivial. They look condescendingly on weaker brothers and sisters who smoke cigarettes or bite their nails. They survive best atop stony cathedral spires where they just stand high in the cold, pure air. They scald in the summer and freeze in the winter, but then saints are supposed to scald and freeze. They enjoy suffering. After all, they are holy people. But is holiness only for those who hurt or wear haloes? If so, why would Jesus say, "Blessed are the pure in heart, / for they shall see God" (Matt. 5:8)? Or why would the writer of Hebrews say, "Without [holiness], no one will see the Lord" (12:14)? Why would Peter quote, "Be holy, for I am holy" (1 Peter 1:16)?

The word *holy* terrifies suburban Christians. After all, they only come to church to hear a little bit about Jesus and play a lot of softball. Who in their right suburbanite minds wants to talk about holiness? Brother Lawrence and God have asked a hard thing of compromising Christians. Let us remember this: Purity of life is not a striving; it is not something we achieve with years of practice, like a 70 in golf. It is the direct, immediate result of confession. Psalm 51 is the heart-cry of a murderous adulterer, whose plea ends in instant purity of life. If David can be made holy in one instant of brokenness, so indeed may all who call upon our God.

> Purge me with hyssop, and I shall be clean:
> Wash me, and I shall be whiter than snow.

Make me hear joy and gladness,
That the bones You have broken may rejoice.
Hide Your face from my sins,
And blot out all my iniquities.
Create in me a clean heart, O God,
And renew a steadfast spirit within me.

(Ps. 51:7–10)

So let us see Brother Lawrence's first means of attaining God's presence as one which is bound up in his cleansing power and not in our struggling power. We do not attain purity of life. Instead, it is God's gift issuing from our yearning to know him. He gives us this gift not because he is impressed with our effort but because he is impressed with our hunger. Cleansing and purity come not because we crave being clean but because we crave being together with God.

The Second Means: Focusing on Him

The second means of attaining the presence of God is in keeping the soul's gaze on him; we must focus on him without giving way to difficulties or worries.[11] This is such a simple rule of presence. It can be mastered by anyone. The gaze of the believer upon the face of Christ is the door to all good things. Notice that Brother Lawrence is concerned that we gaze fixedly upon God. One learns to ride a bicycle by concentrating on the path and not on the trees that flank the trail with hazards. We learn the sin–free union with God not by concentrating on the sin we wish to avoid but by gazing at the God we hope to serve. This God-gazing is the delight of our momentary communion. It is not rote prayers. It is a kind of customary rapture. It is the communion of Creator and creature. It is the silent rapture of lovers. It is the ecstasy of lovers who have spent themselves in wonder, now lying in silence, staring into the glory of their relationship. They speak nothing aloud, but in their hearts they sing, "This is my beloved! I will not abandon this strong togetherness."

Such spiritual bonding between ourselves and our Lord is a

communion of concord, a gathering of grace, an unspoken soliloquy for two!

> Now it should be observed that this communion with God is
> held in the depths of the soul, at its very center; it is there
> that the soul speaks heart to heart with God.[12]

At the heart of this utter presence is silence. In this silence we come to know that he is God (Ps. 46:10). From his side of silence, God sees us as a loving Father sees his children. From our side of silence, we become aware that his presence is an antidote to poisonous noise: the noise of our raucous self-will, the noise of our ambition, the noise of our hurried world calling loudly, "Insist on your rights or you'll never get them!" Gazing on God is a pursuit of quietness seen through the eyes of the soul.

The Third Means: Lifting the Heart Toward God

Worship finds its center in the turning of the heart toward God.[13] Yet the prophet said, "The heart is deceitful above all things, / and desperately wicked; who can know it?" (Jer. 17:9). Brother Lawrence confesses that turning the heart toward God may be the steepest path of our pilgrimage. The sins hidden in our heart are hidden from all but God and ourselves. And since anything hidden may hold deceit, great hypocrisy may hold place within our secret selves. Brother Lawrence of the Resurrection confesses:

> Take care that you begin your actions, continue them, and
> finish them with an inward lifting of the heart to God . . . as
> its formation is difficult, so will your joy be great when it is
> attained. Is it not right that the heart, which is the seat of
> life, . . . should be the first and last to love and worship
> God?[14]

Once more to us comes David's counsel: "Create in me a clean heart, O God" (Ps. 51:10). The clean heart is made ready to worship and practice the presence of God.

The Fourth Means: Praising Your Way Out of Gloom

The use of short inward prayers that focus the heart is the fourth means.[15]

Every spiritual mentor I have ever known has emphasized the "silencing of the mind." This silence which gains the mind of Christ is imperative (1 Cor. 2:16). Brother Lawrence's therapy for the noisy heart is not a silencing of the mind but a replacing of all our noisy thinking with God-directed conversation.

He wrote out his own prescription for directing these prayers:

> It is helpful for those who undertake this practice to use interiorly short ejaculations, such as: "My God, I am wholly yours"; "O God of love, I love you with all my heart"; "Lord, I make my heart like yours"; or any other words as love may suggest at the moment. But care must be taken that the mind does not wander and return again to the world; keep it turned to God only, so that, controlled and subdued by the will, it cannot but rest in God.[16]

In the darkness of my early years I wondered whether God could make a preacher of one so inept as I. I felt that the use of one so void of talent would challenge his omnipotence. I felt dark of soul. Still, I realized the glory of the practical words of Mary Gardner Brainard:

> So I go on, not knowing,
> I would not, if I might
> I would rather walk in the dark with God
> Than go alone in the light.
> I would rather walk with Him by Faith
> Than walk alone by sight.[17]

My darkness, it seemed, would last forever. It is Satan's ploy to make us believe that our disappointment with ourselves will never find release—that our discouragement is permanent. C. S. Lewis has Screwtape advise Wormwood:

Do not let him suspect the law of undulation. Let him assume that the first ardours of his conversion might have been expected to last, and ought to have lasted, forever, and that his present dryness is an equally permanent condition. Having once got this misconception well fixed in his head, you may then proceed in various ways.[18]

Although I knew of neither Lewis nor *Frère Laurenz* in my early years, I was able to break free of Satan's hold by following their advice. I began to break the dark noise of my negative soul by practicing these short prayer bursts that were positive in nature.

In short, what Brother Lawrence is suggesting is that we praise our way out of gloom. But this must be God-directed praise. So much of our praise exalts God but is not directed to him. Praise which practices the presence of God is not that which lets our world know how much we adore him. The praise of practicing his presence breaks from our lips into the throne room of the heavenlies and lets God, our wonderful Father, know how much we adore him. Praise that only exalts God is remote theology. Our praise should adore God. It should be the language of lovers, separated for the moment, but longing to be in each other's presence.

The Fifth Means: Loving the Creator, Never the Created

It is fine for ordinary readers to love a book. But the wife of the writer must love the author. It is fine for ordinary worldlings to worship the created world, but not for a believer. The believer must love the Creator and not the created.[19] Small wonder that Brother Lawrence wrote:

It is impossible for a soul inordinately fond of earthly things to find complete joy in the presence of God, for to be with the Creator it is necessary wholly to give up whatever is created.[20]

How much these words rebuke me. My depression came precisely because I was so in love with sermonizing. When the sermon failed, of course, I was shattered. Had I loved God as much as I loved sermons, then all sense of failure would have been absent. One does not ordinarily fail at loving God, and God has never failed at loving us.

In the years which have followed my haunting first attempts at preaching, I have learned that the secret of happiness is not related to my self-confidence. I now know I can expect to fail when my divine coins are traded in for pointless currency. To love the things of God rather than God himself is to try and spend the currency of earth in his world where our poor monetary system is so deflated it has no purchasing power.

After thirty years in the kitchen, at eighty years of age, Brother Lawrence established what has been called "the little way." William James has extolled his "little way" in these words:

> As for me, my bed is made: I am against bigness and greatness in all their forms, and with the invisible molecular moral forces that work from individual to individual, stealing in through the crannies of the world like so many soft rootlets, or like the capillary oozing of water, and yet rending the hardest monuments of man's pride, if you give them time.[21]

So it is with the "little way." It is couched in a power that seems to say that we are to despise not the day of small things. "If God is for us, who can be against us?" (Rom. 8:31). With God's presence our enemies are of no consequence. Our desperation has lost its sting. The presence of God triumphs over every instance of darkness. Therefore, we have but one single, momentary duty: we must practice that presence.

HEALING

DEPRESSION

Teresa of Avila

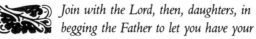 *Join with the Lord, then, daughters, in begging the Father to let you have your Spouse to-day, so that, as long as you live, you may never find yourself in this world without Him. Let it suffice to temper your great joy that He should remain disguised beneath these accidents of bread and wine, which is a real torture to those who have nothing else to love and no other consolation. Entreat Him not to fail you but to prepare you to receive Him worthily.*

As for that other bread, have no anxiety about it if you have truly resigned yourselves to God's will. I mean that at these hours of prayer you are dealing with more important matters and there is time enough for you to labor and earn your daily bread. Try never at any time to let your thoughts dwell on this; work with your body, for it is good for you to try to support yourselves, but let your soul be at rest. Leave anxiety about this to your Spouse, as has been said at length already, and He will always bear it for you. Do not fear that He will fail you if you do not fail to do what you have promised and to resign yourselves to God's will. I assure you, daughters, that, if I myself were to fail in this, because of my wickedness, as I have often done in the past, I would not beg Him to give me that bread, or anything else to eat. Let Him leave me to die of hunger. Of what use is life to me if it leads me daily nearer to eternal death?

If, then, you are really surrendering yourselves to God, as you say, cease to be anxious for yourselves, for He bears your anxiety, and will bear it always. It is as though a servant had gone into service and were anxious to please his master in everything.

—From *The Way of Perfection*

D EPRESSION—WHO CAN escape it? Few of the heroes of the Scriptures did. It caused Naomi to cry from the middle of life's reversals, "Call me Mara, for the Almighty has dealt very bitterly with me" (Ruth 1:20). Hannah cried from the depths of her barrenness, "O LORD of hosts, if You will indeed look on the affliction of Your maidservant and remember me" (1 Sam. 1:11). Job agonizes in his soul, "I loathe my very life; / therefore I will give free rein to my complaint / and speak out in the bitterness of my soul" (Job 10:1 NIV). Spiritual depression is universal; each heart knows its own bitterness, says Proverbs 14:10. David cried often out of great spiritual need, "The troubles of my heart have multiplied; / free me from my anguish (Ps. 25:17 NIV). And although I have examined 2 Corinthians 12 in another chapter, Paul says that the utter pain and need of his "thorn in the flesh" had become the weakness that made him strong (v. 9).

All spiritual pain, depression included, holds this glorious possibility. Depression, like other spiritual needs, becomes the prayer focus that keeps us in touch with God. That touch heals the need from which it cried to be delivered. It is true that contemporary spiritual depression often lacks the grandeur of these biblical afflictions. In fact, much of it may be spiritual at its roots, but it often degenerates to nothing more than poor-little-me-ism. Still, petty or not, few escape it.

Even the giants of the Reformation suffered with depression. Katherine once rebuked Martin Luther for acting as though God was dead. William Cowper, the hymnist who wrote "There Is a Fountain," suffered from such debilitating depression that he was often suicidal. Spurgeon frequently left his pulpit so morose that he would walk directly to his study, desiring to be absolutely alone. The list is endless. Most victims confess, after its passing, that their condition arose out of their own faithlessness. Many, like Paul, would also confess that it was the weakness which, through prayer, made them strong.

Among the Carmelites of Castille in the sixteenth century lived two contemplatives who struggled to be free of crass selfishness and the depression it fostered. John of the Cross was often troubled by what he called the "dark night of the soul." This was no ordinary depression he faced, but a kind of spiritual pain. It was a soul-darkness that came from God as a final step to union with God. It was a depression of spiritual separation, born out of his need to be united with Christ but deepened as he tried to move through it. By contrast, Teresa of Avila does not deal much with gloom in her own life. The attention she gives it, however, may help others deal with it. It certainly suggests that she was no stranger to this common malady.

Dealing with depression is a plight as old as the book of Genesis. Who is to say how Adam felt as he was driven from Eden? What were Lot's feelings as he hurried out of Sodom? When Jacob wrestled with the angel, did he not struggle with his alter ego in the depressive feeling of a lost homeland? Was not his struggle one of an exile caught in the throes of depression? What of Elijah crying out to die and lamenting his lonely defense of righteousness? Is not Psalm 137 the tears of those weeping in exile and hanging their harps on the willows? Jeremiah's entire sojourn of national rebuke is a weeping book. The book of Lamentations is a grieving walk through depression. Hosea laments Israel's loss of soul. Jonah weeps over Nineveh's salvation. The New Testament as well deals with the darkness and loss the disciples felt following the crucifixion of Christ.

But the Bible gives us a purposeful look at "useful" depression. The late Paul Billheimer wrote a most insightful book called *Don't Waste Your Sorrows*. Depression and gloom are not wasted if, in their temporary thrall, our lives are instructed and improved. H. E. H. King wrote:

If He should call thee from thy cross today,
Saying, "It is finished—that hard cross of thine,
From which thou prayest for deliverance."
Thinkest thou not some passion of regret
Would overcome thee? Thou wouldst say, "So
  soon?
Let me go back and suffer yet a while
More patiently—I have not yet praised God."[1]

The key to whether or not we are improved by our depression has to do with whether or not we emerge from our gloom in praise. Long-term depression does not bless God. Nor does it bless us with growth; it rather immobilizes us and leaves us powerless. Then, long-encamped in our souls, it eats away at our dignity and purpose until we are no longer of any use to God or ourselves.

It is here we must distinguish between psychological and spiritual depression. Psychological depression is a form of mental illness; it pervades the mind and must often be treated clinically to find healing. Spiritual depression camps more in the soul than in the mind and always has to do with God and our relationship with him. Generally, spiritual depression focuses on the yearnings of our soul and usually includes feelings of regret that God has failed to meet our needs. From such depression we may dwell overlong on our feelings of disappointment with God. Out of such hostile feelings we even may come at last to an indictment of God.

Needless to say, some of these depressed periods of our lives are evidences of spiritual immaturity. This generally means that we are not being faithful in practicing the spiritual disciplines, of focusing, praying, and personal meditation on the Scriptures. But even when all of these things are in shape, depression will from time to time have its way with most of us. It is not mandatory, just inevitable that it will do so.

One of the best/worst times of my life came in the year 1968, when I was in the second year of a church-planting attempt. I was often so inflated with my own egoistic self-confidence that I felt I could actually do with ease all that God had called me to do. This unbridled confidence would regularly "crash and burn" and send me reeling into long bouts of spiritual depression. These sieges came when I would try to hurry along the growth of the church I was trying to plant. When no one came to church and the attendance was low, I would often look at the big churches around me and compare myself with highly "successful" pastors. Discouragement would set in and then dissolve in depression. There was an odd pattern in my suffrage. I moved between triumphalism and "making God pay." Making God pay is often found in Jeremiah, who indicts God at Benjamin Gate, "O Lord, you deceived me. . . . / I am ridiculed all day long; everyone mocks me (Jer. 20:7 NIV). Jeremiah seems to be saying, "I'm in the pits, God, and it's all your fault!" He was "making God pay."

From my own past struggles I can see that my attempts to "make God pay" had a kind of pattern to them. First, I scolded God for not loving me; next I accused God of deserting me. Then I threatened God with the abandonment of the faith. Finally, by times, I would doubt the existence of God. In this cyclical, predictable scheme, I always moved from spiritual temper-tantrums to the status of a weeping vegetable. The gloom of depression would continue to humble me till I openly acknowledged my need of him. It was usually not long before I, once again, felt my self-confidence surging. In such bilious pride I was once again set up for the depressive cycle I have described.

Teresa of Avila described my situation perfectly when she wrote:

> The devil has yet another temptation, which is to make us appear very poor in spirit: we are in the habit of saying that we want nothing and care nothing about anything: but as soon as the chance comes of our being given something, even though we do not in the least need it, all our poverty of spirit disappears. . . .

But I advise you once more, even if you think you possess it, to suspect that you may be mistaken; for the person who is truly humble is always doubtful about his own virtues.[2]

The only time we can win over spiritual depression is when we are humble. Humility before Christ sets us up to walk in joy. Pride sets us up for defeat and depression. Teresa gives us valuable insights into conquering such gloom. I want to categorize her thoughts under five headings. Consider these five windows of light that dispel our depressive darkness.

Five Windows of Light

The First Window: Defeating the Devil

Among ancient writers, Teresa of Avila seems to take the devil far more seriously than most. Rightly so! For, in one way or another, the gloom that often settles in our souls derives from the prince of gloom. How slow I have been to realize this in my life. So often, when taken with periods of darkness, I seldom remember that Satan, the lord of darkness, is its most probable source. I tend to say, "If only this or that had happened, then I would not have experienced this darkness." In other words, I saw my spiritual status to be the result of my circumstances. How very false! Our darkness is not so much circumstantial as it is personal. It is due to the person of Satan more principally than to the events of our lives.

Treating depression as though it is circumstantial is truly a result of playing "If-only-this-then-that." *If only* I had not committed this blunder, *then* I would not feel so bad. *If only* I had not behaved so selfishly, *then* my friends would not have deserted me. *If only* I had worked harder, *then* my boss would not have fired me. We play this foolish game in an attempt to arrive at a reason as to why we are suffering from depression. The little game of "If-only-this-then-that" always uses our negativity to reinforce our inferiority. Our somber mood leaves us blaming only ourselves for our depression, and we cry, *"Mea Culpa!"* At such junctures we ought to cry, "Get behind Me, Satan!" (Matt. 16:23).

Satan and God are pictured in two different ways in Scripture. God is called the Creator. Satan is called the destroyer. Satan is out to destroy all that God has made to be beautiful and whole. Likewise, Satan is out to destroy the joy that God intends to be customary in our lives. When Jesus teaches us in the Lord's Prayer, "Deliver us from the evil one" (Matt. 6.13), he reminds us that Apollyon, the destroyer, is the true source of all gloom.

Defeating Satan by Praising the Achievements of Others. Teresa of Avila realized that joy is also the creation of God, and that gloom and depression are the ploys of the destroyer to end the glorious possession of joy in our lives. She suggests that there are four ways we may defeat the destroyer before he is able to cause us depression. The first is by learning to praise the achievements of others rather than feeling bad that someone may have "outsucceeded" us. How infernal is our striving after someone else's reputation! How often our inability to celebrate other's successes plunges us into gloom! Teresa writes for us the easy and obvious answer:

> Therefore, sisters, when you see someone to whom the Lord is granting these favors, praise Him fervently, yet do not imagine that she is safe, but aid her with more prayer, for no one can be safe in this life amid the engulfing dangers of this stormy sea.[3]

The sage has so often reminded us that it is easier to weep with those who weep than to rejoice with those who rejoice. But the act of envy keeps us from feeling good about ourselves and our own smaller accomplishments; thus, depression sets in as Satan gains a foothold in our lives.

Predicting Satan's Coming Allows Us to Win Over Depression. Satan may be powerful enough to defeat us, but his coming to us is predictable. We not only know when he is coming, we can guess his tactics. This is nearly always because we have met him before on this same ground.

I have a friend whose life is always being defeated by lust. It is not as though his condition is foreign to any of us; it is just that in his case, he always seems to be drawn into an affair. My number-one question to him is always, "Why?" His affairs follow the same predictable pattern of flirtation, license, and indulgence. He can clearly see Satan moving him toward defeat, and yet he has never developed a strategy for thwarting the enemy. My friend has now moved through a series of marriages because each of his successive mates has at length grown weary of his unbreakable pattern of flirtation and fall.

We ought to be able to see Satan coming and ready ourselves for the onslaught. His coming is obvious. Peter said, "Be self-controlled and alert. Your enemy the devil prowls around like a roaring lion looking for someone to devour. Resist him, standing firm in the faith" (1 Peter 5:8–9 NIV). Teresa warns us that Satan's ever-predictable demeanor should make it easy to destroy his effectiveness before we yield to temptation:

> For it is a characteristic of the true servant of God, to whom His Majesty has given light to follow the true path, that, when beset by these fears, his desire not to stop only increases. He sees clearly whence the devil's blows are coming, but he parries each blow and breaks his adversary's head. The anger which this arouses in the devil is greater than all the satisfaction which he receives from the pleasures

given him by others. When, in troublous times, he has sown his tares, and seems to be leading men everywhere in his train, half-blinded, and [deceiving them into] believing themselves to be zealous for the right, God raises up someone to open their eyes and bid them look at the fog with which the devil has obscured their path.[4]

We are in a sense naïve and childlike when it comes to dealing with Satan.

When my son was four years old, he had a terrible time defending himself against an aggressive three-year-old girl who lived across the street. She would cross the street like a twenty-five-pound marine sergeant on bivouac. She seemed to have no other purpose or calling from God than to stalk other tots. Like "a roaring lion" (to use Peter's image), she attempted to attack and destroy less-aggressive children on the block. She was as fierce as Helga. She was also quite predictable. She would always accost our son in the play pool and take off his bathing trunks in an unseemly discreditation of his manhood that I don't presume to understand. Then she would belt him with her rock-hard little fists. She, at last, left him crying in his wading pool and, happy as Beelzebub, went home.

I would always ask Tim why, when he could clearly see her approaching, did he not simply come in the house. He had no answer. Time and time again, his encounter ended the same way. Finally, I said to him, "Since you refuse to avoid her, I will not have you succumb to her aggression one more time. If she sends you into the house crying, I will spank you as well." This advice probably would not have been sanctioned by the saintly Teresa, but it seemed to work. When the swaggering, militant Helga crossed the street and began to take off his bathing suit, he belted her. Even as she toppled backwards into the wading pool, it was clear that she would not bother him again. She had been countered. She had met her match. I am not necessarily proud of the way Tim solved the situation, but his endless cycle of defeat was over at last.

This kind of deterrence of satanic aggression is clearly what Teresa of Avila has in mind. We are not too smart if we consistently allow Satan to plunge us into a state of spiritual depression. We know his demeanor. He will always leave us crying and defeated—unless we remember that in Christ we have the power to defeat him. He will quickly flee when we stand up to his aggression.

We have already seen how in Luke 10:17 the disciples came back from their preaching tour where Jesus had sent them. They were utterly amazed that they had the power within themselves to rebuke evil spirits. Teresa would call to our minds that we have an authority to rebuke depression before it gains a foothold in our lives. We are foolish not to stand up to Satan in a name greater than our own. With such a deliberate and proven joy, we can gain access to depression-free living.

Defeating Depression by Controlling the Lure of Materialism. Satan's task as the destroyer is to ruin us by causing us to treasure what is worthless. I know of no greater foothold that Satan gains in each of our lives than to convince us that Christ is unnecessary to our happiness. Satan always comes to us, as he did to Jesus in the wilderness, with a whole set of indecent proposals (Matt. 4:1–11). The second and third of Satan's proposals to Jesus had to do with fame and power. The first had to do with the material realm. Jesus is tempted to have "free bread!" For most of the world, daily bread and a bank account are the same thing. We most treasure material things when our appetite is most demanding. But most of us want our Christian friends to believe we are free of materialism. It is, after all, seen as godly to be "detached" from bread. We all want saintly reputations.

How dishonest this snare is. Most often such reputations bind us to ego rather than set us free from it. The church I began was a rather spartan effort to undertake. We had some courage but very little money. We paid, to some degree, the price of sacrifice. There were no financial guarantees. Only as the congregation grew was it able to pay us a better wage. The "bread" and the greater financial benefits was ours.

As the church became larger, however, we began to seek "staff"—other ministers who would help us to continue the work of growing a congregation. We probed seminary placement files and interviewed successive candidates for the new positions. I would often find myself irritated. Those we interviewed made unabashed, "up-front" demands for these fringe benefits it had taken us years to achieve. I never spoke these animosities out loud, but I brooded over them. I resented those who came later. They had almost no concept of what it was like to start a church without any financial guarantees. They were "pushy" in getting what they had coming to them. Then I began to see that in exulting over my own material sacrifices I was, in most cases, far more concerned about "bread" than they were. Materialistic faith may give to Christ, but it rarely gives without gloating.

Teresa warned her nuns that the snare of bread and appetite is grave. In this the poor may be more guilty than the wealthy. Owning something is less consuming than desiring to own it:

> It seems very wrong, my daughters, that great houses should be built with the money of the poor; may God forbid that this should be done; let our houses be small and poor in every way. Let us to some extent resemble our King, Who had no house save the porch in Bethlehem where He was born and the Cross on which he died.[5]

Christ rejected the bread of Lucifer. It was not the bread that he rejected so much as self-gratification. If he makes bread out of one stone, he may create wine from the next and so on, till his self-denial is literally swallowed up in gluttony. Christ freed himself from this material bondage to be the role model for our own self-denial. Materialism does not always consist in what we have, but in what we hunger for. It is not our concern about bread but our temptation to horde it that sins so against our Lord's wilderness example. My staff interviewees gave offense not because they wanted bread, but because they wanted the God of good deals to give them more than bread. They wanted enough to eliminate their need to trust.

Defeating Satan by Not Playing for Sympathy. But most of our depression is not related to material things. We've plenty of bread, but we still feel sorry for ourselves. This self-pity springs from our collapsing pride and subsequent disappointment. But we are unhappy complaining alone. In our misery we must have company. We complain loudly to our friends and thus ensnare others in our sin. We are like a man with a toothache who embellishes his moans and holds his poor jaw. He doesn't do this to heal his toothache. He does it to make sure that he has participants in his anguish.

Poor-little-me-ism makes our depression intrusive into other's lives and demands their focus. Satan is defeated by the believer who gives *to* all and requires nothing *of* others. Teresa warned her comrades of the serious nature of including others in their own private sins of self-interest:

> This human nature of ours is so wretchedly weak that, even while we are telling ourselves that there is nothing for us to make a fuss about, we imagine we are doing something virtuous, and begin to feel sorry for ourselves, particularly when we see that other people are sorry for us too. In this way the soul begins to lose the occasions of merit which it had gained; it becomes weaker; and thus a door is opened to the devil by which he can enter on some other occasion with a temptation worse than the last.[6]

The issue of our sin lies not in what we may be making a fuss about. Rather, it lies in what we see as a legitimate cause of our focus. Satan gains a foothold in our lives. He causes us to stroke our petty pains. Mother Teresa of Calcutta, our own contemporary, forbids her nuns to pray for their own needs, however major. If they are to have release from any area of pain, others must carry their names to the Father. If they do not, there will come no release. Such "other-centered" praying forbids the devil entrance into our egoistic, self-concern.

All of this says that depression springs from self and that we ourselves are the source of such ungodly concern. Teresa reminds us that depression is most often not something that thrusts itself upon us, but something that we invite in. We do this by giving Satan room in our lives through something as simple as self-pity.

The Second Window: A "Crossly" View of Our Suffering

We protestants and evangelicals have perhaps never quite focused on the dying sacrifice of Christ as we should. We are so prone to celebrate his Resurrection that we fail to see the glory of all that his dying provides. We are prone to see the Catholic mass as a morbid focus on the dying Christ. Still, every mass for Catholics has been a way of remembering the Cross and how much their redemption cost. The question we shall have to decide is, Is their focus an exercise in liberty or morbidity? Does it breed or annihilate spiritual depression? Teresa of Avila was convinced that our focus on the redeeming work of Christ saves us from eternal hell. But she believed it also saves us from the hell of spiritual depression:

> Was it not enough, Eternal Father, that while He lived He had no place to lay His head and had always to endure so many trials? Must they now deprive Him of the places to which He can invite His friends, seeing how weak we are and knowing that those who have to labour need such food to sustain them? Had He not already more than sufficiently paid for the sin of Adam? Has this most loving Lamb to pay once more whenever we relapse into sin?[7]

Teresa calls us to remember that our depressive states may only be seen as trivial suffering when we examine legitimate suffering. Elie Wiesel tells about a bystander forced to watch two children executed by Nazis. There is a heaviness that weighs down upon the crowd as they behold the horror. A voice erupts from the crowd, "Where is God in this picture?" The question is meant to imply that God is often absent in human need. "He's on the gallows!" comes the ready answer. How true! We cannot hope to walk meaningfully through our poor issues of depression until we remember that Jesus went through it all first. "We do not have a High Priest who cannot sympathize with our weaknesses, but was in all points tempted as we are, yet without sin" (Heb. 4:15).

How well the apostle testifies of Christ:

> No temptation has overtaken you except such as is common to man; but God is faithful, who will not allow you to be tempted beyond what you are able, but with the temptation will also make the way of escape, that you may be able to bear it. (1 Cor. 10:13)

Christ indeed is the *Archegos,* Greek for *pioneer* or *First-goer* (Heb. 12:2). We can know no suffering on our own that is not bound up in his passion. This is the altogether glorious conquering work of Jesus. His pain to save is the theme of his dying, but his victory over all depression is also a theme of his dying.

This *Archegos Kristos* went through everything—every shade of depression and suffering—while our whole futures were still hidden in eternity past. How powerful to know that the despair of Gethesemane paved our way to victory over our emotional skirmishes. There are those who see only Jesus' humanity to the exclusion of his all-conquering Godhood. He doesn't heal our depression because he was only a hurting human being. He heals us because of his divine power and Godhead (Col. 2:9–10).

I salute only as falseness the song of Mary Magdalene in *Jesus Christ, Superstar.* She counsels her "poor little Jesus" "not to be worried or harried, or sleepless because of [his] rejection." How false it is to see Christ trapped by his neuroses in Gethsemane. To use Moltmais' term, he is the crucified God, not a poor trapped man. He is the *Archegos Kristos,* the *First-goer.* At the cross, he defeats all spiritual depression for all time.

I have a wonderful black friend. When the Los Angeles ghettos were burning in race riots, he taught me the powerful lesson of using Christ's cross to defeat my own insults and depression. It was during that racially tense period that he was out jogging through a largely white, suburban neighborhood. He is a fine physical specimen and would be quite able to handle himself in any direct confrontation. But on this occasion, a carload of angry young whites drove by, rolled down their windows as they passed him, and spit directly into his face. Then they made obscene gestures, called him degrading names, and sped away. A bearded man, my friend instantly felt the stigma and shame of having someone else's saliva drying in his hair and on his face.

He was justifiably angry. "If I could have caught them," he said, "I would have torn the bumper off their car and beaten them severely!" Lucky for them, it was not to be. But as he jogged on and reflected on his degradation, the thought suddenly occurred to him that he was not the first person ever to have someone else's spit drying in his beard. He turned his heart to the cross, and as he mentally fashioned this imaginary Mass, he saw Jesus dying. He realized that here, as in every depressive, dehumanizing aspect of our lives, Jesus Christ is the First-goer. His pain and shame deal with our need well ahead of time. He defeated depression before it came to life. A focus on the redeeming work of Christ is the great balm for any kind of pain, any time it occurs.

Depression may awaken our need for Christ, but it ought not cause us to feel sorry for ourselves. Rather, it should cause us to exult in all that his dying has done to make our living triumphant. Teresa understood this:

> Returning to what I was saying, I should like to be able to explain the nature of this holy companionship with our great Companion, the Holiest of the holy, in which there is nothing to hinder the soul and her Spouse from remaining alone together, when the soul desires to enter within herself, to shut the door behind her so as to keep out all that is worldly and to dwell in that Paradise with her God.[8]

Teresa calls this a "holy companionship." It is a companionship of fellow strugglers, for our depression is defeated by this holy companionship. Our weaknesses disintegrate when bonded to his glorious strength.

But can so much really be accomplished by focusing our heart and mind on the redeeming work of Christ? When I felt called by God to leave the parish ministry and begin teaching, I suddenly had many doubts. I was fifty-five years of age and knew I had not too many years left to serve. I had all the jitters that might accompany such a call. Yet, his love filled my insecurities with confidence.

His love always completes my need for acceptance. I can always see in plentiful light what my young black friend had once seen: I am not the first person ever to feel insecure. In his Cross, the *First-goer* had experienced doubt, denial, and criticism. When I but survey his wondrous cross, my gloom dissolves in joy. I know the truth that sustained Isaac Watts: "Love so amazing, so divine demands my soul, my life, my all." All my feelings of rejection can be swallowed up in joy at any moment I will it so. Every issue of gloom can dissolve in the glorious work of the *First-goer*. Teresa sums up the glory of his work in this way:

> If you are suffering trials, or are sad, look upon Him on His way to the Garden. What sore distress He must have borne in His soul, to describe His own suffering as He did and to complain of it! Or look upon Him bound to the Column, full of pain, His flesh all torn to pieces by His great love for you. How much He suffered, persecuted by some, spat upon by others, denied by His friends, and even deserted by them, with none to take His part, frozen with the cold and left so completely alone that you may well comfort each other! Or look upon Him bending under the weight of the Cross and not even allowed to take breath: He will look upon you with His lovely and compassionate eyes, full of tears, and in comforting your grief will forget His own because you are

bearing Him company in order to comfort Him and turning your head to look upon Him.[9]

How can it be said any clearer? Look on him! If your heart is breaking, look on him! If gloom is sticking to your soul, look on him! If you're down and you can't get up, look on him! Let his redeeming work be for you the serpent in the wilderness (John 3:14). Then you have only to look to live! For when you see the conquest of the cross, then your hurt is healed.

The Third Window: Seeking Union with Christ

Too often we pray for things rather than union with Christ. In our prayers, we often ask God for what we want or want done. It must break the heart of God here and there that we are so busy seeking answers that we almost never seek him. We hunger to have what prayer can provide us rather than have him who could make our prayer effective. There is too little hunger for Union with Christ in our prayers.

The work of achieving this union will often seem grievous to us, because it is based on the disciplines. The disciplines, as I suggest, are called disciplines because they derive from the same stem as the word *disciple,* which means *student.* Students study. Indeed, the hardest work I know is study. As you cannot be a student without study, you cannot be a disciple without discipline. Since all authentic lightness-of-being is so dependent upon our discipline, let us consider the primary discipline. Only those disciplines are primary by which we arrive at Union with Christ. The most primary of all the disciplines is called by various names, but the word I like best is *focusing.* The essence of focusing is the quietening of the heart and stopping the busyness of the mind. We focus in order to give our minds a single, laser-like involvement with Christ. Focusing, which some Christians call centering, is difficult, for it involves our willful detachment from our self-important agendas. Until focus is achieved, we are trapped in lifestyles unfriendly to Union with Christ.

Focusing is a way of breaking the thrall that the world has over us. There are all kinds of devices that help us to do this. Some focus by withdrawing to a quiet place and, if not a quiet place, at least a quiet mode of life. In this self-imposed quietness, they close the eyes and visually shut out the world that is too demanding to allow them any inner vision. In this inner focus, they may concentrate on a verse of Scripture or one of the names of Christ. In this spiritual intensity, the mind can escape its busy captivity. I want to encourage the use of memorized Scripture for every separate period of meditation. After you use one of the many names of Christ to call your mind to attention, you will then want to arrive at a quietness of heart (Ps. 46:10) in which the focused discipline of prayer or Scripture meditation can begin. There is a danger of beginning to meditate upon the Bible without taking the time to focus. You may only introduce Christ into the maelstrom of your busy mind. Without first collecting your soul, his presence will never become concrete in your prayers. The thoughts of the busy heart quickly crowd out our attempts to unite with Christ.

There are two ways any spiritually debilitating busyness may end. First, we may find our busyness interrupted by mandated change to our busy lifestyles. I have a friend who was severely injured in a car accident. His back was broken, along with several of his limbs. When I first saw him in the hospital, bound to a rotating bed—head, arms, and legs strapped immobile—I turned my head to keep from weeping in his presence. Noticing my emotional and agitated state, he said, "Please don't weep for me. I always thought I was too busy to get to know God. Now I am no longer busy. I couldn't get busy even if I wanted to."

The better way our busyness may end is when we elect to pursue the discipline of meditation. We begin to deal with our outer busyness by dealing with our inner busyness. When the heart gives us its hassled agenda, our outer hurriedness is quickly tamed. In *The Table of Inwardness* I spend a great deal of time dealing with what I call "roof-brain" chatter. This is that never-ending, inner conversation that we swim in throughout all of our conscious lives. Psychologists say it never stops even when we are asleep. This ongoing inner dialogue flits from one subject to another, running on and on. If ever we know the focused dialogue of union, however, we must get it stopped. For there can be no meaningful dialogue with Christ when we throw his exalted holiness into the rapids of our ongoing secular lives. Union with Christ means that we must stop the inner "mental noise" so that real inner conversation with Christ becomes possible. But how is this to be done? Is it possible to shut off the "roof-brain" chatter so that our minds may meet with the divine mind of Christ in union?

For a fuller discussion of how this is to be done, consider what I have called "kenotic" meditation. This form of meditation is a "pouring out" (which is the meaning of the Greek word *kenosis*) of the busyness of our souls. In this emptying process, we make room for the quiet coming of his fullness. Emptying and fullness vary inversely. We can only make room for Christ by emptying our heart of its cluttered agenda.

Teresa of Avila says that the actual contemplation of Union is like that of an earthly bride contemplating the consummation of the marriage. We contemplate our Union with Christ by journeying into an inner, bonding relationship:

> He orders all things and He can do all things: with Him to
> will is to perform. It will be right, then, daughters, for us to
> endeavour to rejoice in these wondrous qualities of our
> Spouse and to know Whom we have wedded and what our
> lives should be. Why, God save us, when a woman in this
> world is about to marry, she knows beforehand whom she is
> to marry, what sort of a person he is and what property he
> possesses. Shall not we, then, who are already betrothed,
> think about our Spouse, before we are wedded to Him and
> He takes us home to be with Him? If these thoughts are not
> forbidden to those who are betrothed to men on earth, how
> can we be forbidden to discover Who this Man is, Who is

**His Father, what is the country to which He will take me,
what are the riches with which He promises to endow me.**[10]

Teresa is enraptured like a bride with her bridegroom when she
enters this Union. There can be little doubt that our own Union
with Christ will also produce in us a grand euphoria. We are not
to pursue the euphoria, however. It is enough that we pursue
Christ. The euphoria is the result, not the goal, of our walk.

This is a danger which might not need to be sounded were it
not for the fact that in the West we have become emotional junkies,
always seeking the emotive experience. Culture-wise, we have
become like a girl I knew in adolescence. When rebuked by a
friend who told her she cried too ostentatiously in movies, she
remarked, "I like to cry in movies." But evangelicals and Protestants have often made emotionalism a kind of test of authenticity
for worship. "No crying, no union," or as a friend of mine once
said, "A worship service full of dry eyes is full of dry souls!" To
remedy this dryness, we moisten things up with emotive gigs of
one sort or another to make people cry. Soon, people are condi-
tioned to go to church in search of these feelings rather than
seeking for Union.

Let us understand the necessity of union, with or without this
accompanying emotion. No bride and groom want to be together
primarily to feel emotive. They want to be together because being
apart for them is a waste of time. Union for them is its own
reward. They would prefer to be together, whether or not the
euphoria ever comes. There will indeed come dry times in their
togetherness. In those times they may not even feel "married." At
such times they may forget to celebrate this glorious state they
have embraced. Nonetheless, even then, the prize of union is theirs.

How like an earthly marriage is our Union with Christ: There
will be times of high elation in our relationship. There will be
other times of lesser euphoria. The important issue is not the
mood of our Union but the marriage itself. It is this Union that
produces the overall lightness of being by which our depression
is healed and gloom is barred from ever entering our lives.

The Fourth Window: Selective Listening

The fourth step to acquiring this lightness of being is much easier said than done. There is a childhood taunt that is utterly false: "Sticks and stones may break our bones but words can never hurt us!" Quite to the contrary, words create our potential or destroy it. Affirming words cause us to grow and pry large worlds from their orbits because they have made us believe in ourselves. Negative, critical words, on the other hand, drive us into the darkness of self-doubt. Dispensed to us often enough, such words kill our spirits long before our bodies are ever buried. So hear Teresa's advice:

> Cease troubling about these fears, then, sisters; and never pay heed to such matters of popular opinion. This is no time for believing everyone; believe only those whom you see modelling their lives on the life of Christ. Endeavour always to have a good conscience; practise humility; despise all worldly things; . . . You may then be quite sure that you are on a [very] good road.[11]

Teresa makes it clear that we are not to listen to everyone who brings their opinions against us. As Jesus said in another context, "Therefore consider carefully how you listen" (Luke 8:18 NIV). We are to listen selectively.

We are to give the fullest attention to those whom we can clearly see modeling Christ in their lives. These opinions we are to heed. How destructive is purely negative insight. But how redeeming is godly criticism. A thousand times I have been delivered by the godly severity of wise counsel even when it was not what I wanted to hear. Long ago I preached what I thought was a great sermon. A friend of mine was not so enthusiastic about it. "This I must tell you," he said. "You said, 'y'know' thirty-nine times in your sermon this morning." I, at first, hated him for counting. Then I listened to several of my sermon tapes! Suddenly his criticism came to life: "Y'know" was all I could hear. I had wanted to disregard his opinion, but he was a person desiring conformity to Christ. He had spoken to me in love. His criticism was a harsh but needful correction of a bad sermon pathology. Only after months was I able to muscle the "y'knows" out of my sermons. But once I did so, his godly criticism endowed me with new effectiveness.

So there are times when we are wise to be troubled by godly opinion. But all other criticism must be listened to very sparingly. For that which does not build us up may come from the destroyer. If so, it will render our present lives useless and our future effectiveness impossible.

The Fifth Window: God's Fatherly Faithfulness

If we are ever to enjoy victory over depression, we must learn to trust the faithfulness of God. Above we looked at the glorious promise of 1 Corinthians 10:13. Here is the promise that at last shatters our depression. Whenever our temptations control us, we have given them our consent. If depression is our constant companion, we have agreed to live weakly in the presence of God's power. "You do not have because you do not ask" (James 4:2). Teresa says we *have not* because we are timid. We have not learned to "come boldly to the throne of grace, that we may obtain mercy and find grace to help in time of need" (Heb. 4:16). Our confident spirituality enlightens our darkness. We must simply go to God and say, "I boldly ask you to eliminate my darkness."

But all too often we are guilty of what Teresa calls *bashful praying:*

> Avoid being bashful with God, . . . A fine humility it would be if I had the Emperor of Heaven and earth in my house, coming to it to do me a favor and to delight in my company, and I were so humble that I would not answer His questions, nor remain with Him, nor accept what He gave me . . . and I were so humble that I preferred to remain poor and even let Him go away, so that He would see I had not sufficient resolution. Have nothing to do with that kind of humility.[12]

How we are to depend on bold praying! God has infused us with confidence. He has not given us "a spirit of timidity, but a spirit of power, of love and of self-discipline" (2 Tim. 1:7 NIV). Timidity and bashfulness are unworthy of our relationship with an all-powerful Father. He desires to give us every good thing. I do not advocate a "name-it-and-claim-it" theology. For not all that we want is necessary to our development or our conformity to Christ. But "bashful praying" is unreasonable. I would never have asked my own children to come to me with ducked heads to ask me for something they believed that they needed. Neither does our heavenly Father want us to come to him as though we must grovel before him, suspicious that he will thwart our forwardness. Remember the words of the ever-generous Christ: "If you then, being evil, know how to give good gifts to your children, how much more will your Father who is in heaven give good things to those who ask Him!" (Matt. 7:11). Further, we may trust the generous heart of God. Jesus said, "Which of you fathers, if your son asks for a fish, will give him a snake instead? Or if he asks for an egg, will give him a scorpion?" (Luke 11:11–12 NIV). God is not a devious Father. He will give us all good things as we boldly ask.

He wants to bestow his very kingdom on us. But such a bestowal will not occur in the gaudy and busy moments of our living. His rich light falls best on our inner depression when we come to him in the closet of prayer. There his radiance meets our gloom, and the kingdom of God and the light come through what Teresa calls "the Prayer of Quiet":

> He bestows this Kingdom on them and brings them to this Prayer of Quiet, and yet they deafen their ears to His voice. For they are so fond of talking and of repeating a large number of vocal prayers in a great hurry, as though they were anxious to finish their task of repeating them daily, that when the Lord, as I say, puts His Kingdom into their very hands, by giving them this Prayer of Quiet.[13]

Our depression often issues as a kind of mental noise. It shrieks and howls and drives the last shred of hope from our lives. It makes only raucous demands. Still, his divine fullness is absent. It ingests our noise and returns it as quiet. "Busy-anity" haunts the people of God. The most healing restoration of God is his silence. His holy quiet in wondrous stillness heals the inner discord of our depression. It breathes peace above our stormy wranglings. And this peace comes, rebuking our dark seas and crying, "Peace be still!" The light of God then drives out the darkness. These five great windows of healing open. His splitting sunlight washes over our darkened moods. Joy is born, for Christ is all-sufficient.

WINNING

BY

ONEING

*Julian of
Norwich*

And when I was thirty and a half years old, God sent me a bodily sickness in which I lay for three days and three nights; and on the fourth night I received all the rites of Holy Church, and did not expect to live until day. But after this I suffered on for two days and two nights, and on the third night I often thought that I was on the point of death; and those who were around me also thought this. But in this I was very sorrowful and reluctant to die, not that there was anything on earth that it pleased me to live for, or anything of which I was afraid, for I trusted God. But it was because I wanted to go on living to love God better and longer, and living so, obtain grace to know and love God more as he is in the bliss of heaven. For it seemed to me that all the time that I had lived here was very little and short in comparison with the bliss which is everlasting. So I thought: Good Lord, is it no longer to your glory that I am alive? And my reason and my sufferings told me that I should die; and with all the will of my heart I assented wholly to be as was God's will.

So I lasted until day, and by then my body was dead from the middle downwards, it felt to me. Then I was moved to ask to be lifted up and supported, with cloths held to my head, so that my heart might be more free to be at God's will, and so that I could think of him whilst my life would last; and those who were with me sent for the parson, my curate, to be present at my end. He came with a little boy, and brought a cross; and by that time my eyes were fixed and I could not speak. The parson set the Cross before my face and said, "Daughter, I have brought you the image of your Savior. Look at it and take comfort from it, in reverence of him who died for you and me." It seemed to me that I was well as I was, for my eyes were set upwards towards heaven, where I trusted that I was going; but nevertheless, I agreed to fix my eyes on the face of the crucifix if I could so as to hold out longer until my end came. . . . Suddenly in that moment all my pain left me, I was as sound, particularly in the upper part of my body, as ever I was before or have been since.

—From *Showings*

IT IS NOT possible to estimate all that Jesus did for us on the cross. In his living he took the pain out of living. But in his dying he took the sting out of death (1 Cor. 15:55). At Calvary, Christ tasted death for all of us, once for all. While I was a pastor, I don't think I ever met a Christian who was terrified of death. Considering all of the funerals at which I have officiated, this statement alone would make it a wise decision for all to become converted to Christ. But while I never met anyone afraid of death, I have met many a Christian who was afraid of dying. We do not fear death as an event, only as a process.

Dying is often bleak work. It is sometimes accompanied by the most shattering pain, and it is always accompanied by that uncertainty every traveler feels when crossing borders into uncharted kingdoms. Yet it is not a fear of meeting the King that dogs us. It's the business of "going through customs." We are uncertain of the language and the topography of the new country. The children of Narnia referred not to heaven but to earth and our leaving it as "Shadowlands." But the Shadowlands are the inevitable terrain of everyone. Our conquest of heaven is only made possible by leaving earth.

One thing that never leaves a Christian in whichever world he or she resides is the accompaniment of Christ. Between 1342 and 1420, an Anchorite nun lived and prayed in a small cell attached to the Church of St. Julian in the English shire of Norwich. If she had a name, it has been lost to us. She was simply given the name of the church where she served. Holy men and women of old never quibbled much about their names. Their names were not of much importance to them when they considered the mighty, transforming name of Christ. Julian's name is like that of the author of *The Imitation of Christ*. The name of Thomas à Kempis was assigned as the author of *The Imitation of Christ* as the most likely monk to have written the piece, but this is by no means certain. Julian's name also is uncertain.

In our day we are more ego-driven. We are so afraid that our names will be missed by our peers and that our small place in the sun will be lost. It may strike us as odd that *The Showings of Revelations,* Dame Julian's master work, comes to us from a woman whose name is registered only as the name of her church. Julian's way was exactly the way that John the Baptist replied when they asked him who he was:

> He confessed, and did not deny, but confessed, "I am not the Christ."
>
> And they asked him, "What then? Are you Elijah?" He said, "I am not." "Are you the Prophet?" And he answered, "No."
>
> Then they said to him, "Who are you, that we may give an answer to those who sent us? What do you say about yourself?"
>
> He said, "I am 'The voice of one crying in the wilderness.' . . . but there stands One among you whom you do not know. It is He who, coming after me, is preferred before me, whose sandal strap I am not worthy to loose."
>
> (John 1:20–23, 26–27)

John the Baptist may have been the very role model for Julian of Norwich. As she cared nothing for her own name, John seemed to have no particular affection for his. When they pressed him to tell them who he was, he replied that he was a crying voice (John 1:23). In effect, John was saying, "My name is unimportant. When a herald plays a fanfare, none need ask, 'Who is the man on the trumpet?' They rather ask, 'What great person does the blare of trumpets announce?' My name matters not; I am but a trumpet. I am a voice crying in the wilderness. Jesus is the only important name you need to remember. Remember Christ; forget this poor and unimportant herald."

Dame Julian would not have been terribly disturbed that we really don't know her name. But God spoke to her in a very special way on May 8, 1373. In this very special revelation, she was given some sixteen "showings." Although she never received any later revelation, the strength of what she saw from God at that time would continue to fuel her hunger for Christ and would be the basis of her writing for the next twenty years. She would have been thirty-one years of age at the time, and by her own admission she was reluctant to mention these "showings" at all. This was a day when women generally left all religious writing to men. Many women—Joan of Arc, for instance—had been accused of witchery for even suggesting that they had special revelation. Nonetheless, she tentatively offered the world these "showings" as she disclosed the intense hunger in her life for union with Christ.

She called this yearning for union with Christ, *Oneing*. Becoming one with her Savior dominated the last forty-five years of her life. In her mind, *Oneing* was all that mattered. It made life in this world sensible and life in the world to come possible. Her *Oneing* became heightened when she began to pray for the ultimate steps of mortification. She had been inspired by the example of Cecilia, whose martyrdom came by being stabbed three times in the neck. Thus, Dame Julian prayed to receive each of the three wounds. Symbolically, and for herself, she renamed Cecilia's wounds, *contrition, compassion,* and *longing with her will for God*.[1]

This longing after God is not peculiar to Dame Julian, for all who ever walk with Christ desire it at their best moments. Further, the apostles and holy souls of old also desired it. Julian's hunger came as she endured a great illness that all but claimed her life. While that illness was stalking her very existence, she writes of her decision to make *Oneing* the passion of her life. There is nothing like a near-death experience to teach us what really matters. Still, hear what she writes of that experience:

After this my sight began to fail, and it was all dark around me in the room, dark as night, except that there was ordinary light trained upon the image of the cross, I never knew how. Everything around the cross was ugly to me, as if it were occupied by a great crowd of devils.

After this I felt as if the upper part of my body were beginning to die. My hands fell down on either side, and I was so weak that my head lolled to one side. The greatest pain that I felt was my shortness of breath and the ebbing of my life. Then truly I believed that I was at the point of my death. And suddenly in that moment all my pain left me, I was sound, particularly in the upper part of my body, as ever I was before or have been since. I was astonished by this change, for it seemed to me that it was by God's secret doing and not natural; and even so, in this ease which I felt, I had no more confidence that I should live, nor was the ease complete, for I thought that I would rather have been delivered of this world, because that was what my heart longed for.[2]

The glory of Julian's experience must be noted: She not only learned the art of "dying ahead of time," she learned the art of *Oneing* as well. Her devotion teaches us to seek her same three "wounds" and to hunger after Christ. Contrition is that first wound, by which we long for holiness. Compassion is the second wound, by which we see our needy world as Jesus did. Once we see the spiritually needy people of our world, then we may long to see Christ touch their lives. But the third wound, longing with our will after God, causes us to cry out for union with Christ.

During a particularly severe period of spiritual depression in my teens, the emotional pain I felt caused me to think about ending my life. I suppose my bout with depression is not all that unusual, for many teenagers toy with the idea of suicide when adolescent woes become severe. In fact, suicide is the number-one killer of teenagers in the West.

One day as I thought of ending it all, I had the following experience. I was driving alone on a desolate highway turning Hamlet's "to be or not to be" over in my mind. Upon crossing a railroad track, I heard the sudden, blaring whine of a diesel horn. I was horrified at seeing the huge black front of a train bearing down on me. The light, blinding in its intensity, flooded the inside of my car. I have no idea how I escaped death. The train must have missed me only by inches.

I was honestly trembling as I moved to the side of the road and stopped the car. I saw in an instant that I had not wanted to end my life nearly as much as I had thought. Further, the experience, vivid to this day, marked me in a way that I shall never forget. I saw that life is fragile. I decided to find some way to make life meaningful. That night Julian's third wound was born in a special kind of reality. Then and there, I realized that the only answer for reasonable living is Union with Christ.

The entire medieval church talked about three steps to this Union. The process began with the step of *purgation,* in which the soul recognized its inherent depravity and worthlessness and ridded itself of all sinfulness. The second step was *illumination,* in which the soul, being cleansed of all sin and desire for sin, began to see the nature of true reality. At this step the soul could see what really mattered and what did not—which things were eternal and which were not. The final step was that glorious phase in which the soul, cleansed of sin and clearly grasping reality, reached out and apprehended Union with God. Of course, the three wounds for which Julian prayed align with these three values: contrition, compassion, and hungering with the whole will after God.

Gerald May has well integrated psychology with the role of the Holy Spirit. Psychiatry might profit from understanding this psychiatrist. In a much different way from Julian, he speaks of the hunger in his heart to submit himself to entering a new spiritual dimension. He is refreshingly honest when he confesses:

We all have secrets in our hearts. I will tell you one of mine. All my life I have longed to say yes, to give myself

completely, to some Ultimate Someone or Something. I kept this secret for many years because it did not fit the image I wanted to present—that of an independent, self-sufficient man. The desire to surrender myself had been at least partially acceptable when I was a child, but as a man I tried to put away childish things. When I became a physician, and later a psychiatrist, it was still more difficult to admit—even to myself—that something in me was searching for an ultimate self-surrender.

Society, to say nothing of medical and psychiatric training, had taught me to say no rather than yes, to try to determine my own destiny rather than give myself, to seek mastery rather than surrender.[3]

How odd these words may seem to us. In some sense the very idea of Union with Christ sounds like something that would fit only a pre-modern world. Back then, people may have had more time to sit around and think about God. Perhaps even as you are reading these words, you are thinking that *Oneing* is more interesting than vital to you. You may feel it is something you could never make work in your life. It is spiritually high brow. It should be left to occupy the minds of the saints, who never had to prepare casseroles for the Wednesday-night church suppers. Still, Lady Julian's pursuits *should be* ours. If we are not marked by her "three wounds," then our lives will only parallel life in Christ; we can never intersect it. For, if the contemporary church with all its "surface demands" only keeps us busy without conforming us to the image of Christ, it has miserably failed in all that God has called the church to do. Churches often teach us only program-tending, disinterested in our conformity to Christ. Serving fast-paced church programs more quickly develops the legs than the heart. Let us, therefore, consider why Julian's "three wounds" are quite practical and altogether essential to our own spiritual development.

Contrition. First, Dame Julian's hunger for God ought to call us to *contrition.* There are pages of medieval definitions of this word, but simply put, *contrition* asks: Are you taking your sin seriously? Is there grief in your life over your sins? Or have you learned to tolerate these sins by renaming them "little permissions"? I believe that the heart of God must be grieved that so little personal repentance has survived the psychologized morality of our times. In our march toward the Nirvana of self-esteem, we jettisoned everything that got in our way. Belief in sin, we were told, was bad conditioning, and if we took it too seriously, we could never be free of damaging guilt. Bit by bit we forgave ourselves as we slowly moved away from ever acknowledging that sin could exist within our souls. Never having sinned, there was no need to repent, and Narcissus moved into our B. F. Skinner theology. For a while, we asked Menninger's question: "Whatever became of sin?" The question helped us remember that originally our sin was the reason for the Cross. We examined with rubber gloves those old ideas that, until we dealt with our sins, we could not be saved. In the pre-Jungian world, redemption followed contrition. But we Christians seem to have joined our odd world. Now, even Menninger's question is gone. Neither Christians nor non-Christians are seriously concerned with contrition. Those who wept their way to church altars in the '50s and '60s now sit in the pew smiling. They await those "practical" sermons that tell them how to get ahead in the world without anything so medieval as repentance. Brokenness, a side product of contrition, has also gone. After all, how can we weep over something that doesn't exist?

Lady Julian is still right! Contrition is and always will be the first step toward Union with Christ. What is to make us think that God in his utter holiness will be one with our unredeemed lifestyles? "As obedient children, do not conform to the evil desires you had when you lived in ignorance. But just as he who called you is holy, so be holy in all you do; for it is written: "'Be holy because I am holy'" (1 Peter 1:14–16 NIV). Hebrews 12:14 reminds us that "without [holiness] no one will see the Lord." Paul, admitting that he was "chief of sinners" (1 Tim. 1:15), said God

THE UNCHAINED SOUL

has called each of us to a "holy life" (2 Tim. 1:9). How far his church has slipped in her understanding of his expectation of her. But if we lose this first step toward *Oneing,* we shall never be able to arrive at the final stage of being united with Christ.

Compassion. Secondly, Julian's hunger for God ought to call us to *compassion.* As contrition begins with our consideration of ourselves, compassion begins with a consideration of others. Contrition is a "looking in." Compassion is a "looking out." It is interesting that the Bible calls us to our ministries by examining our lives in this way. We are not to look out till we have looked in. There is no use, in the name of mere, soiled humanitarianism, to export a tainted concern. When we are clean then it will be time to minister to the dirty. We are not to flaunt our "cleanness" in their faces, but neither are we to presume we can help the sick while we are still infected. Until the plank is out of our own eye, then we shouldn't deal with the specks of anybody else's need (Matt. 7:3).

Compassion is not merely a helpful act. Compassion is a way of seeing. Jesus would often look on the crowds and feel compassion welling up within him (Matt. 9:36). He testified to his disciples, "I have compassion for these people" (Mark 8:2 NIV). Dame Julian herself spent time listening to others, sewing vestments for the priests and clothing for the poor. Mother Theresa of Calcutta has long instructed her nuns that they are not to keep their hands so folded in prayer that they cannot open their hands and use them to serve others. But let us make it very clear to our world that compassion without contrition is but a kind of do-goodism, for it tries to serve man without measuring his standing before God. We must first know contrition and then we can become the arm of God in ministry. We become credible to others when we have compassion for them. But we become credible to God when we see that we take our own immorality seriously and remember what our sins cost our Lord.

Hunger with Our Whole Heart After God. The third wound—hungering with our whole heart after God—is one that ought to mark our lives. Jesus said in his Sermon on the Mount, "Blessed are those who hunger and thirst for righteousness; / for they shall be filled" (Matt. 5:6). How this hunger for God is to mark the person of God! Paul's hunger for union caused him to cry out, "For to me, to live is Christ, and to die is gain" (Phil. 1:21). The hunger for the final crossing of this barrier of separation is Dame Julian's finest contribution to our lives.

As her own near brush with death joined her longing to be one with Christ, her teaching on the matter became dynamic. But rest assured, her confidence in Christ at the hour of her dying was expressed totally in terms of her longing. Consider her account of the time when she faced death:

> Then suddenly it came into my mind that I ought to wish for the second wound as a gift and a grace from our Lord, that my body might be filled full of recollection and feeling of his blessed Passion, as I had prayed before, for I wished that his pains might be my pains, with compassion which would lead to longing for God. . . . I desired to suffer with him, living in my mortal body, as God would give me grace.[4]

But even here, Julian's view of death should not be seen as a different kind of event. Dying is to be experienced as a kind of living and passing with Christ. There is no sense of interruption as though one is either living or dead. One is always living somewhere, and the word *death* does not occur. To be one with Christ is to walk in a kind of entwined, absorbed existence that holds no place for separating words like *dead*.

Her whole life is a kind of call to winning by *Oneing*. Death is not to be a grave matter. *Oneing* is pure joy. It is losing our gloom and littleness in the wider categories of praise and largesse. I believe that Julian has given us three great gifts for our ongoing discipleship. These ideas are not stated as gifts in her work. I have extrapolated them for our consideration. But I believe they are found in her writing. I want to be sure that I don't give her more credit for the ideas in this book than she would like. Still, her concept of *Oneing* holds three very useful and practical ideas for our lives.

Julian's Three Gifts

The First Gift: Laughing Satan Out of Our Lives

Praise is a kind of divine laughter. Julian believed in laughter, and while this may not seem unusual to us, it represents a wide divergence from where the medieval church lived and thought. Laughter among nearly all of the various orders of monks and priests was strictly forbidden. It was seen to be frivolous and improper *in lieu* of the high purposes of God. But Julian understood that it is all right to laugh, both in comforting ourselves and in rejoicing in God.

Julian attaches laughter not only to the wholesome enjoyment of life, but also as a natural part of praising God. There are many biblical verses that encourage the use of laughter in praise: "Then our mouth was filled with laughter, / and our tongue with singing" (Ps. 126:2). Or, "He will yet fill your mouth with laughing, / and your lips with rejoicing" (Job 8:21). Or, "He who sits in the heavens shall laugh" (Ps. 2:4). But the most interesting facet of Julian's doctrine of laughter seems to be the way that she viewed it as a weapon against Satan who is ever the father of gloom.

Augustine used Psalm 2:4 to point out that God derided his enemies with laughter. Does not the psalmist's commentary set the stage for Satan's being laughed out of heaven? Certainly there is no more powerful way to ridicule anyone than to laugh at them.

Many a schoolchild has left the playground reduced to tears by the mocking laughter of her playmates. Who has not known this pain? In some ways it may seem to belittle the dignity of God by seeing him laugh his enemies to scorn, but laughter always reminds us that the one who laughs is the one with absolute power. Underlings do not laugh at monarchs, only vice versa. Christ alone gives us the power to laugh at the enemy of God. John reminds us in 1 John 4:4: "You are of God, little children, and have overcome them, because He who is in you is greater than he who is in the world." When we are living in Union with God, he who indwells us may use our lives to deride the devil.

Julian sensed the presence of the devil in the foul smell of brimstone that surrounded his coming. But Satan's coming did not make her afraid. Instead, it called her sleeping soul to "bless" his coming. Satan's coming was but another opportunity to prove that God was in charge.

> This ugly apparition came when I was sleeping, as none of the others did; and in all this time I trusted to be saved and protected by the mercy of God. And our courteous Lord gave me grace to wake, more dead than alive. The people who were with me watched me, and wet my temples, and my heart began to gain strength. And then a little smoke came in at the door, with great heat and a foul stench. And then I said: Blessed be the Lord! Is everything on fire here? And I thought that it must be actual fire, which would have burned us all to death. I asked those who were with me if they were conscious of any stench. They said no, they were not. I said: Blessed be God! for then I knew well that it was the devil who had come to tempt me.[5]

It is clearly in this encounter that Julian saw the fiend as being overcome. She felt as though she was about to break into laughter. Julian did not see Christ as laughing just to have a good time, but she did see him laughing to mock the powerlessness of Satan in a universe that belonged to God. All Christians should learn to laugh in such wholesome joy that their laughter drives the Prince of Darkness from their lives:

> God showed me that the fiend has now the same malice as he had before the Incarnation, and he works as hard, and he sees as constantly as he did before that all souls who will be saved escape him to God's glory by the power of our Lord's precious Passion. . . .

> Also I saw our Lord scorn his malice and despise him as nothing, and he wants us to do so. Because of this sight I laughed greatly, and that made those around me to laugh as well; and their laughter was pleasing to me. I thought that I wished that all my fellow Christians had seen what I saw. Then they would all have laughed with me; but I did not see Christ laughing, but I know well that it was the vision he showed me which made me laugh, for I understood that we may laugh, to comfort ourselves, and rejoice in God, because the devil is overcome.[6]

If we apply this "laughing at the fiend" principle, it can be a great liberation from gloom and doom. How can it liberate us? Remember that Satan never comes to us to bring us any authentic happiness and joy. Such a gift is not possible for him to give. He only comes to us to bury us in depression and gloom. As it is true for us individually, it is true for the entire body of Christ, the church, as well.

I well remember going to serve a congregation for a while that was torn by inner division. They had no pastor at the time, and there was a quarrel raging in the power vacuum left by the departing pastor. Satan had been having a field day. Brother was set against brother and sister against sister. Faces were grim. Church business conferences had become shouting matches.

It is customarily my style to use humor when I speak. Since I had no idea that they had been having such a powerful personality struggle, I entered their service preaching in my oft-lighthearted manner, oblivious to the tension. Beginning with the very first service, many in this large congregation began telling me "how good it was to laugh in church again!" As the weeks progressed with generous doses of laughter, the animosity receded. The church forgot its interiorated quarrel. It was then able to return to a sharp focus on reaching out to their community.

If Julian's manner of encountering Satan was to laugh in his face, Martin Luther had an even more contemptuous method. For years visitors were shown an ink blot on the wall of Wartburg, where Luther had once thrown an inkwell at the devil. Dame Julian and Martin Luther, being from separate and warring traditions, would never have been able to hold each other in much esteem. But Martin Luther also said in *Table Talk* that one way to handle the fiend was to "break wind in his face."[7] This way of humiliating Satan would have outdone even Lady Julian's denigrating way of dealing with the devil.

The ultimate point of either method is that *Oneing* is not possible while Satan is in control of our lives. If we are to drive him from our lives then we must break his bondage over us. Julian's great "laugh-out" sets us free to proceed toward unbroken union. We can live victorious over Satan and every negative circumstance he throws between us and our hunger for Union with Christ.

But I must sound one final warning: We are not to use laughter demonically to defeat the prince of demons. We are not to take something as holy as laughter and cheapen it by making it a kind of "gig for the frogs of hell." Our laughter is to be directed toward God. Ours is not a hellish laughter but a heavenly laughter. It is its heavenly ring that so intimidates the tempter and drives him from our lives. Such laughter is the laughter of praise that wakes the joy of heaven. It is the intensity of this heavenly joy that makes it impossible for Satan to come near us. He always flees from true joy, for such joy resides so near the presence of God. Satan cannot stand the glare of pure divinity in which the laughter of praise is packaged.

In the case of the church mentioned earlier, we did not laugh to exorcise the devil from our midst. We laughed to celebrate our community in the body of Christ. We laughed to praise his name. We laughed and gave our laughter to God as an offering. Nonetheless, the effect was the same. Its joy drove the fiend from our midst and left many in a state of closer Union with Christ. Satan loves the sound of hopeless crying. We serve him only when we abandon God and agree to "weep as those without hope" (1 Thess. 4:13). When we laugh we participate in the spirit of heaven, where "God will wipe away every tear from their eyes; there shall be no more death, nor sorrow, nor crying" (Rev. 21:4). Heaven's laughter will at last define the dwelling place of God and all his saints.

Gift Two: Seeing Ourselves as the Prize of His Passion

Oneing is not just the pursuit of saints. The Father also yearns for union with his children; he longs for us to long for him. We evangelicals have talked about and preached the importance of making Jesus "our personal Savior." Just how personal is the love of God? According to Dame Julian, he loves each of us individually—so individually that if I had been the only soul who needed the cross, Christ would still have died. God longs so to save to the uttermost every single, suffering human being:

> We know in our faith that God alone took our nature, and no one but he, and, furthermore, that Christ alone performed all the great works which belong to our salvation, and no one but he; and just so, he alone acts now in the last end, that is to say he dwells here in us, and rules us, and cares for us in this life, and brings us to his bliss. And so he will do as long as any soul is on earth who will come to heaven; and so much so that if there were no such soul on earth except one, he would be with it, all alone, until he had brought it up into his bliss.[8]

The glory of our possibilities lies in the fullest love of God. Dame Julian will not have us unite with a God who loves moderately, but one who loves us passionately.

Many years ago it became clear to me how much God craves

this *Oneness* with his children. When my only son was a child, he and my mother became separated from the rest of the family on a Disneyland outing. I can't remember exactly how or where it happened. But my wife and I, clutching tightly to our little girl, began to search for them amongst the crowd. We divided into two frantic teams, agreeing to meet back at the foyer-patio of the "people mover" after our search. I remember running through same-faced crowds of people. From Frontierland to Fantasyland I flew, looking for a divine old woman with her precious little one. I remember thinking how much all people looked alike, except for the two I desperately needed to find. On and on I tore madly, until at last I spied them waiting on a bench. Even before I found them, I saw this as a marvelous parable of waiting lovers. They had no panic. They knew I, the father, would be looking, hungering. They knew I would have no peace till I found them. Thus they sat while hordes of people passed by.

There and then, I loved them. Not just for knowing I would come, but for knowing I would have no peace until my family was gathered back together. They were to be commended for understanding how much they meant to me. They could wait, knowing that I longed for this familial oneness as much as they. No wonder Dame Julian writes:

> For the first heaven, Christ showed me his Father, not in any bodily likeness but in his attributes and in his operations. That is to say, I saw in Christ that the Father is. For the Father's operation is this: He rewards his Son, Jesus Christ. . . .

> For he is well pleased with all the deeds that Jesus has done for our salvation; and therefore we are his, not only through our redemption but also by his Father's courteous gift. We are his bliss, we are his reward, we are his honor, we are his crown.[9]

We truly are his joy and his crown. Union is his near obsession for all whom he loves.

How disappointed he must be when we do not crave what he craves. Let us suppose that on that awful night of separation, my son had said to his grandmother, "Let us go on and enjoy the park. My father's love doesn't matter." Let us say they had wandered off and carelessly tossed my desire to be with them aside. Is not this the spiritual case with so many these days? Next to blaspheming the Holy Ghost, I think spurning the Father's love must be the most grievous of sins. Not to want to be found must torment our seeking Father. Not to want for ourselves that same longing union that God wants with us must surely grieve him. Not to be thankful for the Father's willingness to send his Son as the means of this union is the scourge of the human soul. Much to be pitied are all God's ungrateful offspring. King Lear well defines God's thankless children: "How sharper than a serpent's tooth to have a thankless child."[10]

Oh, let us rather praise him that he has died to provide for us this union with the Father. Let us praise him that *Oneing* is as much his goal for us as it should be our goal for him. How glorious is the laughter with which we praise him! Praise is a sacrifice well pleasing. For he considers us to be the prize of his passion. He has raised us from sin and death to union:

> Therefore we were buried with Him through baptism into death, that just as Christ was raised from the dead by the glory of the Father, even so we also should walk in newness of life.

> For if we have been united together in the likeness of His death, certainly we also shall be in the likeness of His resurrection. (Rom. 6:4–5)

Our Union with Christ is both the prize of his passion and the trophy of his resurrection. What can it mean to speak of his suffering as the prize? Just this: If ever you are prone to doubt that Christ loves you, simply ask him for evidence. He will show you his scars and say, "These I had in loving you! I beg you enter into my wounds and find in our union all that both of us desire. Be one with me and my dying will have meaning in your life. If you prefer to live without me, making your own way in this pointless world, then my passion will be as empty as your soul. My dying is pointless till you can celebrate my wounds as your greatest joy. Be assured of this: *You are the prize of my dying!* As my dying is the prize of your living."

Gift Three: Eternity, the Ultimate Oneing

The prophet Amos rallied his most threatening and his very wisest word when he called to Israel, "Prepare to meet your God" (4:12). All of life is a time of preparation. This present desire for Union with Christ is precedent to our ultimate, grand, and finishing desire. This smaller, token marriage to our Lord declares our ultimate, eternal union. How odd this argument must seem to a culture well fed on pheasant and creme tortes. We have lost our taste for "pie in the sky, by and by." Our glut is now. Our diets rank by comparison. It is difficult these days to attract much interest in the subject of heaven. So Julian will seem odd to many of today's here-and-now Christians who are in love only with the moment. But Christ came to deal with the temporariness of life. He came to teach us to avoid trading the temporal for the eternal.

Julian's brush with death should remove all doubt from our minds that she was tied to little definitions of *Oneing.* Julian believed that Christ saved all who will believe. To these, Christ will give birth anew in heaven. How glorious and transcendent this new life will be:

> In this we should truly see the cause of all the deeds which God has done; and furthermore, we should see the cause of all the things which he has permitted; and the bliss and the fulfillment will be so deep and so high that, out of wonder and marvelling, all creatures ought to have for God so much reverent fear, surpassing what has been seen and felt before, that the pillars of heaven will tremble and quake. But this

kind of trembling and fear will have no kind of pain. . . . For the contemplation of this, makes the creature marvelously meek and mild. . . . For it leads us in the right way, and keeps us in true life, and unites us to God.[11]

This "interweaving with God" is suggestive of the final triumphant work of *Oneing*. In this wonderful and final act of *Oneing*, God will, at last, restore everything fallen. The significance of this is that everything which has been separated by time in eternity will be unified once again. The universe itself is headed for this wonderful union, for in Adam's transgression, the issue of union became a horrible "great divorce." But in the final reaches of heaven, the apocalyptic God will have ended the separation of all things in an all-encompassing unity. The best part of this will be the ultimate togetherness of God and man:

See I lead everything to the end I ordained it for from without beginning—by the same power, wisdom, and love by which I made it.[12]

What is most glorious about this? All of this new union, or *Oneing*, will be accomplished by Christ.

Julian consistently thought of Christ in terms of motherhood. This must not be read as some kind of medieval feminist attempt to write gender into the Godhead. Julian prefers the term to speak of the tender attributes of Jesus. She is not saying that in any way Christ is a redeeming woman. But she is saying that his tenderness with which he folds us to himself is as a mother would fold her child to her bosom. To be one with that child, a young mother literally merges with her infant during feedings. Thus, the ever-loving and ever-nourishing Christ is motherlike. He draws us tenderly to the Father. Julian tends to build this powerful metaphor in the same way that Isaiah exults over the gentle keeping of God (Isa. 66:10–13). The Father exhibits motherlike concern for his infants:

But Zion said, "The LORD has forsaken me;
And my Lord has forgotten me."

"Can a woman forget her nursing child,
And not have compassion on the son of her womb?
Surely they may forget,
Yet I will not forget you."　　　　(Isa. 49:14–15)

In this glorious and protective metaphor, the mother Jesus intercedes for the Father's children. A mother will viciously and vigorously fight for her offspring. She will lay down her life for them. So this glorious Jesus fights for and defends his children in the church. He brings them from oneness with himself to oneness with his Father. Anselm wrote of this motherly, protective side of Jesus:

He [Jesus] put Himself between us and His Father who was threatening to strike us, as a mother full of pity puts herself between the stern angry father who is going to strike it.[13]

How Julian too writes splendidly of the loving and protective office of our Lord:

And in our spiritual bringing to birth he uses more tenderness, without any comparison, in protecting us. By so much as our soul is more precious in his sight, he kindles our understanding, he prepares our ways, he eases our conscience, he comforts our soul, he illumines our heart and gives us partial knowledge and love of his blessed divinity, with gracious memory of his sweet humanity and his blessed Passion, with courteous wonder over his great surpassing goodness, and makes us to love everything which he loves for love of him, and to be well satisfied with him and with all his works. And when we fall, quickly he raises us up with his loving embrace and his gracious touch. And when we are strengthened by his sweet working, then we willingly choose him by his grace, that we shall be his servants and his lovers, constantly and forever.[14]

111

. . . As regards our substance, it can rightly be called our soul, and as regards our sensuality, it can rightly be called our soul, and that is by the union which it has in God.[15]

The final work of protection of our "mother" Jesus will be to bring the entire family into union with God in eternity.

But how is the true person, our soul, to change worlds? Julian says that it will be accomplished as she saw it. Her word picture is remarkably like Paul's who says:

> But someone will say, "How are the dead raised up? And with what body do they come?" . . .
>
> In a moment, in the twinkling of an eye, at the last trumpet. For the trumpet will sound, and the dead will be raised incorruptible, and we shall be changed. For this corruptible must put on incorruption, and this mortal must put on immortality. So when this corruptible has put on incorruption, and this mortal has put on immortality, then shall be brought to pass the saying that is written: "Death is swallowed up in victory."   (1 Cor. 15:35, 52–54)

How powerful is the image of the clothing of mortality with immortality! Julian writes of it this way:

> And in this time I saw a body lying on the earth, which appeared oppressive and fearsome and without shape and form, as it were a devouring pit of stinking mud; and suddenly out of this body there sprang a most beautiful creature, a little child fully shaped and formed, swift and lively and whiter than a lily, which quickly glided up to heaven.
>
> The pit which was the body signifies the great wretchedness of our mortal flesh; and the smallness of the child signifies the cleanness and the purity of our soul.[16]

This clothing of mortality with immortality is most graphic: the description of the tired old bag of bones being honored as a new being, alive in Christ and young, moving into the presence of the Father. How it is like the promise in Revelation, "Behold, I make all things new" (21:5). The ultimate renovation is when the mortal is at last dressed in immortality for an eternity with Christ.

It is Julian's gentle view of Christ that appeals to me. My mother was a shy woman, a single parent of nine children, who felt intimidated in the world of men and their oft-swaggering manhood. I like the idea that Jesus was so tender and motherlike that his own powerful manhood would acceptably deliver my mother to the keeping of his Father. She went to be with the Lord more than fifteen years ago, her body ravaged by poor circulation. Indeed, she had undergone the amputation of a part of one leg, and the many surgeries required had at last rendered her most frail. But in reading this picture of the renewal of her brief mortality with unending immortality, I know that her newness must have astounded her as she reached the bosom of her Father. She found out, as all of us shall, that heaven is the coming of newness, the best part of which is a new oneness with Christ.

When I first learned of my mother's passing, the darkness of our separation settled hard upon me. But the bright eclipse of the glory of God soon enveloped me. I understood then the greatest promise of the Scriptures: Those who crave spiritual oneness while they walk through their earthly years are destined to experience a final, glorious, unending *Oneing*.

To date, the passing of my mother remains the single greatest loss of any earthly relative. The salvaging of my hope was not so difficult as I had imagined that it would be. All of my despairing was not long-lived. To be one with Christ is, after all, the goal of all living and an instant payment upon dying.

Still, I must be candid. My wife and I have often talked about which of us shall move first into death. Neither of us likes the idea of leaving the other behind. But I do believe that both of us are resolved that the doctrine of his overcoming oneness is the greatest hope. And we can say of this struggle, as Paul instructed us, "[I have] a desire to depart and be with Christ, which is far better. Nevertheless to remain in the flesh is more needful for you" (Phil. 1:23–24). Our fear of separation is always wrapped in his all-sufficiency.

We are not hung up on the nature of heaven. Heaven is to be one with Jesus. So much as a heaven can occur here on earth, our Union with Christ has already made it so. So much as heaven is possible in heaven, our Union with Christ will make it so. The strength of our final Union with Christ we know will be so firmly fixed that the union will never be broken. "Who shall separate us from the love of Christ?" (Rom. 8:35). Nothing, for this is an inseparable union. Ritamary Bradley sums up the Lady Julian's benediction on our foreverness with these words:

> Further, we may be able to commune, delightedly, with our own soul—that innermost life which is our substantial soul, strong in its oneness with God (LT 56). Where shall we seek for that soul? Only in God, wherein it is rooted in endless love—knit to God like branches knotted to the tree.[17]

PILGRIM'S PROGRESS

John Bunyan

Now I further saw that betwixt them and the gate was a river; but there was no bridge to go over; and the river was very deep. At the sight, therefore, of this river the pilgrims were much stunned. . . . The pilgrims then, especially Christian, began to despond in his mind, and looked this way and that, but no way could be found by them by which they might escape the river. Then they asked the men if the waters were all of a depth. . . . They then addressed themselves to the water, and entering, Christian began to sink, and cried out to his good friend Hopeful.

Christian: I sink in the deep waters; the billows go over my head; all the waves go over me!

Hopeful: Be of good cheer, my brother; I feel the bottom and it is good. . . .

And with that a great darkness and horror fell upon Christian, so that he could not see before him. Also here he in a great measure lost his senses, so that he could neither remember nor orderly talk of any of those sweet refreshments that he had met with in the way of his pilgrimage. But all the words that he spoke still tended to discover that he had horror of mind, and heart-fears that he should die in the river, and never obtain entrance in at the gate. Here also, as they that stood by perceived, he was much in the troublesome thoughts of the sins that he had committed both since and before he began to be a pilgrim. It was also observed that he was troubled with apparitions of hobgoblins and evil spirits; for ever and anon he would intimate so much by words.

Hopeful therefore here had much ado to keep his brother's head above water; yea, sometimes he would be quite gone down, and then, ere awhile, he would rise up again half-dead. Hopeful also would endeavor to comfort him, saying:

Hopeful: Brother, I see the gate, and men standing by to receive us. . . . Be of good cheer; Jesus Christ maketh thee whole.

And with that Christian broke out with a loud voice, Oh, I see Him again! and He tells me: "When thou passeth through the waters, I will be with thee; and through the rivers, they shall not overflow thee" (Isaiah 43:2).

Then they both took courage, and the enemy was after that as still as a stone, until they were gone over. Christian therefore presently found ground to stand upon, and so it followed that the rest of the river was but shallow; thus they got over.

—From *Pilgrim's Progress*

PILGRIMAGES ARE TRIPS made to shrines out of reverence for some life to which the shrine is dedicated. I have never made a pilgrimage as such, for I have never felt free to "enshrine" mere earthlings for any exalted reason. I did once travel to Stratford, England, to celebrate my esteem for the literary genius of William Shakespeare. I have traveled to Tintagel to define some of my vague Arthuriana. At Walden, I sought better to define Thoreau. And I once visited that small cemetery in Rome where Keats and Shelley sleep.

I have driven through Avila, Spain, in the heart of Old Castille to try to understand the Carmelite contemplatives, Teresa and John of the Cross. While there (and somewhat before arriving there), I read as much of their works as possible. I wanted to find their secret of pursuing the heart of God and the lifelong passion they gave their pursuit.

Yet I have never made a pilgrimage as such, for pilgrimages too much focus on events—they enshrine the past. Jean-Pierre de Caussade is right to have asserted that the present moment is the only place where our spiritual ardor can be spendable currency. How true! Still, reading the devotional classics gives me that needed framework into which I can insert the present moment, a well-tried yardstick I can trust to measure the direction of my life.

I recently turned back to *Pilgrim's Progress*. As I reread it, I knew why I had never made a special, religious pilgrimage. It is because life *is* a pilgrimage. The journey is fueled by our hunger of heart. For when we have at last sated our souls with all of Jesus there is, our journey to him will have ended.

Yet it cannot end here, can it? We do not yet have all of God that we want. We cry out with Job: "If only I knew where to find him; / if only I could go to his dwelling!" (23:3 NIV). Often, as the hunger of our pilgrimage grows desperate, God hides himself deeper and deeper. He also lures our pursuits of him into twilight longings, where we grope and grasp but cannot reach. Still, in these reaching times, we build our own interior shrines.

Shrines have, for their noblest virtue, the fact that they mark off spiritual geography. Abraham built altars as he traveled through the land (Gen. 12). As we follow his well-marked trail through Canaan, we see that he cried out as he passed through the new land. He built an altar. He moved on. But not only did Abraham move on, so did God. God is always on the move.

Later in Israel's history the ark of the covenant—the dwelling place of the mobile Jehovah—was moved with rings and staves. God, like the nomads who worshipped him, moved around a lot. He warned Israel against shrines, knowing that shrines get too anchored in stone to be his dwelling place.

We will never find enough of God at any single place of prayer to satisfy us long. Why? Because he moves! We, too, must journey, ever following the ark, ever holding on to God as we journey toward him. We travel toward him for two reasons. First, we will find all of him someday at that glorious place where life's journey ends. But second, as we travel toward him, the journey itself brings him near. Jesus is the Emmaus Christ (Luke 24:13) who both walks us along the journey and reveals himself to us at the journey's end (v. 32).

How often in life have I constructed some imaginary shrine where I would pray and there, at the place I designated, God would come. Once or twice in my life I have joined with other brothers and sisters to beg the coming of the Spirit on some event that we had designated as appropriate.

I remember a time in our church's history when many became desirous of revival. We began to ask God fervently to fall upon our congregation in an undeniable event of power, so that many in our community might come to Christ. We prayed, the event came and went, but the "fire did not fall." We felt at first that God had betrayed us. Then, as I remembered both the prayer and the event, I recalled that during our prayer, we were all impressed by the nearness of God. God did not answer us with the fire we required, but he warmed us with fire unseen. When I thought back on it, his nearness at those prayer times was so overwhelming that I was often afraid to open my eyes. I was terrified by the idea that I might actually "see" him.

One other grace was given to me when God did not answer our prayer for revival. As I set the disappointment of the "unanswered" event alongside the overwhelming power of his reality, suddenly I understood Emmaus. We are the shrine. But more than this, the pilgrimage is the shrine. If "our hearts burn within us along the way" (Luke 24:32), is it necessary that the end of the pilgrimage be marked by a shrine?

Maybe this is what is wrong with Job's search: "If only I knew where to find him" (23:3 NIV). While God is everywhere present, he becomes elusive when we lower our spiritual guns and focus the cross hairs on our need for him. We will not ever find him if we force him to be "dug up" by the treasure maps we invent. He is not out there waiting for our zeal to discover him. He is too much with us while we search for him. It is as though we hear God speaking to us, "What are you looking for?"

"God," we reply.

"Ah, it is good to look for God," our Father answers. "I'll join you in your search."

One Christmas Eve in 1964, I felt that I needed to tell the story of Christ to whatever man in our town needed him most. I asked God who this man might be. A name came immediately to my mind. It was cold in the little Nebraska town where I then served as pastor. It wasn't snowing at the time, but there was a great deal of snow on the ground. I bundled myself in a warm coat and boots and set off walking toward the house of that man who I had decided needed Christ most. It wasn't far to his house, and along the way, I imagined how it would be at the precise moment when this "Christ-needy" man would offer himself to the incarnate Lord of Christmas.

I arrived at his house and knocked on the door. He welcomed me in. He took my coat and offered me a hot cup of coffee, and I accepted. But when I began to talk to him of his need for Christ, he became angry and told me that if Christ was all I had to offer him, I could leave.

"I am in no mood to be converted!" he shouted.

"But it's Christmas and I thought . . ." I stopped short as he stood up, scowling darkly.

I stood up too. He gave back my coat and I stepped outside his door. It closed, all too rapidly, behind me. Humiliation and the biting cold felt like prickly little needles in my flushed face. "But who is to win the most spiritually needy man in town?" I asked God.

I crunched on through the snow.

God was silent.

Then in one of those moments when truth overwhelms us, I suddenly saw that *I* was the spiritually needy man! My host needed Christ but did not see his neediness, and no man's needs can be met until he confesses his neediness. Nor can we rescue the needy without their confession of need. No, it was not this man who most needed Christ, it was I. I was the pilgrim, and pilgrims are by very definition longing for some journey's end. I knew, too, that on this particular night, my need for Christ was far greater than my host would have ever confessed.

Let us move to consider what grace is, what it used to be, and how the pilgrimage of life must reckon with the Bible, or the grace of God is lost. I have drawn from *Pilgrim's Progress* the seven stations of our pilgrimage.

Seven Stations on the Journey of Life

Station One: Beginning the Journey
Bunyan wrote of Christian at the outset of his journey:

> Now over the gate there was written: "Knock, and it shall be opened unto you" (Matt. 7:7). He knocked, therefore, more than once or twice, saying, May I now enter here? . . .
>
> *Christian:* Here is a poor burdened sinner. I come from the city of Destruction, but am going to Mount Zion, that I may be delivered from the wrath to come: I would therefore, sir, since I am informed that by this gate is the way thither, know if you are willing to let me in.
>
> *Goodwill:* I am willing with all my heart.
>
> And with that he opened the gate.[1]

Need comes not from discovering Christ's all-sufficiency; it comes from stumbling upon our insufficiency. But in this self-congratulating day in which we've come to live, we've congratulated ourselves completely out of spiritual neediness. It is rarely possible to save the "un-needy," since honesty and need are what bring us to Christ in the first place.

But the problem is even more serious than this. It is not only need which causes us to come to Christ for salvation, it is need which causes us to return to him again and again as we continue life's pilgrimage. Spiritual need is rooted in our honesty. And spiritual need is all that can put vitality in our relationship with him.

Station Two: The Deadly Pitfall of Trifling with Grace

There is only one sin unto death. It is the sin of playing lightly with the beckoning of God.

In *Pilgrim's Progress*, Christian comes to a poor man in an iron cage. The man is grievously lost because he has lived so long in rejection that he has grown immune to the Spirit's wooing. He has refused to confess and repent of his sins. Consider the poor soul's reply:

> *Caged Man:* I left off to march and be sober. I laid the reins upon the neck of my lusts. I sinned against the light of the Word, and the goodness of God. I have grieved the Spirit, and He is gone. I tempted the Devil, and he is come to me. I have provoked God to anger, and He has left me. I have so hardened my heart that I cannot repent.

> *Christian:* For what did you bring yourself into this condition?

> *Caged Man:* For the lusts, pleasures, and profits of this world; in the enjoyment of which I did then promise myself much delight; but now every one of those things also bite me, and gnaw me, like a burning worm.

> *Interpreter:* Let this man's misery be remembered by thee, and be an everlasting caution to thee.[2]

How are we to apply this? The iron cages that now house the self-esteemers of our generation must stretch between the very gates of heaven and hell. The sadness is that those who are too arrogant to admit their sins may never come to know the sweetness of God's forgiveness. When I think back over my own repentance and coming to Christ, it stirs my heart to singing. I grieve for all of those who will never sing redemption's song because they have never faced the discord of their own repentance. The church in our day must quickly return to preaching the truth. Sin is never beautiful, but it is the first face we ever see in God's mirror of grace. It is a medusan face. It freezes hopes. Yet until once we face it down, we cannot be re-created in the likeness of Christ (Rom. 12:1–2). Someday the cry of the psalmist will be ours: "As for me, I will see Your face in righteousness; / I shall be satisfied when I awake in Your likeness" (Ps. 17:15). Such Scriptures are beyond all possibility for Narcissus, who is too content with his own likeness to crave any greater identity in Christ.

Station Three: Facing and Receiving the Cross

The Cross, too, is a subject which has lost its luster for Narcissus. To the self-sufficient, the Cross is always pointless. If there is any change that needs to be made, Narcissus will manage his own reformation. If there are any exorcisms to be done, he will purge his own demons. He will heal his own wounds. Jesus once told a parable about a man, who, freed of demons, later found himself even more mired in sin than when he started. "When an unclean spirit goes out of a man, he goes through dry places, seeking rest; and finding none, he says, 'I will return to my house from which I came.' And when he comes, he finds it swept and put in order. Then he goes and takes with him seven other spirits more wicked than himself, and they enter and dwell there; and the last state of that man is worse than the first" (Luke 11:24–26). Narcissus can never know the glory of Christian's experience. Listen to his tale of forgiveness:

> Now I saw in my dream that the highway which Christian was to go was fenced on either side with a wall, and that wall was called Salvation (Isa. 26:1). Up this way therefore did burdened Christian run, but not without great difficulty, because of the load on his back.

He ran thus till he came to a place somewhat ascending; and upon that place stood a cross, and a little below, in the bottom, a sepulcher. So I saw in my dream that just as Christian came up with the cross, his burden loosed from off his shoulders, and fell from off his back, and began to tumble, and so continued to do till it came to the mouth of the sepulcher, where it fell in, and I saw it no more.[3]

This euphoric sense of lightness marks the experience of all who really consider their estate before God. Their need is Christ. He comes. They yield. It is more than a lovely experience. It is as close to splendor as a human being can come. It was John Newton who used the adjective *amazing* to describe God's grace. And well it marked his life. In his younger years, Newton had been a sailor. Even his shipmates agreed that he was the vilest of sailors. He could use more "cuss words" in a row than any of them. He could also drink more than any of them. He was, by all the standards of his day, a sinful man. Several accounts abound concerning his sinfulness. One of the most curious tells of his being in a drunken stupor during a storm at sea. In this experience his whole life flashed before him, and he came face to face with the Cross. When Newton cried out to Jesus, his sins—like Pilgrim's—rolled off his back and tumbled downward into the empty tomb. How glorious is Newton's testimony, sung now by Christians everywhere:

> Amazing grace! how sweet the sound,
> That saved a wretch like me!
> I once was lost but now am found,
> Was blind, but now I see.

Christian in *Pilgrim's Progress* sings a similar anthem to the glory of the all-sufficient cross:

> Thus far did I come laden with my sin;
> Nor could aught ease the grief that I was in,
> Till I came hither: what a place is this!

Must here be the beginning of my bliss?
Must here the burden fall from off my back?
Must here the strings that bound it to me crack?
Blest cross! blest sepulcher! blest rather be
The Man that there was put to shame for me![4]

No one can fail to be touched in reading Charles Colson's testimony of being born again in his book by that title. He languished in prison, shut up with guilt. Beyond his prison experience, he was given a copy of C. S. Lewis's *Mere Christianity* and came most gloriously to faith in Christ. Again, Bunyan's description of the euphoria of Christ swept over Colson. From the apostles until now, this experience characterizes all who begin their Christian life. They begin this pilgrimage by facing their own depravity at the cross. The Cross answers our sin with the utter forgiveness of God and the indwelling Spirit.

Station Four: Clothing Ourselves with Christ (to Do Battle with Apollyon)

Paul, in Ephesians 6:10ff., suggests that the warfare of the Christian is awesome. We must dress to do battle, for the enemy is real. One of my greatest fears for contemporary Christianity is that we are failing to take Satan seriously. If there is no sin and no reason for the cross, then there may be no father of lies. Remember that Jesus said of Satan that he was a liar and the father of lies (John 8:44). Is it sensible to do battle with Apollyon? Is he not too powerful for us? Of course, he is. But he is not too powerful for God. In the eyes of God, he is but a small, fallen angel. He has been judged already and cast out of heaven (Rev. 12:12). We are now living in the interim between his sentencing and his final incarceration in the bottomless pit. Apollyon is defeated already. The battle is ours, or rather, God's.

Then did Christian draw, for he saw it was time to bestir him; and Apollyon as fast made at him, throwing darts as thick as hail; by the which, notwithstanding all that

Christian could do to avoid it, Apollyon wounded him in his head, his hand, and foot. . . . This sore combat lasted for above half a day, even till Christian was almost quite spent. For you must know that Christian, by reason of his wounds, must needs grow weaker and weaker. . . .

Then said Apollyon: "I am sure of thee now." And with that, he had almost pressed him to death; so that Christian began to despair of life. But, as God would have it, while Apollyon was fetching of his last blow, thereby to make a full end of this good man, Christian nimbly reached out his hand for his sword, and caught it saying: "Rejoice not against me, O mine enemy; when I fall, I shall arise" (Mic. 7:8).

With that he gave him a deadly thrust, which made him give back, as one that had received his mortal wound. Christian perceiving that, made at him again saying: "Nay, in all these things we are more than conquerors through him that loved us" (Rom. 8:37). And with that Apollyon spread forth his dragon's wings, and sped him away, that Christian saw him no more (James 4:7).[5]

Notice that Christian is victorious over Apollyon because he accosts the prince of demons in a stronger name than his own. He rebukes Satan with the use of Bible passages. James 4:7 clearly tells us to resist the devil and he will flee from us. William Peter Blatty, in his popular novel *The Exorcist,* has this right. The demons of hell are always subject to the indwelling power of Christ in the Christian's life. But those demons must be ordered from our lives in the powerful name of Christ. Even so, let us not presume that we are to use the name of Christ as an *abracadabra* or a cheap magical trick to order the tempter from our lives. Some demons are hard to drive out. So strongly do they camp in the human heart that they require the powerful name of Christ, coupled with a life of prayer and fasting, to be cast out (Mark 9:29). Still, the power of Satan must always make a reply to the authority of

Christ as it is manifested in the life of the believer (Luke 10:17). During a student convention which I attended some time ago, some students brought in a young man who was helplessly caught in some kind of trance. His gaping shirt revealed a pentagonal crystal hanging from a leather strap. His mind seemed as vacant as his eyes. He spoke words that were gibberish and sometimes became so wildly erratic in his flailing and thrashing that we had to restrain him. In the name of Christ we rebuked the demons that seemed to be holding his mind in thrall. Then one of the students in the prayer circle reached up and grabbed the crystal from his neck and pulled it free. At the mention of the strong name of Jesus, Satan's hold on the boy released itself, and he began to breathe regularly and became calm. It seemed to all of us who were surrounding him in prayer that after the tempter was gone, "angels ministered to him" (Mark 1:13). When Jesus cried, "It is finished" (John 19:30), the conflict between kingdoms was effectively over. Satan was forever defeated. The Christian may now, at any moment, appropriate his defeat and be free of the abuse of Satan.

Station Five: The Nine-Step Path of the Backsliding

Christians are ever in danger of losing their first love (Rev. 2:4). The fervent joy of receiving Christ is always in jeopardy. *Backsliding* is a word that seems quaint, old, and a bit revivalistic. Perhaps we are prone to think that it does not hold place in the Christian lexicon any longer. Is it possible that we have dismissed it at a time when the church is in great need of universal repentance? Backsliding begins at the point when we begin to think it humorous. In the true believer, it never begins in intention. It is a state we arrive at because we let slip those glorious disciplines of prayer and meditation. Satan is a gradual deceiver. He never comes to us in the height of our devotional life and suggests that we blaspheme Christ. As Valiant says (in *The Valiant Papers*), Satan himself first fell by skipping his morning alleluias. It may have been further down the road of gradual degradation that he demanded his own throne and cast God completely out of his life. I can still remember a teacher of mine who taught us that Macbeth was the tale of the gradual degradation of a willfully sinning soul. Ah, how this description fits the path of all backsliders. Notice how gradual are the steps we take to walk away from God:

Hopeful: Now I have shown you the reason of their going back, do you show me the manner there of.

Christian: So I will willingly.

(1) They draw off their thoughts, all that they may, from the remembrance of God, death, and judgment to come.

(2) Then they cast off by degrees private duties, as closet prayer, curbing their lusts, watching sorrow for sin, and the like.

(3) Then they shun the company of lively and warm Christians.

(4) After that, they grow cold to public duty; as hearing, reading, godly conference, and the like.

(5) They then begin to pick holes, as we say, in the coat of some of the godly, and that devilishly, that they may have a seeming color to throw religion (for the sake of some infirmities they have espied in them) behind their backs.

(6) Then they begin to adhere to, and associate themselves with carnal, loose, and wanton men.

(7) Then they give way to carnal and wanton discourses in secret; and glad are they if they can see such things in any that are counted honest, that they may the more boldly do it through their example.

(8) After this they begin to play with little sins openly.

(9) And then, being hardened, they show themselves as they are. Thus being launched again into the gulf of misery, unless a miracle of grace prevent it, they everlastingly perish in their own deceivings.[6]

Whether or not Bunyan suggests complete apostasy here, it would be hard to say. But one thing is not hard to say: Whether or not people literally "perish in their own deceivings," the effectiveness of their lives is lost. Whether they be irreparably dead in hell, or whether they are only dead to every great use God might make of their lives, their end is still tragic. Apostasy knows some passing point of no return. Mark this: "It is impossible for those who were once enlightened, and have tasted the heavenly gift, and have become partakers of the Holy Spirit, and have tasted the good word of God and the powers of the age to come, if they fall away, to renew them again to repentance, since they crucify again for themselves the Son of God, and put Him to an open shame" (Heb. 6:4–6). I find no real companionship with those who use their license to sin "as a cloak for vice" (1 Peter 2:16). Paul makes it clear that our license to sin begins in our willfulness. He further intimates that apostasy resides in the heart of Satan and that, when believers enter into league with Satan, they often depart the faith. "Now the Spirit expressly says," said Paul, "that in latter times some will depart from the faith, giving heed to deceiving spirits and doctrines of demons" (1 Tim. 4:1). Apostasy is the lesson of Jude to be reminded that our sin has consequence and that back-sliding is a serious offense that may lead there. Jude bids us remember that those angels that "kept not their first estate" God now keeps in everlasting chains (Jude 7 KJV). He further reminds us that while God saved Israel out of Egypt, he later destroyed those who did not believe (Jude 5). These Scriptures are not given to refute the prosaic issue of "once-saved-always-saved." God's grace is everlasting. But these verses in Jude exist to remind us all that apostasy is serious business, that apostasy begins in backsliding, and that backsliding begins in slipshod spirituality. The refusal to love God with all our hearts in any single moment may give place to the devil (Eph. 4:27). With such a little entrance, he may in time wreck our lives.

Station Six: Facing Death

Perhaps the strongest and most beautiful part of the *Pilgrim's Progress* comes at the end of the piece. Notice this powerful list of Scriptures which are given here to affirm our final crossing of the river of death:

> *Men:* There is the Mount Zion the heavenly Jerusalem, the innumerable company of angels, and the spirits of just men made perfect (Heb. 12:22–24). You are going now to the Paradise of God wherein you shall see the Tree of Life, and eat of the never-fading fruits thereof: and when you come there, you shall have white robes given you, and your walk and talk shall be every day with the King, even all the days of eternity (Rev. 2:7; 3:4,5; 22:5). There you shall not see again such things as you saw when you were in the lower region upon the earth: to wit, sorrow, sickness, affliction, and death, "for the former things are passed away" (Isa. 65:16,17).[7]

It is a benediction of grandeur. Jesus once said, "He who endures to the end will be saved" (Matt. 10:22). But consider the glory of our salvation:

> There your eyes shall be delighted with seeing, and your ears with hearing the pleasant voice of the Mighty One. There you shall enjoy your friends again that are gone thither before you, and there you shall with joy receive even everyone that follows into the holy place after you. There also you shall be clothed with glory and majesty, and put into an equipage fit to ride out with the King of Glory.[8]

There I must confess the sixth station of life's pilgrimage comes alive for me. When I think of all of those I have been forced to part with, I confess my solitary need of Christ. These images of seeing those who have gone before me fuel me with a sense of joy. I cannot escape it. The day is coming when, completely restored in his presence, I shall see again all those at whose gravesides were yielded up to God. Once parted, we shall someday claim all of the joys of heaven together. It shall be even as John wrote: "And I heard a loud voice from heaven saying, 'Behold, the tabernacle of God is with men, and He will dwell with them, and they shall be His people. . . . and God will wipe away every tear from their eyes; there shall be no more death, nor sorrow, nor crying; and there shall be no more pain, for the former things have passed away'" (Rev. 21:3–4).

Station Seven: The Final Union

None can fully imagine the glory of that final union. Perhaps we should let Bunyan end this chapter with his discussion of all that Pilgrim saw and rejoice in the final union promised to every pilgrim whose journey is faithful and whose life is committed to Christ:

> Now, when they were come up to the gate, there was written over it in letters of gold, "BLESSED ARE THEY THAT DO HIS COMMANDMENTS, THAT THEY MAY HAVE RIGHT TO THE TREE OF LIFE, AND MAY ENTER IN THROUGH THE GATES INTO THE CITY" (Rev. 22:14). . . .

> Now I saw in my dream that these two men went in at the gate. And lo, as they entered, they were transfigured; and they had raiment put on that shone like gold! There were also that met them with harps and crowns, and gave them to them; the harps to praise withal, and the crowns in token of honor. Then I heard in my dream that all the bells in the City rang again for joy and that it was said unto them: "Enter ye into the joy of our Lord" (Matt. 25:23).[9]

THE
PENIEL
GOD

The Unknown
Author of The Cloud
of Unknowing

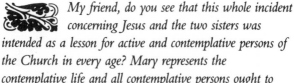 *My friend, do you see that this whole incident concerning Jesus and the two sisters was intended as a lesson for active and contemplative persons of the Church in every age? Mary represents the contemplative life and all contemplative persons ought to model their lives on hers. Martha represents the active life and all active persons should take her as their guide.*

Just as Martha complained about Mary, so in every age active persons have complained about contemplatives. How often it happens that the grace of contemplation will awaken in people of every walk and station of life, both religious and lay alike. But when after searching their own conscience and seeking reliable counsel they decide to devote themselves entirely to contemplation, their family and friends descend upon them in a storm of fury and criticism severely reproving them for idleness. These people will unearth every kind of dire tale both true and false about others who have taken up this way of life and ended up in terrible evils. Assuredly, they have nothing good to tell.

It is true that many who seemingly left worldly vanities behind have afterward followed evil ways. There is always that danger. These people who ought to have entered God's service as his contemplatives became instead slaves of the devil and the devil's contemplatives because they refuse to listen to the counsel of authentic spiritual guides. They became hypocrites or heretics and fell into frenzies and other wickedness which led them to slander Holy Church. I hesitate to go on about this right now lest I obscure our subject. But later on, God willing, if I see it is necessary, I shall tell you some of the causes and circumstances of their downfall. Let us leave the matter for the time being and continue with our subject.

—From *The Cloud of Unknowing*

FOR ANY WHO have ever tasted of the grace of Christ, there is no appetite so demanding as the hunger for God. There is no taste of joy quite as sweet as that momentary splendor that comes to us when we first savor the fullness of the everlasting God. But the days of these euphoric glories do not come often. For many of our days, God is elusive and leaves our hunger for him unappeased. For much of our lives, it seems, our quest for his presence is but a ritual of absence. Jesus said to his disciples, "A little while, and you will not see Me; and again a little while, and you will see Me" (John 16:16). This separation describes our inner yearning. But here and there our hunger and thirst for him is rewarded. He comes *to* us.

The Cloud of Unknowing seeks to answer one question: How does one go about loving God? This is the issue which haunts all who meditate on God's love. It is a fair question—an important question. But it is not the most prior question of our love affair with God. The prior question is: What about God's loving us? The Gallup Poll affirms that nine out of ten Americans believe that God loves them.[1] This is most striking when you consider that only four out of ten claim to have had a uniquely personal encounter with Christ. We are loved by God. We all feel that to be the case. But how do we express our longing toward him? This is the theme of *The Cloud of Unknowing.*

What strikes me as strange is that many are content to receive God's love and remain unchanged. They are loved but never become curious about their Lover. Their contented ignorance leaves them always unhappy. Their misery is all-engulfing. This misery results from an odd, double love: They are loved by God and yet they love only themselves. Harold Bloom observed that freedom in American religion means being alone with God or Christ; the soul hungers for this communion, he says.[2] How well his idea jibes with Blaise Pascal's God-shaped vacuum. This vacuum, said Pascal, lies at the heart of every person. It is God-shaped and only God can fill it. Yet the God-shaped vacuum cannot define his "shape." His greatness eludes our small human senses. Only our longing brings him near. Then we can see the unseeable and touch the intangible. Then our lives are forevermore an unending quest to have more of him. The reward of this yearning is his presence, which guarantees us that our life is not to be lived in loneliness. Our hunger to devour the things of God may not find everything on the table that it longs for. Still, that hunger tells us that the universe is not empty. *Gloria in excelsis!* God inhabits *our* universe. He stalks *our* lives. He is there and he is not silent. Our prayers are not dull auto-suggestion. They are the reaching words of lovers, begging, "Even so, come, Lord Jesus!" (Rev. 22:20).

Still, the face of God is an awesome reality. As Moses learned on the mountain of God: "No man shall see Me, and live" (Ex. 33:20). But we are all a little like Jacob in his flight from Laban to meet his brother Esau, whom he had wronged. Like Jacob, we are often in flight from one peril enroute to the next. For Jacob fled from a father-in-law who would like to destroy him, to a brother, Esau, whom he suspected would like to destroy him. What dismal alternatives? Not at all! For between the proverbial rock and the hard place is often the place where God at last speaks. But, more than speak, it is here God comes down and wrestles with us as he did with Jacob.

What is the glorious end of this wrestling match? Jacob cried the name of God, only to be reproved and congratulated: "Your name shall no longer be called Jacob, but Israel; for you have struggled with God and with men, and have prevailed. . . . And He blessed him there. So Jacob called the name of the place Peniel: 'For I have seen God face to face, and my life is preserved'" (Gen. 32:28–30). Which of us in fleeing from the circumstances of life do not hunger for such a corroborating vision? It is almost delicious to fear God. We are so in need of knowing that God *is* that we would as soon be suddenly and violently destroyed by his awesome presence as to be slowly eaten away by our fear of his absence. "Come,

God, show us your face," we beg. "Kill us with the very sight of it, but do not leave us alone to fight with our circumstances, unsure about whether you are there or whether or not you love us."

In the fourteenth century there lived a holy man whose name we shall never know. He, like so many of the devotional writers of days gone by, was not out to make a name for himself in the publishing world. He, therefore, left his work unsigned. For like John the Baptist, he saw himself only as a voice. His words were not his own. His name, for him, held no consequence. His life held only one meaning: to contemplate God. He wanted to offer the light he had discovered to others who yet hungered for his own face-to-face experience. If any human life holds a reason to exist, the reason must be union with Christ. This nameless author believed that only when we are united with Christ does life have purpose.

St. John of the Cross once cried, "O life, how canst thou endure since thou livest not where God livest?"[3] In every heart that names the name of Christ, this cry exists. But our hungering after God is sometimes flawed. Most believers only hunger for the *Peniel* experience when they are locked in paralyzing circumstances. But there are those who have an unquenchable ever-present need for God. These needy ones do not cry, "God show me your face, I'm in deep trouble." For them, the *Peniel* hunger is a way of life, a continuous cry of the soul. They remain unsatisfied unless they are always face to face with Christ.

Distinguishing Active and Passive Christianity

How we deal with this hunger of soul will involve our discernment in several areas. We must learn to define and clearly differentiate between the active and passive life, based on the Mary/Martha model. Not only should we know which of these two women best defines our own spiritual mystique, we must also be able to define our detachment from worldly entanglements. Finally, we must be able to distinguish between the power of knowing and the power of loving. The power of knowing leads to intellectual reputation within the church. The power of loving God leads to an utter passion for union with Christ.

Distinguishing Between the Active Life and the Passive Life

Martha and Mary (Luke 10:38–42) are different kinds of people. In examining this account, one cannot help feeling that Martha is trying to discredit Mary. She feels Mary should help with the immense work of hostessing Jesus and his friends. But if there is ever to be any peace in the church, the active people must not discredit the contemplatives. Each group is to be respected for their differing spiritual mystiques. The author of *The Cloud* takes the position that the servant's service, while utterly important to the church, begins and ends on earth. It is quite another matter with the contemplative person:

Let me begin by saying that in the Church there are two kinds of life, the active and the contemplative. The active life is lower, and the contemplative life is higher.

The active life is such that it begins and ends on earth. The contemplative life, however, may indeed begin on earth but it will continue without end into eternity. This is because the contemplative life is *Mary's part which shall never be taken away.* The active life is troubled and busy about many things but the contemplative life *sits in peace with the one thing necessary.*[4]

The illustration I am about to use may be a weak one to get at the heart of this distinction, but here goes. In the church I was very fond of the deacon council. They were men who prayed for the health and welfare of the congregation. The trustees and the finance committee were less favorites of mine. These "secondary" committees dealt with the nuts and bolts of church business issues. In spite of my preference for the work of prayer in the church, which of the two groups was more necessary to God? No answer can be given to this. If the church loses its financial credibility, who would maintain any interest in its spiritual credibility? Nor is it fair to say that the trustees were all ponderously *Martha* while the deacons were gloriously *Mary.* The church needs both the contemplative and active members to define itself. It is important to realize in this passage that Jesus does not rebuke Martha for not being like Mary, only for criticizing Mary for not being more like *her.* Activists are prone to cry that contemplatives are "super-spiritual" and useless in the *real* world. Contemplatives are prone to criticize activists as people of trivial passions. Contemplatives snub the church's casserole-bakers. They view these "Marthas" as spiritually flat as the pancakes they fry for the brotherhood. Obviously, such mutual snobbery cannot build the body of Christ into a loving missionary enticement to a lost world.

Distinguishing Between Detachment from Our Present World and the "Cloud of Forgetting"

The author of *The Cloud* says that we are to separate ourselves from our earthly attachments in a most unusual way. We are to construct a second cloud, beneath our position in Christ. This is a *cloud of forgetting*. This cloud obscures our world of earthly attachments. In this cloud we forget all that hinders a focus on God. It goes without saying that we are to forget those sins that God has forgiven; even God has forgotten those (Isa. 43:25). We are even to forget the glory of that forgiveness, not because it is not wonderful to think about, but because in thinking of that glory, we cannot pursue the greater glory of knowing Christ. Both our sin and our material attachments are to be voluntarily hidden in this cloud of forgetting. We are not to give attention to what we own or those busy agendas that fill our days with empty hurriedness. But the *cloud of forgetting* does more than just obscure the sins of materialism and busy-ness. This *cloud of forgetting* should be allowed even to cover our religious thoughts and our saccharine devotionalisms. Our hungers should be those of union with Christ, not a hunger for merely knowing more about him or praising his goodness. Even our good and holy thoughts should not be allowed to take the place of our pursuit of union with Christ:

> Actually, they were good and holy thoughts, so valuable, in fact, that anyone who expects to advance without having meditated often on his own sinfulness, the Passion of Christ, and the kindness, goodness, and dignity of God, will most certainly go astray and fail in his purpose. But a person who has long pondered these things must eventually leave them behind beneath a *cloud of forgetting* if he hopes to pierce the *cloud of unknowing* that lies between him and his God.[5]

This may seem almost severe to us. How, indeed, are we to separate our thoughts of the glory of Christ from Christ himself?

But it is possible to separate from others without hungering for God.[6] I know many Christians who must have their "me time." They want to be alone with themselves to end the stress in their lives. But they are not craving that aloneness that invites Union with Christ. Rather, they crave that aloneness that gets rid of all cumbersome involvements. Loving aloneness sometimes is only selfish individualism.[7]

Distinguishing the Knowing Power and the Loving Power

Most of the great devotional classics of Christianity were not written by scholars or theologians. Indeed, these writers often played down their true knowledge of theological things. They were bent on loving God, not knowing him in an intellectual sense. They weren't championing ignorance in their pursuit of Union with Christ, but they emphasized *apophatic* or "non-rational" meditation. The author of *The Cloud* admits to being influenced by Dionysius who had written of this distinction in the sixth century. The way of knowledge (the *logos* way) as an approach to God should be seen as inferior to the way of love:

> According to Dionysius, there are two ways in which man can know God: one is the way of reason *(logos);* the other is the way of mystical contemplation.
>
> Rational knowledge of God is obtained through speculative theology and philosophy; but mystical knowledge is greatly superior to this, giving a knowledge of God that is intuitive and ineffable. Hence, it is called "mystical" or "hidden."[8]

The author of *The Cloud of Unknowing* states several times that the pursuit of God's love is a gift.[9] Those who have it have been given the gift of seeking divine love. All who do not seek God's love should remember that his love may be wounded. Consider the following tale.

An African myth tells of a tribe whose people noticed that their cows were not giving as much milk as they once did. In spying on their cows at midnight, they noticed a beautiful young woman carrying a large pail and floating down to earth on a moon ray. She milked their cows and went back to the skies. On the following night, when they trapped this thieving goddess, they discovered that she was the Sky Maiden, a member of a sky tribe who had no other way to get food for themselves. The man who had trapped the Sky Maid promised to release her if she would return and marry him. She agreed, but only if he would allow her to return to the sky for three days and prepare herself. When she returned, she brought with her a large sealed box. She told the man that she would now marry him, but he must promise her he would never look inside the box. They were married and for many weeks lived happily together, but one day when his wife was away from their hut, the bridegroom's curiosity got the best of him. He opened the box and looked inside. He was amazed. The box was empty.

When the Sky Maid discovered that he had looked inside, she refused to be married to him any longer. Her earthbound husband did not understand why she would leave him for so trivial a matter as an empty box. She replied to him with these words:

> I'm not leaving you because you opened the box, I thought you probably would. I'm leaving you because you said it was empty. It wasn't empty; it was full of sky. It contained the light and the air and the smells of my home in the sky. When I went home for the last time, I filled that box with everything that was most precious to me to remind me of where I came from. How can I be your wife if what is most precious to me is emptiness to you?[10]

This parable explains the plight of God. How is it that, when we mean so very much to God, he means so little to us? Yet his love is wonderful because it is unconditional. It flows eternally toward us, whether or not we ever stop to love God in return.

For when we were still without strength, in due time Christ died for the ungodly. For scarcely for a righteous man will one die; yet perhaps for a good man someone would even dare to die. But God demonstrates His own love toward us, in that while we were still sinners, Christ died for us.

(Rom. 5:6–8)

God loves us to the extremity of the cross and says to us, "Look in the box." Grace fills the treasure chest of God. Is his love glorious or of no value? Do you experience this love beyond all telling, or are you incriminated by Jeremiah's cry, "Is it nothing to you?" (Lam. 1:12).

But sometimes we come to the treasury of God, and it appears empty. Our hunger has driven us to his treasure chest, and yet his presence seems elusive. He hides himself, it seems. We need the *Peniel* experience, but find ourselves face to face with emptiness.

Is it for our own good that the face of God is veiled? Perhaps it is because, as we have said, no man can see it and live. The *shekinah* of his face is so laser in its glory that it would sear the human retina to darkness. But this unknown fourteenth-century mystic taught that the fullness of union that we hunger for is veiled by a cloud of unknowing. The only thing that can pierce this veil is our desire for *Peniel*—that driving hunger that brings us face to face with him. Until the intensity of our love for God is greater than all other earthly concerns, *Peniel* is impossible.

I need to say that *Peniel*, in the way I am using it, is unused by the author of *The Cloud of Unknowing*. Even though this devotional classic does not use the term, I believe the book hungers for its reality. Let me define the two sides of this hunger. First, there is a crisis hunger for relationship. Second, there is also the lover's hunger for *Peniel*.

When our son Timothy was born, his first weeks of life were tenuous. He suffered repeated attacks of pneumonia. Often his little body would lie so still that my eye was not able to discern by the rising and the falling of his coverlet that he was even alive. Those days were days of silent suffering. In that season of

143

despairing, Barbara and I always prayed each night that he would be alive the next morning. How often my faith seemed smaller than the crisis. I needed to know God felt what I felt. I wanted to see him. I cried for *Peniel*. But the crisis so blinded my spiritual vision that I could not see God. I wanted him to come to me as he came to Jacob. I yearned to be a prince who "struggled with God and . . . prevailed" (Gen. 32:28).

Our Tim gradually grew stronger. Today he lives to bless us by being so involved in our lives. Now I celebrate yesterday's lost moments. Those bygone days taught me that those who hunger for *Peniel* in a crisis usually pray with the crisis in mind. Their prayers are so focused on their needs that they talk to God without seeing him. While I prayed, "God, save our baby," I confess that my mind was more focused on our baby than on Christ. God did answer our prayers, but he did not show himself to us. He couldn't. Our eyes were downcast and he stood above us. Instead of piercing the cloud of unknowing, we were still muddling beneath the cloud of forgetting. So the crisis obscures our hunger for *Peniel*.

The second hunger for *Peniel* is the hunger of separated lovers. Heaven promises to end our separation with God ultimately as it provides us with glorious union. Till then our hunger must endure the pain of separation that only lovers know.

Shortly after our marriage, I moved to Kansas City, where I was a "middler" in seminary. During our first few weeks of marriage, I had made good money at my job as a chemist, but I had been remiss in saving the money I made. Had I saved that money, it would have allowed us the convenience of moving together to the seminary. Since we did not have the capital to move and set up our home together, we both agreed that I would move to Kansas City alone. I would work there for a period of weeks until I had saved enough money to allow Barbara to join me. The idea seemed like a good one at the time.

What I had not reckoned on was the pain of separation that we would endure for several weeks. I took care of the first two assignments: I found a small affordable apartment and a job, run-

ning a press at Hallmark Cards Manufacturing Corporation. It
was in waiting through the first few paydays that I found I was
not able to manage. At twenty-three years of age, the three weeks
I had to wait until my first payday seemed more time than the
entire Pleistocene Age had once consumed.

What were the lessons of God during these days? I learned the
lessons of the city. I was from the country and the country was
warm. The country was caring. The country knew neighbors and
smiles and community. The country loved me as I loved it. My
new bride was still in the country, but I was in the city. Here no
one knew me, no one smiled, no one spoke. In our separation I
learned Sandburg's truth about cities:

> Of my city the worst that men will ever say is this:
> You took little children away from the sun and the dew,
> And the glimmers that played in the grass under the
>   great sky,
> And the reckless rain; you put them between walls
> To work, broken and smothered, for bread and wages,
> To eat dust in their throats and die empty-hearted
> For a little handful of pay on a few Saturday nights.[11]

I knew why Jesus, himself from the country, laid out the work
of the kingdom to be done in the cities. Just as he was about to
leave this earth in ascension, he told them not to go back to their
comfortable rural lives; rather, he told them to wait in the city till
the Spirit came (Luke 24:49). Barbara's absence took all the country out of my worldview. I, like those frightened apostles, had to
wait in the city where life was depersonalized by the very crush
of urban heaviness. There in the city would the kingdom of God
be born. I was lonely. I was bored. Boredom is the curse of empty
people. I can understand why Kierkegaard wrote that boredom
built an "urban Babel":

> Adam was bored because he was alone, and so Eve was
> created. [From that moment on] boredom entered the world,

145

and increased in proportion to the increase of population. Adam was bored alone; then Adam and Eve were bored together; then Adam and Eve and Cain and Abel were bored *en famille;* then the population of the world increased, and the peoples were bored *en masse.* To divert themselves they conceived the idea of constructing a tower high enough to reach the heavens.[12]

Babel had an urban tower. *Babel* has come to mean "unintelligible, guttural nonsense." Babel is man's poor attempt to communicate when life itself is meaningless.

I knew the pain of Babel. They who had made themselves "urban" were out to make a name for themselves (Gen. 11:4). But it is hard to make a name for ourselves in the city, for the city steals our stamina with empty anonymity. Emptiness is the parent of boredom. Emptiness fosters such expensive ideas as Epcot and cruises. But the plastic faces of all in the plastic kingdom tell the real truth. Millions of people live in sterile desolation. Cities are not really crowded; they are moonscapes of emptiness and vacant hopes. Only a loving God can refresh the empty soul.

Even though I was a Christian, I was not appropriately the receiver of God's love. My loneliness in Kansas City was telltale. Day by day I found myself inventing things to do to avoid the early bedtimes. I found myself totally absorbed in thoughts of my absentee bride. It seemed that the long days and slow nights would never allow us to be together again. But the agonizing weekdays faded into even more intolerable weekends. Finally in desperation, I called Barbara's home in Oklahoma. She was not home, so I talked to her aunt. In a kind of force I rarely use, I all but threatened her aunt, "Tell Barb I have only about $40.00, so I cannot afford to mail her the train ticket I promised to send. But tell her I refuse to wait till our poverty eases. I intend to meet the train at Union Station on Saturday morning. I have no idea where she will get the money for the fare, but *I want her to be on that train!"*

"Well, well . . . uh . . ." stammered her aunt. "All right, I'll tell her!"

For the next few days of my life, I prepared the apartment. I worked, trusting that somehow Barbara would find money— perhaps from some compassionate relative—and she would indeed be on the train. We never talked (I couldn't afford a phone). I had no real assurance that she would be able to beg, borrow, or steal the money she needed. Thus my early rising on Saturday and my driving to Union Station was entirely an act of faith and love.

I stood at the top of an escalator in Union Station on the fateful day. I waited out the preoccupation of my faith in our common love. Suddenly I heard the rumble of the train's arrival on tracks below. My senses froze on autopilot. I stared down the dark opening of the rising belt of silver stairs. In a moment, people began floating up the stair belt. Never had I realized how many unnecessary people there were in the world: noisy children, over- weight women, paunchy, red-faced men in hats and boots. Then in the never-ending queue of pointless people, I saw a white glove on the escalator belt. What of it? Many people wore white gloves in those days. Then I saw a blue dress just like the one she had worn away from the church when we began our honeymoon. And so what? Others might have blue dresses. But when I saw her face and those bewitching brown eyes that had first drawn me into their ensnaring magic, I knew the force of our love. The gloves, dress, even the mystique might belong to someone else, but not those eyes. What a reunion was ours. A new and glorious doctrine was written that day into my theology of marriage. God does not give us poverty to separate us but to unite us in the facing of our joint neediness. Poverty is an asset of togetherness in marriage: To be poor together is much better than being poor separately. But our longing to be together remains for me a kind of allegory of all that Christians should feel for Jesus. The restless souls of all who know Christ should reach ever upward with longing. Jesus is in heaven and we remain his earthly servants.

The longing of lovers is as near as I can get to explaining the kind of hunger that believers ought to feel for their separated Lord. There is a German theologism, *sensucht,* that comes close; the best translation of the word would be something like the word *homesickness.* Yet this word, in reference to eternity, is still not strong enough for those possessed of a *Peniel* hunger. The yearnings of some who walk with Christ is a dogging kind of hunger that is not willing to wait for eternal union. It wants to know Christ *now*.

There is all too little of this in the contemporary church. We love church, Christian reputation, the programs that involve our lives and order us to serve them. We love teaching, preaching, camp programs, prayer circles, etc. In short, we love the things of God, not God.

The anonymous author of *The Cloud of Unknowing* speaks of this hunger for *Peniel* as a passion of the heart. It is a passion which remains firm in spite of the fact that our love affair with Jesus is blocked. The mystical barrier that exists between our physical natures and the spiritual nature of our lover must be crossed. This barrier, this cloud of unknowing, keeps us from union.

Let me return once more to my illustration of early marriage. Missing my wife was not a matter of summing up intellectual categories of love. Nor could missing her be expressed by explaining the chemistry of love. Rather, this ache was an intuitive meditation of passion:

> He whom neither men nor angels can grasp by knowledge can be embraced by love. For the intellect of both men and angels is too small to comprehend God as he is in himself.
>
> Try to understand this point. Rational creatures such as men and angels possess two principle faculties, a knowing power and a loving power. No one can fully comprehend the uncreated God with his knowledge; but each one, in a different way, can grasp him fully through love.[13]

Knowledge may write theology, but only love can spell Union with Christ. Yet in that separation from Barbara to which I earlier alluded, I wanted no remembrance of the little pet peeves of our early days. I wanted to forget any pain I might ever have caused her, lest I blunt my desire to be with her. But this "cloud of forgetting" in our relationship went even further. I was not even willing to content myself by pondering her virtues. Just as forgetting her bad points would not make me happy, neither would celebrating her good points. Only her presence could make me content. Thus it is with Christ and his lovers. Tragically, Christians do not all seem to be possessed with this ardor of soul. Some seem to care far more about churchy things than they do knowing Christ at this face-to-face level. It is to clarify this difference in Christians that the author of *The Cloud of Unknowing* turns to the biblical example of Mary and Martha. The author finds no fault with those in the church who are honestly Mary or genuinely Martha. Neither does he believe that the Marthas of the church (those possessed with active Christian lifestyles) should be critical of the Marys (those who are more turned toward the pursuit of Union with Christ). In fact, every Mary should have a little of Martha in her, and vice versa. Every activist should have a prayer life. Every contemplative should be active in ministry. As *The Cloud* unfolds, the writer makes it clear that in some sense all Christians can only be defined as *Christians* if they are in love with Christ, their separated Lover. Let us turn now to the issue of how much we should desire knowing God face to face. Only then can we know who we are and what we have been called to do. Only then will we understand whether we are more like Mary or more like Martha. Only then will we know whether we should serve first and pray as we serve, or pray first and serve as we pray.

Are We Spiritual Activists or Contemplatives?

One of the greatest sins in the church is the refusal of Christians to seek to define their spiritual gifts (1 Cor. 12, Rom. 12, Eph. 4). To fail to seek out what we have been called to do keeps the church hamstrung. This is its equivalent: Consider a hospital of a thousand employees who have never made decisions as to which of them will be surgeons and which will be the janitors. Both are essential to a hospital. But without self-definition, who will meet the ambulances and who will care for sanitation?

If there is a second sin, it may be the sin of failing to define these key categories of activism and contemplation. Neither category is inferior. We are all God's children—missionary healers and teachers. But it would be best to isolate whether or not we are Mary or Martha. Then we can round out the kingdom of God with our best self-definition.

The Martha Christian. Again, as the Marthas of the church take their place in the world, they need to understand that their position is not inferior. The author of *The Cloud* counsels:

> You are busy and troubled about many things. This indicates that active persons will always be busy and concerned about countless diverse affairs pertaining first of all to themselves and then to their fellow Christians as love requires. He wanted Martha to realize that her work was important and valuable to her spiritual development.[14]

To accept our calling, as God has made us, is commendable. But as I have already said, to judge contemplatives as spiritually useless is beneath the dignity of Marthas:

> I think that those striving to be contemplative should not only pardon all who complain about them, but be so occupied with their own work that they do not even notice what is said or done around them. That is what Mary Magdalene did and she is our model. If we follow her example Jesus will surely do for us what he did for her.

> And what was that? You recall that Martha urged Jesus to reprimand Mary; to tell her to get up and help with the work. But our blessed Lord Jesus Christ, who discerned the secret thoughts of every heart, understood perfectly that Mary was deep in loving contemplation of his divinity and so he himself took her part.[15]

The Marthas are ministers, and Jesus made it clear that the priority of the kingdom of God is ministry. After all, where would missions and evangelism be if everybody's gifts were contemplation and continual prayer for union? Someone must get out, touch the dying, and tell them of Jesus.

Jesus clearly said that he had come to be a servant (Matt. 20:28). One catches in Jesus what must be the perfect balance between the servant and the meditative lifestyle. The best of all possible approaches must be, therefore, the person who can be both Martha and Mary. There must be intermittent spaces in our prayer lives when we begin to minister with our hands. Hans Urs von Balthasar says that pressed between contemplating Christ and showing mercy in his name, we must first choose the showing of mercy. For it is on the basis of our merciful acts, and not our aloof meditations, that we shall ultimately be judged by a needy world.

> How the Lord will judge, no one knows in advance; he tells us just one thing, namely, what he will judge about: "I was hungry, and you gave me food (or you gave me no food)." Me, in the least of my brethren. Have we shown mercy, or only loved ourselves? Once the documents have been presented, there is no longer any need at all to pronounce the verdict: "I will condemn you out of your own mouth, you wicked servant!" (Luke 19:22). "Should not you have had mercy on your fellow servant as I had mercy on you?" (Matt. 18:33). "Judgment is without mercy to one who has shown no mercy; yet mercy triumphs over judgment" (James 2:13).[16]

All who are satisfied to contemplate Jesus as the sole activity for life should see their contemplation as a ministry. Martha's ministry to Jesus and his followers must have said that everyone can't sit around being holy all the time. The world without Marthas is unfed and uncared for.

Contemplation in terms of union is a kind of servanthood.

But consider all the kinds of servanthood that radiate from direct commandment of the Scriptures:

> Matthew 20:27: "And whoever desires to be first among you, let him be your slave."

> Matthew 25:21: "Well done, good and faithful servant."

> Philippians 2:5-7: "Let this mind be in you which was also in Christ Jesus, who, being in the form of God, did not consider it robbery to be equal with God, but made Himself of no reputation, taking the form of a bondservant."

If, as Jesus suggests, Mary has chosen the best part (contemplation), then it must be that her commendation by Christ comes in terms of her servanthood. Contemplation, then, is not the opposite of ministry. It is but another kind of service.

The Mary Christian. The essence of this chapter may seem to argue that a Christ-focused life is a gift. To some degree, I believe that it is true. Perhaps here the author of *The Cloud* will bear me out:

> Contemplative prayer is God's gift, wholly gratuitous. No one can earn it. It is in the nature of this gift that one who receives it receives also the aptitude for it. No one can have the aptitude without the gift itself. The aptitude for this work is one with the work; they are identical.[17]

During the sixties and seventies, I used to take various "deeper-life" discipleship programs and try to make them universal within the church I served. Inevitably, only 15 to 20 percent of the people would get very excited about these programs. Across the pole from this 15 percent was another 15 percent who seemed to have no interest in these "contemplative" programs at all. Scattered along the gradient between these no-interest and deeper-life poles was all of the rest of the congregation. I used to think of these poles as the "busy people" and the "godly people." I now believe these early categorizations were erroneous.

The Broadway play *Agnes of God* makes the point that people like Agnes, or in the case of this book, the author of *The Cloud of Unknowing,* do in a sense possess a special gift. They have a kind of romantic drivenness to know God. I believe the author of *The Cloud* is trying to say this when he makes a special category for the active people. The author readily admits that the stringent demands of the contemplative life are not suited for all:

> I have in mind a person who, over and above the good works of the active life, has resolved to follow Christ (as far as is humanly possible with God's grace) into the inmost depths of contemplation. Do your best to determine if he is one who has first been faithful for some time to the demands of the active life, for otherwise he will not be prepared to fathom the contents of this book. . . .
>
> This applies, also, to the merely curious, educated or not. They may be good people by the standards of the active life, but this book is not suited to their needs.[18]

So, at the risk of saying it too often, Marys must be content with loving God through the inward yearnings of the heart. Marthas must be content to love God through more frequent acts of ministry and service.

It was a great lay friend who once taught me the simple power of this truth. I saw this man whom everyone respected as a great servant of the kingdom. He never really did get into the prayer ministries of the church. Yet under his leadership, our educational organization grew. It advanced from only a few souls to an enrollment of nearly two thousand people. He worked tirelessly. At first I said that he did it because he was ego-driven. He wanted to build a huge organization. Later, I came to the conclusion that no one worked that hard just to build an organization. He was a man committed to the principle that loving Christ was a matter of "actively" serving Christ. He was a Martha, his adoration naturally coming in a way that he appropriated and understood life. Even today he still has the greatest respect of the congregation he serves.

But as we have said, active persons must also have a prayer and study life. In a sense I see them as persons who are more "intermittent" in their contemplation of Christ. Active persons pray; indeed, their whole life may be a prayer. In truth, they may pray without ceasing. But they rarely "stop" and pray. They pray while they serve. I am brought back again to the "little way" of Brother Lawrence. Remember that he prayed as he did dishes. Yet his minimal religious writings indicate that he was a contemplative as well as an active. Great servants of God can not be neatly divided into Marys and Marthas. Brother Lawrence, to all who worked around him at the monastery, may have appeared to be a Martha, "always busy about many things." In reality, he was a Mary whose inwardness never lost its focus.

Directing the Hiding Yearnings of the Heart

But for the Marys who serve in a visibly more passive way, it must be said that these hiding yearnings of the heart must find a quiet place to take their exercise (Ps. 46:10). The church must make place for them, not just to tolerate them but to apprise and esteem their devotion. When Malcom Muggeridge visited the monks of Nunraw, he expected to find men whose lives were wasted because all they did was pray. After a little while in their presence, he saw them in a new light. He became convinced that it was their prayers that made the world possible. He ultimately believed that without their fervent prayer, national deficits and international wars would be more severe. These devout men convinced Muggeridge that their prayers undergirded world peace.

In a more practical vein, I have known great pastors who lived busy and activist lives. Forthrightly, they admitted that the power of their ministry was often traceable to a single person. They knew of someone in their church who loved Christ and prayed for them night and day. All that these great pastors accomplished was made possible by those whose praying lives were committed to them. Charles Haddon Spurgeon once told about a visitor to his church. The man was taken on a tour of the great metropolitan tabernacle. The tour was extensive, taking in every nook and cranny of the church. It ended at the church's "boiler room." The visitor was confused as to why he was being shown the boiler room. Spurgeon then opened the door to the private closet off to one side of the room. There the visitor saw a number of churchmen kneeling and praying. Here, said Spurgeon, was the power plant of the church. Behind Spurgeon's oratory was a circle of contemplatives making his very ministry possible.

At the risk of sounding sexist, praying wives and mothers serve their activist sons and spouses in remarkable ways. As we saw in chapter 1, R. A. Torrey readily admitted that his mother's unceasing prayers hounded him to conversion. Augustine confessed the same thing of Monica's prayers. Some pastors I know are married to powerful women of prayer. It would be impossible for them to achieve anything less than dynamic, world-changing ministries. Thus, it is often the unrelenting Marys who create the achievements of super-productive Marthas.

The Marys must be given room for their devotion. They should be appreciated, even if they seem "off on a cloud of their own spirituality." The busier Marthas of the kingdom must be prayed for so that their lives will remain in touch with God.

Accepting Our Hunger for Christ

Since Marys are so essential, they must not allow the criticisms of the "busybody" Marthas to bring them to an untenable low point in their own self-esteem. The author of *The Cloud of Unknowing* seems always to confuse Mary Magdalene with Mary of Bethany. Few reliable biblical scholars would agree with his confusion of the two Marys. But let's grant him this error for the sake of his argument. Magdalene is the woman first to see earth's greatest truth. If we can accept Mary's weeping hunger, the glory of her need makes her a heroine for the entire world. How glorious is her role that first Easter morning. It is Mary who finds the tomb empty and is first to discover that great, all-glorious Resurrection truth: He is risen:

> This is the same Mary who sought him weeping at the tomb that first Easter morning. The angels spoke to her so gently then. "Do not weep, Mary," they said. "For the Lord whom you seek is risen as he said. He is going on before you into Galilee. There you will see him with his disciples, as he promised." But even angels were powerless to reassure her or stop her tears. Mere angels could hardly comfort one who had set out to find the King of Angels.[19]

Finding Our Completeness in God

But whether Mary or Martha, all of us are called to find our completion in Christ. If we seek that completion in any other way, we sin. Jesus reminded us that if our eye is single, our whole body shall be full of light. We must all, Mary or Martha, focus our eyes on completion in Christ:

> And so I say again to anyone who wants to become a real contemplative like Mary, let the wonderful transcendence and goodness of God teach you humility rather than the thought of your own sinfulness, for then your humility will be perfect.[20]

Whoever possesses God, as this book attests, needs nothing else in this life.

This single-eye devotion is the basis of the kingdom of God (Matt. 6:33). If indeed we seek *only* the kingdom, it will matter little whether we do it in active or contemplative ways. Purity of heart will fall upon the church, baptizing it in purpose and joy.

This final all-consuming joy will be marked for either Mary or Martha in three developmental stages of entering into Christ:

Nevertheless, although the active and the contemplative are the two ways of life in the Holy Church, yet within them, taken as a whole, there are three parts, three ascending stages. These we have already discussed, but I will briefly summarize them here. The first stage is the good and upright Christian life in which love is predominately active in the corporal works of mercy. In the second, a person begins to meditate on spiritual truths regarding his own sinfulness, the Passion of Christ, and the joys of eternity. . . .

In the third stage a person enters the dark *cloud of unknowing* where in secret and alone he centers all his love on God. The first stage is good, the second is better, but the third is best of all. This is the best part belonging to Mary. It is surely obvious now why our Lord did not say to Martha, "Mary has chosen the best life."[21]

It is to the glory of Mary's *best* part that we should all commit our days. For in the light of eternity to come, entering into Christ is the only part that will have mattered.

CONQUERING
PRIDE

Bernard of Clairvaux

Avoid what is forbidden, lest you lose what has been given to you. Why do you look so intently on your death? Why are you always glancing at it? What is the good of looking at what you are forbidden to eat?

"I reach out with my eyes, not my hand," you say. "I was not forbidden to look, only to eat. Can I not look where I like with the eyes God gave me?" To this the Apostle says, "I may do anything, but not everything is good for me" (1 Cor. 6:12). Even if it is not a sin, it hints at sin. For if the mind had not been failing to keep a check on itself your curiosity would not have been wandering. Even if there is no fault, there is an occasion of sin and a prompter to sin and a cause of sin. For when you are looking intently at something, the serpent slips into your heart and coaxes you. He leads on your reason with flattery; he awakes your fear with lies.

"You will not die," he says (Gen. 3:4). He increases your interest while he stirs up your greed. He sharpens your curiosity while he prompts your desire. . . . You too, Satan, were made in the likeness of God, and you had a place not even in the Garden of Eden but in the delights of God's paradise (Ezek. 28:12). What more ought you to ask? Full of wisdom and perfect in beauty, "Do not seek what is too high and try to look into what is too mighty for you" (Sir 3:22). Stand in your proper place, lest you fall from it, by walking in the great and wonderful which is beyond you (Ps. 130:1). Why are you looking toward the north? I see you now. I do not know what you are thinking, except that it is about something which is beyond your reach. "I will place my throne in the north," you say (Isa. 14:13). Everyone else in heaven is standing. You alone affect to sit. You disrupt the harmony of your brothers, the peace of the whole heavenly realm, and, if it were in your power, you would disturb the tranquility of the Trinity.

O wretch, is this what your curiosity has led to, that all by yourself you do not hesitate to offend the citizens of heaven and insult its King? "Thousands of thousands minister to him. Ten times a hundred thousand stand before him" (Dan. 7:10). In that court no one has a right to sit, except he who sits above the cherubim (Ps. 79:2), and whom the others serve. You want to distinguish yourself from others. You want to pry with your curiosity. You want to push in disrespectfully. You want to set up a throne for yourself in heaven so that you may be like the Most High (Isa. 14:14).

With what purpose? On what do you rest your confidence? Measure your strength, you fool. Think about the purpose of what you are doing; consider the manner in which you are doing it. Are you presuming to do this with the knowledge of the Most High, or does he not know? Is he willing for you to do it or are you acting against his will? His knowledge extends to everything. His will is for the best. How can you contrive any evil of which he is ignorant or in which he supports you? Do you think he knows and is against what you do, but cannot prevent it? Unless you believe that you are not his creature, (Job 36:4) I do not think you can be in any doubt about the omnipotence and universal knowledge and goodness of the Creator, for he was able to create you from nothing and he knows how to make you as he willed.

—From *Selected Works of Bernard of Clairvaux*

ONLY ONCE HAVE I been hated! That hate, like all hate, came from a proud person. The humble are prone to hate nothing but their pretensions. The proud find contempt more second-nature. The person who hated me gave rise to a single response within me: I made a commitment never to answer hate in kind. Hate engenders hate. But hate is never born of itself. It springs from pride. To be hated almost always triggers one immediate defensiveness within us, "I'm not so bad. In fact, deep down, I'm a wonderful person. Actually, I'm splendid. So, why am I hated?" Inflated self-assessment often gives rise to vengeance. We hate back. It is our reasoning that if we are as wonderful as we proclaim ourselves to be, then we have every right to answer hate in kind. As hate and pride always keep company, humility and love do too. Pride is the fruit of conceit. Conceit is bilious self-love, too airy to keep its feet on the ground. It worships its own opinions. "Don't become set in your own opinions," said the apostle (Rom. 12:16 PHILLIPS). Paul said this because he knew the love of self-infatuation is too small a package for great souls.

In 1090 Bernard was born and, by his twenty-first birthday, he had founded a Cistercian monastery in Aube, France, in the valley of Clairvaux. He was deeply offended by the monks of Cluny for grand permissions they gave themselves in surfeiting and high-court living. Bernard could see that materialistic indulgence came with pride and that pride was the spoiler of our journey toward God.

How truly has Bernard advised our lives. For when we are hated, we come across Satan's most serious temptation: not the temptation merely to return hate but to plunge ourselves into defensive pride. In my case it was certainly true that I was not as despicable as my enemy painted me. Still, I should have been content to let God answer my critic. I decided that the only way

I could withstand his demeaning attacks was to try and build myself up in my own eyes. But Bernard warns us about arriving at such self-contrived esteem:

> When I was still in ignorance of the truth, [I] thought myself something when I was nothing (Gal. 6:3). But after I had come to believe in Christ, that is, to imitate his humility, I learned the truth and that truth is raised up in me by my confession. But "I am profoundly humbled," that is, I have been greatly lowered in my own estimation (Ps. 115:10).[1]

The worst feature of trying to build ourselves up in our own eyes is that we become like the Pharisees. The Pharisees, proud of their own humility, were excoriated by Jesus because they were "braggy" about their virtue. They could hate enough to trump up a crucifixion, yet they walked with downcast eyes so that all would notice their humility. Jesus spent a lot of time helping them define who they really were. Humility is easily complimented into pride. But once we agree to the compliment of humility, we own it no more. The Pharisee's definition was quite the opposite. Bernard described the devouring scourge of crass pride: "Pride in the mind is a great beam which is bloated rather than heavy, swollen rather than solid, and it blocks the mind's eye and blots out the light of truth, so that if your mind is full of it you cannot see yourself as you really are."[2]

Pride has for its worst fault the obscuring of everything but the self and its agenda. There exists everywhere about us the myth of the free spirit. America has become fertile ground for the development of the individual extremism. Tim Bascom describes a real-life event of the eighties. Like so many of us who heard of the "flying lawn-chair man," Bascom was both amused and instructed:

> One of my personal heroes is a man hardly anyone has ever heard of. I don't even remember his name. But ten years ago, he decided to fly. He got his hands on a bunch of

weather balloons, tied them to a lawn chair and took off. All he carried with him was a soda and a BB gun. . . .

This fellow toasts himself, the only man to have flown a lawn chair. Then a plane passes a half-mile away, and he waves. Inside, packed in with hundreds of other conventional travelers, a worried businessman sees him and sucks in his breath. *It's impossible. I can't be seeing what I'm seeing.* He says nothing, but wishes it *were* true. Wishes he were out there too, flying a lawn chair, completely free, no longer bound by his responsibilities: a job, a house, a church, a family.

The lawn-chair man is elated. *Forget the rules. Nobody can touch me now.* . . .

In this country, we are rich with such free spirits. . . . "Be whatever you want to be," we say. "Just do your own thing."[3]

Great disciples become great because they have never done their own thing. "God's thing" is "their thing." They have no desire to be "free spirits," yet oddly they find personal freedom by surrendering compulsive individualism. Self-denial is the agenda of those who have escaped all need to "be themselves."

Nike has sold a lot of tennis shoes by saying, "Just do it." America has become the world's largest gathering of the indulgent. From many billboards comes the grand doctrine of "feel good." Its popular proverb is, "If it feels good, do it." But those who "feel good" are often materialistically sick. Richard Foster confronts those who hunger for this "feel-goodism": "It is time we awaken to the fact that conformity to a sick society is to be sick."[4]

This spirit of indulgence is a sickness. It has bred a kind of captivity for all of us. We live in the world without ever joining it. We live in the big world without ever leaving our own microcosms of pride. We go to church and hear sermons on the sacrificial life, but those sermons are delivered within the framework of our if-it-feels-good-do-it lives. Again, Tim Bascom instructs us. He went to worship God in a well-attended megachurch. Upon leaving it, however, he still felt bundled up in the small confines of his own ego:

> When I enter that church, there is the feeling that something exciting is going to happen—a real event. Why else would so many have gathered? I look around to find somebody I know, and I recognize one or two familiar faces in the huge crowd. I can only wave since there are so many people in the aisles. I sit down and wait for the action to begin, and when it does, I am not disappointed. The service is full of well-rehearsed performances by musical ensembles and drama groups. The sermon is dynamic, delivered like lines from a play. I walk out, feeling lucky to get all this for free, a bit as if I'd been to a very good benefit concert. . . .
>
> I once asked an acquaintance who is a long-time member there why that church has grown so large. He replied, "Because it puts no obligations on anyone. I can be perfectly anonymous."[5]

Many churches today have majored on this very point, permitting everyone to be perfectly anonymous. But take care. Many church-growth experts encourage those who want to grow a large church quickly to champion this "protective" anonymity. Yet Jesus said that the church is to confess him openly (Matt. 10:32–33). We must be careful in our desire to protect people's privacy lest we "protect them from confessional, authentic discipleship."

I have come to feel very badly about many church-growth moguls. There is often little of Jeremiah in their message. The thorny personal requirements of Amos or John the Baptist have been traded for a velvet togetherness. In fact, megachurch messages are all too often contrived to attract the largest possible crowds. The scriptural feeding of these thousands is often accomplished by keeping the soup so bland that no one is offended by the taste. If any significant content arises, it is put aside lest anything doctrinal or demanding get in the way of building a large crowd. In such a milieu we never talk about the quality of the soup, only how many we serve. One church in New Jersey has now instituted "Express Worship":

> "Express Worship, 22 minutes" advertised the sign outside the township's First Lutheran Church. The Minister is attempting a new way to draw people into the fold—limit the service to 22 minutes by omitting sermons and sacraments.
>
> The shortened service started January 9. It includes a greeting, statement of faith, apology for sins, prayer, an interpretation of the weekly Bible reading and a song without accompaniment. . . .
>
> Parishioner Penny Bonawitz said she attended the service with her two young children. "You get it all in 20 minutes, and that's just about the time the kids start acting up," she said. "You don't feel like you totally missed church."[6]

Some soup is both fast and thin. Some clergymen have described this nonnourishing, widely-served broth as being ashamed of the gospel. They have warned us against every attempt to build robust disciples with watery truth and bland confessions.

Again, Bernard of Clairvaux warns us that we can only think ourselves to be very important when we remain in ignorance of the real demands of the gospel. How demanding is this gospel? Listen to Jesus:

> He who loves father or mother more than Me is not worthy of Me. And he who loves son or daughter more than Me is not worthy of Me. And he who does not take his cross and follow after Me is not worthy of Me.   (Matt. 10:37–38)

Did it ever occur to Jesus that his church would in time actually devise a mystique that would allow the lost to come and go, while cowering under the armor of anonymity? I think not. If so, he would have said, as he said to the woman with the issue of blood, "Who touched me?" The Bible records:

> Now when the woman saw that she was not hidden, she came trembling; and falling down before Him, she declared to Him, in the presence of all the people the reason she had touched Him and how she was healed immediately.
>
> (Luke 8:47)

When God begins to touch our lives there should be no hiding. Open confession, and not anonymity, is the business of the church. Who are we to declare ourselves anonymous in lieu of Jesus' great benediction, "Blessed are you when men hate you,/ and when they exclude you, / and revile you, and cast out your name as evil" (Luke 6:22).

We never see any evidence of the church being a place to be comfortable while those who go there remain unchanged. Nor are we anywhere commanded to major on church growth at the expense of truth and commitment and confession. We need to hear our Lord say again, "Many are called, but few chosen" (Matt. 20:16), or hear him say, "Narrow is the gate and difficult is the way which leads to life, and there are few who find it" (7:14). Charles Wesley had ego in mind when he wrote of his surrender:

> My chains fell off
> I was set free
> I rose, left all
> and followed thee.[7]

We will have no more talk of protective anonymity as though it is a biblical doctrine. It may be effective church growth psychology, but it leaves the ego too unchallenged to belong to Christ.

Modern church growth psychology may be too weak to understand the strong wisdom of Bernard of Clairvaux.

Bernard defined the humble this way: "Humility is the virtue by which a man recognizes his own unworthiness because he really knows himself."[8] It is hard to practice condescension when we are hated. What this means is that it is hard to put ourselves down when our enemies are already doing such a good job of it. Let's consider again the time I was victimized by hatred. As the brunt of gossip, I was at first prone to "gossip back." It was hard not to tell my friends at church what my accuser was really like. I wanted to answer accusation with accusation.

The image that meant the most to me in those days was the image of Christ before his accusers at his trial. Philip read to the eunuch the Isaiah 53 passage describing a kind of condescension that makes no place for hate: "He was led as a lamb to the slaughter, / And as a sheep before the shearer is silent, / So He opened not His mouth" (v. 7). How is it that Christ could bless his hate-filled crucifiers? There is but one answer: He would not sin the sin of pride. He was not proud of being Jesus. He found no need to be praised. His Father requires this same condescension of all who would be saved. How well Bernard of Clairvaux captures his willing submission:

> I do not say that he was made wiser by the experience, but he came to seem nearer to us weak sons of Adam, whom he did not disdain to make and to call his brothers (Heb. 2:11). . . .

> And the Apostle says, "We do not have a high priest who is unable to feel for our weaknesses" (Heb. 4:15). He adds, to indicate how he is able to do so, "He was tempted at every point like us, but without sin" (Heb. 4:15). . . .

> He became not only lower than himself, but also a little lower than the angels (Heb. 2:9; Ps. 8:6), for they too are impassible, though by grace not by nature. He lowered

himself to that form in which he could suffer and be in subjection, for, as it is said, what he could not suffer in his divine nature he learned by the experience of suffering: mercy, and to be obedient in subjection.[9]

If I consider all that Christ accomplished on the cross, I realize humiliation always fashions humility. It is easy for the proud to be proud for they know so little anguish. But humiliation always hurts. It tears at us like Good Friday. It is all thorns and nails. It exposes us with the shame of naked crucifixion. We hang and hurt and weep.

We have already scorned the lie that teaches: "Sticks and stones may break my bones, but words will never hurt me." When my enemy had practiced his haughty hatred, I was all but driven from the pulpit of our little church. At night when I was most discouraged, I would stare disconsolately into the darkness, wondering how I could survive. How I could ever support my wife and children. Still, everything, good or evil, may serve those who are called according to his purposes (Rom. 8:28). Those horrible days of fear taught me the difference between being humble and being whipped. God is for all those who are beaten up by life. No wonder God told Moses he had heard the cry of his people (Ex. 3:7). God always hears the cry of the underdog; yet, said Bernard, it is the "bread of sorrow" (Ps. 127:2) that is the meal of our best relationship with Christ. Let us break bread with the Savior whose loaf is enriched by the spices of all those hurtful circumstances we prayed to avoid. We are to share this loaf with Christ in a fellowship of suffering (Phil. 3:10). Bernard describes this exquisite simple table I discovered:

"Come to me all who desire me, and be filled with my fruits" (Sir 24:26). "Come to me all who labor and are heavy-laden, and I will refresh you" (Matt. 11:28). "Come," he says. Where? "To me, the truth." How? by humility. For what reward? "I will refresh you."[10]

And refresh me Christ did. I learned in times of need that both humility and pride are not merely *points* in our pilgrimage, they *are* our pilgrimage. Humility is the harder pilgrimage. It separates us from our grasping egos. It is stepping back and looking at ourselves. It is being so rebuked at what we see that we yield to a better self.

Pride, on the other hand, never requires self-scrutiny. In fact, pride cannot stand the bright light of self-study. Pride has a fear of seeing what ego really looks like. Pride is a generous self-portrait. Humility shuns such portraiture. Humility fosters the art of loving. Loving fosters the art of adoring Christ.

Secular atheistic evolution is a happy doctrine for our age. If, as Huxley theorized, life springs *sui generis* from chains of unlinked causes, then humankind is happenstance. The race owes its existence to good fortune alone. God either isn't there or doesn't matter in such a view.

There are only two possible options to explain why we are here. One is that we are a happy accident, owing *nothing* to God. The other is that we are fearfully and wonderfully made (Ps. 139:14), owing *everything* to God, wholly responsible for his service in the world. Sir Fredrick Hopkins, the great British scientist, once said that the possibility of life just happening was the most unlikely event in the history of the universe. Fred Hoyle and Elenora Wickramasinghe said the possibility of a chance cosmic origin was one in ten, raised to the power of 40,000.[11]

Those who hold to chance as the explanation of cosmic origin believe that natural selection results from trial and error. After all, they reason, put an infinite number of monkeys on an infinite number of typewriters and one of them would write a Shakespearian play. Michael Cassidy isn't quite sure:

> One story tells of such an experiment. The monkeys had been typing for decades with no orderly statement appearing. Finally one ecstatic professor saw something emerging and rushed through to his colleagues with the typescript which read:

To be or not to be . . .
That is the umzinsquatch!

Oh well! You can't win all the time![12]

By the same theory an infinite number of baboons on an infinite number of instruments would play Beethoven's "Ninth." There's no guarantee of that either. A conscientious objector to the baboon theory wrote:

> There once was a hairy baboon
> Who always blew down a bassoon
> For he said, "It appears
> that in billions of years—
> I shall certainly hit on a tune!"[13]

The Bible, quite to the contrary, starts and ends with God. Seeing God as both Creator and Final Reckoner is quite a problem for ego-positivists. Once you admit that there is a universal God who made heaven and earth, you have to abandon your own godlike status. Every narcissist knows he can only really remain almighty in his own system if there are no contenders.

But once you have a God and you admit that he had a Son who died for you, then you are obliged to reckon with your own foolish and finite limitations. The next step after saying, "I believe" is to bow the head and say, "What wilt thou have me to do?" The answer is a ready-made "You shall worship the LORD your God, and Him only you shall serve" (Matt. 4:10). Humility at such a moment is only natural.

It is hard to hate our fellow creatures once we arrive at created status. No animosity has force for all who partake of the same creatureliness. When my enemy forced me to endure his hate, he was doing me a favor. I later blessed him for it. It was indeed his serving of the bread of sorrow that furnished the meal for both myself and my Lord. But this is a meal we would rather eat with companions close at hand. Christ often waits till our self-pity has

170

lost all human counsel. In my need, I came to exalt in the truth of St. John of the Cross: We should never pray for God to give us friends, only enemies. As long as we have even one earthly friend, we will fly to that one friend to bandage fresh wounds and showcase old scars. But when we have not even one earthly friend, we have no retreat but to the bosom of Christ.

Humility is the tutor he sends to teach us love. Bernard says we can always avoid hate if we learn to feast on three foods. His recipe knows but three ingredients:

The first food, then is humility. It purges by its bitterness. The second is the food of love, which consoles by its sweetness. The third is the food of contemplation, solid and strengthening.[14]

This is always the pattern: We pass from bitterness to love to the glorious contemplation of Christ. But bitterness and humiliation can push us in very opposite directions. It is not out of concert with the teachings of Bernard of Clairvaux to say that when we are humiliated by hatred, we may sometimes flee from the presence of Christ.

We must never forget that at the point of our greatest humiliation there is a fork in the road. At this fork we issue one of two cries. Either we declare: I am so destroyed that I must have all of God I can hold. Or we abdicate faith, saying: I know there is no God or he would not let me hurt like this! At this juncture of despair, we either fly to or from Christ. But the very pain that drives us from God often becomes the balm that heals our despair. How often in my brokenness have I fled from him, praying the words of Francis Thompson:

> And smitten me to my knee;
> I am defenseless utterly.[15]

I cried first like the psalmist, "That the bones You have broken may rejoice" (Ps. 51:8). And then, like Ezekiel, I asked, "Son of man, can these bones live?" (37:3). My friend who hated me must have done it in this arid valley of pride. For pride and the hate it spawns makes valleys dry. How is it that pride is born and grows until it makes brittle the bones and drags this arid arrogance out of which it is possible to hate? Pride moves through twelve steps in the decadent pilgrimage of our lives.

The Descent into Decadence

Step One: Curiosity

Bernard suggests that pride begins in our curiosity about things which are not our duty. Our duty is to serve God and not be overtaken by undue concerns about others. Bernard says that Eve's besetting sin was curiosity:

> IX.30. You, too, Eve. You were placed in paradise to work there and look after it with your husband (Gen. 2:15), and if you had done what you were told you were to have passed to a better life in which you would not have to work or be concerned about gardening. Every tree of paradise was given you to eat, except the one which was called the tree of the knowledge of good and evil (Gen. 2:16). For if the others were good and tasted good (Gen. 2:9), what need was there to eat of the tree which tasted bad? "Do not know more than is appropriate" (Rom. 12:3).[16]

This curiosity has us all wondering if we shall get "all that's coming to us." We do this right in front of the Savior. Peter, after learning that he will be martyred, asks Christ as he points to

John, "But Lord, what about this man?" (John 21:21). Spiritual one-upmanship reigned in his life! Competition was his insatiable curiosity. Peter wanted to be sure he got God's best deal.

In my earlier ministry, we listed our house for sale. It was on the market for a year. At the same time we listed ours, another couple in our church listed their house, and it sold in three days. When anyone asked this man how he sold his house so fast, he would always say, "I just put that house in the hands of the Lord and the Lord sold our house in three days." Each time I heard him say that, I would always say secretly to God, "Hey, God, what have you got against me?" I reacted defensively to this man's three-day-sale brag. Our house stayed on the market. Very few people even came to look at it. As the months dragged by, I would remind God how very unlike this surface man our deep spirituality really was. We had led many people to Christ in our long-unsold home, while the braggart three-day-deal man never had led anybody to Christ. Further, in our unsold house, we had held many Bible studies and receptions for urban newcomers. This man, this god of the three-day deal, never "used his house for Jesus" at all.

It was not till I read Bernard of Clairvaux that I realized my own curiosity was an occasion to sin. I was too concerned about the good deals God gave others. This concern was championing my own spiritual defeat. I was too much asking, "Lord, what about this man?" and it took me a little while to hear Jesus say— in loose paraphrase, "None of your beeswax" (John 21:22). In Christ, all competition is ruled out. Light is to be every Christian's product. And as the old proverb teaches, there is no competition between lighthouses.

While I was pastor of a suburban congregation, I often saw churches competing with one another. I saw pastors who couldn't afford to like each other, lest it blunt their competitive edge to outgrow each other. To be the best in the city fueled their suburban, church-growth game. They were so obsessed with being number one that they saw other churches only as contestants and never as kingdom comrades. They believed that they would spend eternity with those comrades, but they were in no sweat to practice that distant koinonia. There would be time for loving each other later. For now they must outdo each other in member-recruitment wars. They were competing lighthouses.

Cain's competition with Abel began in curiosity but ended in incrimination and murder. It was Cain's curiosity that kept asking, "How come Abel gets all the good deals in life?" Curiosity not only killed the cat, it was the beginning of humanity's competitive spirit. It teaches us first to compete and later to hate.

Step Two: Light-Mindedness

The second step has to do with light-mindedness. Once curiosity gets us looking around to compare ourselves with others, we begin to mock the estates of others:

> XI.39. For the monk who instead of concentrating on himself looks curiously at others, trying to judge who is his superior and who is his inferior, will see things to envy in others and things to mock. Thus it is that the light-minded follow their roving eyes and, no longer pinned down by proper responsibility, are now swept up to the heights by pride, now cast down into the depths by envy. Now the man is consumed by foolish envy; now he grows childishly pleased about his own excellence. . . . Now his words are few and grudging; now numerous and trivial; now he is laughing; now he is depressed; but there is never any reason for his mood.[17]

This is such a deadly pitfall in church. I never cease being amazed at the large number of different denominations in the world. Each of these was started by sincere believers who believed they were sincerely right. Nothing is more beautiful than a martyr suffering for what he believes. Nothing is more ugly than one who jeers the beliefs of others and tries to belittle their faith with mocking humor.

Many denominational names have come about from the mockery of largely "Christian" enemies. "Baptists" was a slur like the word *Dunkards,* uttered in contempt by those who held another view of baptism. "Methodists" was a label given to people who taught and preached their doctrines in an orderly fashion. "Holy Rollers" was a nickname bestowed on sincere people because of the informal way they worshipped. But the worst part is that such names were applied by those who were light-minded in the jealous way they viewed their brothers. This light-mindedness, said Bernard, led to the third step of pride, merriment.

Step Three: Merriment

Perhaps there is nothing more harmful than laughing at our enemies. Nothing quite so wounds a child's self-esteem as being laughed at. But it is the arrogance of those who laugh that will so condemn them on Judgment Day. I was speaking at a seminary not so very long ago. Far more often than I might have wished, I felt like these high-churchmen were scoffing at my Southern Baptist heritage. I sensed their disdain for Baptists, as though we were historically uncouth with too short and too naïve a history to be considered worthy scholars. I endured their Baptist jokes and their doctrinal contempt till mercifully it was time to go home. But even as I left them, I couldn't help feeling sorry for them.

Elitism is self-esteem whose schoolmaster is unkindness. Even Christian scholars may feel so much pride in their prestigious schools that they allow snobbery to steal courtesy in their treatment of others. I have a friend who went to study on a well-known New England campus. Two other post graduate scholars arrived on campus at the same time. When the three of them were introduced at a scholar's colloquium, the two others were greeted first and received a welcome of thunderous applause. But my friend's introduction was met only by a searing elitist silence. He was from our Baptist tradition and apparently deemed less applause-worthy. He confessed to me later how this gathering of Christian scholars had stripped him of personhood and dignity.

Shakespeare wrote in another context:

When in disgrace with fortune and men's eyes,
I all alone beweep my outcast state,
And trouble deaf Heaven with my bootless cries,
And look upon myself, and curse my fate,
Wishing me like to one more rich in hope,
Featured like him, like him with friends possessed,
Desiring this man's art, and that man's scope,
With what I most enjoy contented least.[18]

Who hasn't known the contempt of snobbery? Who hasn't here and there felt the painful insolence of rejection? But Christians have only to remember Christ's all-consuming love and we are healed:

For thy sweet love remembered such wealth brings,
That then I scorn to change my state with kings.[19]

Truly Christ's love sustains us when insolence and rejection come to call.

Next, we are never free to hate in return. We are to love those who belittle us, remembering that out enemies are not Christ's enemies; he has none. We are to reach for those who would slice the very arms from our entreaty. We are to practice inclusion of all who would exclude us. Edwin Markham ordered us to obedience when he wrote:

He drew a circle that shut me out—
Heretic, rebel, a thing to flout.
But Love and I had the wit to win:
We drew a circle that took him in.[20]

In the meantime, we are never to answer snobbery with snobbery. It is always better to be despised than to do the despising. It is God's habit to scatter the proud and lift up the humble (Luke 1:51-52). "Mockers" usually appear in the Scriptures as ugly people who ultimately reap the judgment of God. Paul reminds the

Corinthians: "Not many wise according to the flesh, not many mighty, not many noble, are called. But God has chosen the foolish things of the world to put to shame the wise, and God has chosen the weak things of the world to put to shame the things which are mighty; and the base things of the world and the things which are despised God has chosen . . . to bring to nothing the things that are, that no flesh should glory in His presence" (1 Cor. 1:26–29). It is better to be the laugh*ee* than the laugh*er*. How unbearably ugly are those who laugh in pride to sting others with utter humiliation. How contemptibly Bernard paints these proud mockers:

> Note the signs, which you can recognize in yourself or in anyone else. You will rarely or never see in such a man any signs of groans or tears. You would think to look at him that he was not giving himself a thought, or that he had no sin on his conscience, or that he was purged of his sins. He makes scurrilous gestures. He giggles. He preens himself. He is always joking and ready to laugh at the slightest thing. If anything has happened which would bring contempt on him or cast him down, he wipes it from his memory. And if he notes any good things in himself he will add them up and parade them before his mind's eye. He thinks only of what he wants and he does not ask himself whether he ought to want it. At times he is seized by fits of laughter; he is unable to suppress his foolish mirth. He is like a blown-up bladder which has been punctured and squeezed. As it goes down it squeaks, and the air does not come out everywhere but whistles through the little hole in a series of shrieks. So, the monk who fills his heart with vain and scurrilous thoughts cannot let them out all at once because of the rule of silence, so they burst out at odd moments in giggles. Often he hides his face for shame, purses his lips, clenches his teeth. He still cannot stop laughing and giggling. When he puts his hand in front of his mouth the giggles can still be heard popping out through his nose.[21]

Step Four: Boastfulness

After we finally are so callous as to laugh at others, we come to the place where we are selfishly arrogant and boastful. All unlovely, arrogant souls stay too near the center of their ambitions. They swagger into conversations and with loud opinions refuse to let others talk. Really, to such ego-centered persons there are no others. Excessive self-esteem is an unkind shrine attended by insensitive priests.

It must grieve God to know that many of these selfish souls are in the chief seats of congregational prestige. The church's leadership can be filled with high-minded people who thrive on ungodly contempt. But the contempt usually begins in seeking out the Almighty as the "God of Good Deals." Ronald was a man converted through the outreach ministry of our church. His conversion at first gave him a radiant zeal for the things of God. He was a man made humble in his own eyes by all the glorious things Christ had done for him. But he soon became friends with a long time Christian and super achiever named Geoffrey.

Ronald admired Geoffrey's wealth and entrepreneurial mind. It was inevitable that they would soon become partners in various business ventures. Ronald soon claimed that Goeffrey had swindled him out of his fair share of the company profits. There seemed to be little doubt that Geoffrey was guilty of most of Ronald's charges. Still, Geoffrey's deportment remained gracious and warm. Ronald, who had begun his Christ-life desiring to be nothing, suddenly exhibited lots of pride—a fierce pride that Geoffrey had wounded. Ronald felt that Geoffrey was a hypocrite, trying to appear as a gracious and godly servant in the church. Ronald became incensed at Geoffrey's double life—a swindler at his business and a saint in the church. He then declared all-out war on Geoffrey—a *blitzkrieg* of fiery, braggy gossip. He tried to get everybody on "his side" of the congregational quarrel. Ronald's lost Christlike humility became venomous and spiteful. Ronald, even though he was probably right, still remains a prime example that arrogance and humility are odd bedfellows in the human heart.

The church officer who once hated me so furiously was the vice-president of a large company. He flew cross-country to any number of prestigious assignments. His degrees and certificates were also impressive. His house was not only large, it was in the proper subdivision. He enjoyed the thrall of civic leadership in our city. Long before I would learn of his potential to destroy by hate, I had often heard him tell others—usually young aspiring executives—of all the things he had accomplished. He had achieved status by being a "sharp executive and good company man." But the area of his boasting that seemed to me to be most unnecessary had to do with the roles he played at church. There in his church world, as in his business world, his achievements were many. He taught a huge Bible class, which was full of his admirers. He held the reigns of administration in the church by being chairman of the board. But mostly he held the center of congregational esteem for being so great a Christian.

All of these accolades went awry. He did not draw people close to God. He really did not draw people close to himself. Like most boastful persons, he was too ego-centered to have any idea about how others really did see him. Bernard says the arrogant have to live on an inflated cloud of their importance to remain central in their own lives:

> He hungers and thirsts for listeners to whom he can make empty boasts, to whom he can pour out all he feels, and whom he can tell what he is and how great he is.

> He finds an occasion to speak. Let us say the subject is literature. He says new things and old (Matt. 13:52). His opinions fly about. His words tumble over one another. He butts in before he is asked. He does not answer other people's questions. He asks the questions himself and he answers them, and he cuts off anyone who tries to speak. When the bell rings for the end of the discussion, even though it has been a long one, he asks for a little more time. He asks permission to come back to the stories later, not so

as to edify anyone, but so that he can show off his knowledge (1 Cor. 8:1). He may say something edifying, but that is not his intention. He does not care for you to teach, or to learn from you what he himself does not know, but that others should know how much he knows.

If the subject is religion, at once he has dreams and visions to offer. Then he praises fasting, commends vigils, enthuses above all about prayer. He discusses patience, humility, and all the other virtues at great length, but in utter emptiness. Yet if you were to hear him you would say that he "speaks from the fullness of his heart" (Matt. 12:34), or "A good man brings forth good things from his good treasure" (12:35).

If the talk turns to lighter things, he is discovered to be even more talkative, because this is something he really knows about. You would say if you heard him that his mouth was a stream of vanity, a river of scurrility, so that he stirs even solemn and grave minds to merriment.[22]

Gradually, from this point in arrogance, the heady believer slips out of all usefulness in church. Paul here reminds us that these arrogant despisers will be the typical Narcissus of the last days: "But mark this: There will be terrible times in the last days. People will be lovers of themselves, lovers of money, boastful, proud, abusive, disobedient to their parents, ungrateful, unholy, without love, unforgiving, slanderous, without self-control, brutal . . . rash, conceited, lovers of pleasure rather than lovers of God" (2 Tim. 3:1–4 NIV). It is verse 5 that so attracts the mind: "Having a form of godliness but denying its power." Moffat's outstanding translation of this verse reads: "For though they keep up a form of religion, they will have nothing to do with it as a *force* in their lives." When godliness is rejected as a force in our lives, then ego is set free to behave as it will. Bernard says that there is a continual slide from occasional pride to habitual sin.

Bernard lists the last eight steps of this arrogant degradation in this way:

Step Five: Trying to Be Different

When a man has been boasting that he is superior to others it is galling to him not to outdo them in performance, so as to make it obvious that he is more advanced than they are. . . . He acts not so as to live better but so as to seem to triumph, so that he can say, "I am not as other men" (Luke 18:11).[23]

Step Six: Arrrogance

He believes the praises he hears. . . . When he hears something said in his own praise he thinks it comes not from the ignorance or kindness of the speaker, but from his own merit, and he arrogantly takes the credit.[24]

Step Seven: Presumption

He judges the judges and prejudges every case. . . . If obedience imposes some humble task on him he is indignant . . . for he feels himself to be fitted for great tasks.[25]

Step Eight: Self-justification

There are many ways of making excuses (Ps. 140:4) for sin. One person will say, "I did not do it." Another will say, "I did it, but it was the right thing to do." Another will admit that it was wrong but say, "It was not very wrong." Another will concede that it was very wrong, but he will say, "I meant well."[26]

Step Nine: Insincere Confession

How great do you think will be the confusion in the heart of the proud man when his deception is discovered, his peace gone, his praise diminished, and his sin is still not purged?[27]

Step Ten: Rebellion

This step is so obvious, Bernard does not define it.

Step Eleven: Freedom to Sin

> Then he begins to travel roads which seem good to men (Prov. 14:12, 16:25) and, unless God blocks his way (cf. Hos. 2:6), he will come at their end to the depths of hell, that is, to contempt for God. . . . Like someone entering a river, he does not plunge but goes step by step into the torrent of vices.[28]

Step Twelve: Habitual Sin

> He cannot tell good from evil now. Nothing holds him back. . . . He conceives an idea. He chatters about it. He carries it out. He is malevolent, evil-speaking, vile.[29]

Finally, of course, the life separates from all desire for Christ's control.

These, if saved at all, become the lost saved. When my friend's hatred for me had run its gamut, he left behind a wide swath of spiritual confusion. When anyone would ask me if he were really redeemed, I never knew how to answer. Fortunately, it was not my place to answer. But I found it most difficult to correct the destruction his spite left behind him. We can never change hatred directly back into love. We must deal with it more basically by trying to love pride back into humility. For only when humble persons take time to study their own violent judgments do they discover that their hate came first from self-concern. We must allow Christ to say to our haters, "My good man, your hatred comes not from the fact that you love me too little, but that you love yourself too much."

Inordinate self-love begins when we look away from Christ. Peter, on the waves of Galilee, was at first amazed at what he could accomplish when he kept his eyes on Jesus. It was an easy transfer for him to move from what Christ enabled him to do, to the feeling that he could do it as well on his own. It was at that point that he began to cry, "Lord, save me!" (Matt. 14:30). But his desperation, at least, kept him from pride.

Our own willpower is a force that God gives us. Still, we are left with his call to deny ourselves. It is tempting to want to be in charge, for the joy that comes from trying to walk on the water is immense. But what would have happened had Peter been able to walk Galilee with no help from Jesus? We have only to write our own epilogue to the story. What had begun with much tentative faith might have ended as a sideshow: "Come one, come all, see Peter of Capernaum, walk, run, do handstands on Galilee! *Amazing* former fisherman defies buoyancy and gravitational forces. Come one, come all! Bring your Auntie Alice! Only two denari for all-day passes!" The tabloids would have had a field day!

The idea seems a little farfetched to me until I remember that I once was too terrified to preach until gradually I lost my fear of it. Now I enjoy it. I do like being told, however, that I have preached a great sermon (even if it wasn't). Worse, in my depravity, I sometimes suffer when others criticize my messages; in fact, criticism can bottle me up in self-pity for days. Why this overreaction? I hate life when others do not esteem me in the same inflated way as I esteem myself. How much I need to rebuke those demons of pride that stand around me in long red lines to congratulate me into impotence. Such demons make tyrants who believe themselves kind.

Humility is a discipline. It is the daily exercise of standing next to Christ, whose wonderful light illumines our sin and all our humanity. No wonder Paul counsels us, "Let nothing be done through selfish ambition or conceit, but in lowliness of mind let each esteem the others better than himself. Let each of you look out not only for his own interests, but also for the interests of others. Let this mind be in you which was also in Christ Jesus, who, being in the form of God, did not consider it robbery to be equal with God, but . . . humbled Himself and becme obedient to the point of death, even the death of the cross" (Phil. 2:3–8).

Christ humbled himself by becoming a man. We humble ourselves by standing close enough to Christ that his towering presence teaches us who we really are. In learning who we are, our own spiritual poverty should teach us a love for other needy beggars. There is no one whom we are above. The undue reverence we hold for ourselves leads first to arrogance and last to hate.

Humility is the first virtue of the Christian, said Bernard. The second greatest virtue is also humility. The third greatest virtue is, likewise, humility. So is the fourth. Since the four greatest virtues of the faith are all humility, the subject ought to receive our full attention. Only when we have put our humility into practice will we learn our place before God and our ministry to our world.

SANCTIFYING

THE

SECULAR

*Jean-Pierre de
Caussade*

Is not a picture painted on a canvas by the application of one stroke of the brush at a time? Similarly the cruel chisel destroys a stone with each cut. But what the stone suffers by repeated blows is no less than the shape the mason is making of it. And should a poor stone be asked "What is happening to you?", it might reply "Don't ask me. All I know is that for my part there is nothing for me to know or do, only to remain steady under the hand of my master and to love him and suffer him to work out my destiny. It is for him to know how to achieve this. I know neither what he is doing nor why. I only know that he is doing what is best and most perfect, and I suffer each cut of the chisel as though it were the best thing for me, even though, to tell the truth, each one is my idea of ruin, destruction and defacement. But, ignoring all this, I rest contented with the present moment. Thinking only of my duty to it, I submit to the work of this skillful master without caring to know what it is."

—From *The Sacrament of the Present Moment*

THE WORLD GIVES Jesus little serious consideration. How shall we escape denying our Lord? Our witness is challenged. Have we the stamina to sing God's tune in the devil's land? Yet we are resolved. Our lamp shall not be snuffed by the gloom of those who care nothing for God. We are like Israel in Egypt—the Land of Ra and Isis. But our charge is larger than Israel's. Israel was charged only with remembering the covenant. We are to proclaim it as well.

Secularism has grown fierce.

When we start preaching what we believe, we are assaulted. If a Christian child affirms creationism in a biology class, the child is often scoffed at or ridiculed by a teacher. How true Jean-Pierre de Caussade's words, "Everything in the present moment does tend to draw us away from the path of love."[1]

We have arrived at a day when, if you dare to speak your religious convictions, you are slandered as a "fundamentalist." What a dreaded word this is. It is usually a libel rather than a label. H. L. Mencken slurred fundamentalists as those who assert themselves against the whole course of learning. "Fundamentalists," he said, "are everywhere where learning is too heavy a burden for mortal minds to carry."[2]

To believe the Bible has become a kind of grand slur—an antiquated stumbling stone in the path to the brave, new, liberated world. Christians have been accused of being a non-thinking people ever since the "Monkey Trial" at Dayton, Tennessee. In the 1925 trial, the State of Tennessee, represented by William Jennings Bryan, prosecuted schoolteacher John Scopes for violating the state law that prohibits the teaching of Charles Darwin's theory of evolution. In the play, *Inherit the Wind*, Clarence Darrow, Scopes' defense, questioned William Jennings Bryan about Noah's flood:

Darrow: But what do you think that the Bible itself says? Don't you know how it was arrived at?

Bryan: I never made a calculation.

Darrow: A calculation from what?

Bryan: I could not say.

Darrow: From the generations of man?

Bryan: I would not want to say that.

Darrow: What do you think?

Bryan: I do not think about things I don't think about.

Darrow: Do you think about things you do think about?[3]

Christians have been accused of being a nonknowing people in a world where knowledge is exploding.

If we tend to feel it is too hard to believe, we need to heed the wonderful counsel of Jean-Pierre when he says, "It requires heroic courage and self-surrender to hold firmly to a simple faith and keep singing at the same time."[4] These words do not mean that Jean-Pierre lived in the same secular wasteland in his day that we do in ours. But he did understand that the present moment is the only place we can live with our convictions.

Does the present moment seem too dark? Never mind, God is with us in that darkness. I remember a winter storm in 1964. My son was two years old. We were having a dinner party, a cozy time of laughter, hot coffee, and dessert, while outside the gales flung stinging sleet and dusty snow against our gathering. No matter, the furnace worked, the lights were blazing, the kettle steamed.

We were down to strawberry shortcake and coffee when the lights were suddenly killed by the storm. Oh, it was dark! One moment we were eating strawberries, the next, our world went black. My two-year-old son could not fathom where the party went. Worse, he could see nothing. He began to cry, rather loudly, in the darkness. I struck out across the room, reaching for him across the gloom. I followed the wail, seeking his cry. I stumbled over all that came between us in the darkness. I tripped over someone's legs. I fell over the coffee table that lay like a final barrier between myself and my child. Then reaching in the darkness, I found him. I picked him up, crushed him to me, and said, "Now, now, it's not so bad . . . I'm here . . . you can quit crying."

He did.

Then the lights came on.

My entire suit and shirt were red with strawberries. His little jump suit was also berry-stained. We fell to laughing. Some seemed to be pointing at me, broken up in mirth as they pointed at my stained shirt. (Our guests laughed a little more than necessary, it seemed to me!) But best of all my son began to laugh.

Darkness is never so deep that it obscures the coming of his presence. But what does it mean to try to be a Christian in such a day as ours? What is this "new-agey" day doing to our belief system? The secular moment is ever trying to steal the content of our faith. The great teachings of the church are being scoffed at. Multiculturalism is saying that Jesus is like Buddha, is like Confucius, is like Osiris, is like Thor. Marketing God in individual boxes is a "fair" way to sell divinity. The new Jeremiahs no longer sell such difficult products as repentance. They are the Howdy-Doody hucksters, hawking Brand X religion. Come! they cry. Come to the cafeteria of deity. Pick up the god of your choice, on sale, mind you. When grace was costly, it was free. Now it is merely cheap.

Critical Christian doctrines of transcendence have eroded and we don't quite know how or when it happened. In spite of all the transcendent references to heaven and salvation, both categories have suffered. Hell has nearly disappeared. John Blanchard cites in his book *Whatever Happened to Hell?*:

[When] Martin Marty, a professor at the University of Chicago Divinity School, was preparing a Harvard lecture on the subject [of hell], he consulted the indexes of several scholarly journals dating back over a period of a hundred years to 1889, and failed to find a single entry. His conclusion was that "hell disappeared and no one noticed." Gordon Kaufman, a professor at Harvard Divinity School, says that hell has been in decline for 400 years and is now so diminished that the process is irreversible: "I don't think there can be any future for hell."[5]

Heaven still exists under a thousand secularized movie definitions. Films like *Ghost*, *It's a Wonderful Life*, or *Chances Are* tend to define heaven for most Americans. Secularians glutted on movie theology continue to remain ignorant of the biblical categories.

Second, traditional doctrinal values have been shot full of holes with the cannonade of multiculturalism. Salvation itself has been widened far beyond the definitions of Scripture. Hell for the culturally elite isn't there anymore. As hell has disappeared, heaven is generally broadened to include everyone who dies. In *The Problem of Pain*, Lewis knew the plausible pain of taking a biblical stand when he said:

> I willingly believe that the damned are, in one sense, successful, rebels to the end; that the doors of hell are locked on the inside.[6]

All of this dialectic goes to say that the secular realm will require our lives to be a sacrament. But his burden is light. There are strawberries in the darkness. We whistle in the darkness; indeed, we must or the old tune will be lost.

But what is that tune?

The tune is the unchanging nature of spiritual reality. This unchanging truth is grounded in God's Word. Nay, it *is* God's Word!

However, God sent out his warnings against time as it operates to change the content of his timeless truth. Jude 3 asks us to "contend earnestly for the faith which was once for all delivered to the saints." The holy Scriptures are "given by inspiration of God" (2 Tim. 3:16); they are there to make us "wise for salvation"

(v. 15). They were given to us both through the prophets and by Jesus (Heb. 1:1–2).

But the apostle warns us that a secular climate will prevail in the "end times." We who follow Christ must then learn to sing Paul's tune:

> But know this, that in the last days perilous times will come: For men will be lovers of themselves, lovers of money, boasters, proud, blasphemers, disobedient to parents, unthankful, unholy, unloving, unforgiving, slanderers, without self-control, brutal, despisers of good, traitors, headstrong, haughty, lovers of pleasure rather than lovers of God, having a form of godliness but denying its power. And from such people turn away! (2 Tim. 3:1–5)

But what of the best/worst days of our lives motif? Perhaps in this chapter alone we must see that we who live for Christ and whistle the tune he gives us consecrate the worst days by obedience. To live in an unbelieving world causes us to walk in dependency and neediness. How does our faith sanctify the present dark moment?

> Therefore He says:
>
> > "Awake you who sleep,
> > Arise from the dead,
> > And Christ will give you light."
>
> See then that you walk circumspectly, not as fools but as wise, redeeming the time, because the days are evil.
> (Eph. 5:14–15)

It is ever as Jean-Pierre de Caussade said in another context: "Each moment inspires a virtuous obligation in us which committed souls faithfully obey."[7] This secular age has plunged us into moral night. But God is here. Let us fish out the strawberries and rejoice. We have a Father who sanctifies the present moment, baptizing our fear in laughter. Our fear of culture nibbles away at our testimony. Jon Mohr wrote a verse whose words speak of the necessity of making our lives a "sacrament of the present moment":

> Oh may all who come behind us find us faithful
> May the fires of our devotion light the way
> May the footprints that we leave
> Lead them to believe
> And the lives we lead inspire them to obey.[8]

There is no question about it: The past few decades have goaded Christians out into the open. We must live increasingly closer together with secularians in an increasingly secular world. Further, we must live and function in the sunlight. We don't always know what to do with this openness. Evangelical Christians are, for the most part, "secularphobes," committed to living in the open world, but afraid of it.

I think I have also detected an equal and opposite fear among secularians. Non-Christians simply do not understand people who love God and want to go to church all the time. They cannot imagine themselves singing hymns, saying prayers, and ministering to hurting people in the name of—as they see it—a long-dead Carpenter. One only has to look at a network newscast, where commentators comment on abortion or cult mass suicides, to see that anchorpersons are so secularized they are both ignorant and afraid of anything that smacks of faith.

I believe that a part of the mania which fuels both the private school movement and the home-school movement is caused by our fear of the secular world. The antipathy that Christians feel for the cultural sanction of immorality makes us wonder at what point even reasonable believers will appear to secularians as the Amish do. Our separation from culture is not so self-proclaiming. Our black hats and bonnets are totally internal, less apparent than those of the Amish. But as society is further secularized, we will feel more and more the anti-Amish stigma of its scorn.

Further, the secularians seem to be in charge of the world

where we must live. They run our schools, filling it with books we disagree with. They seem to have the upper hand in Congress, enacting laws that Christ would never allow us to sanction. They overwhelm the arts and entertainment industry, infiltrating our morality with bogus definitions of power, sex, pride, and narcissism.

How are we to confront this world's value systems?

First of all, we need to admit that Christians are often uncomfortable trying to live in a secular world because we have forgotten that we are not to consider this world our home. It may have been a major fault of evangelicals ten years ago that they thought they could actually Christianize the secularians and build the kingdom here on earth. Now it seems clear we cannot. Perhaps this loss of influence will make our thinking clearer. We have been called by Christ to redeem the world. We are called neither to Christianize nor control it.

Do not misunderstand me. We are not to abandon our faith to enjoy the world's bogus morality and destructive philosophies. But we are not to live in fear of those philosophies either. We are the children of the light. God is our Father. Christ is our Brother. The Spirit is our seal and security. With assets like these, we are to advance and challenge all godlessness. We are to be the aggressive vanguard of righteousness. *Carpe Diem* is our cry. It should be *Carpe Diem in Christo*. We follow Christ and are under obligation to challenge and change the secular world where it needs change. We are not to hate it or ignore it. We are debtors to it. Jean-Pierre speaks to that debt:

I also have a duty which I joyfully fulfill: to weep with those who are weeping, to rejoice with those who rejoice, to talk with the simple-minded in their language and to use the most erudite and learned terms with sages. I wish to make all see that everyone can aspire, not to the same specific things, but to the same love, the same surrender, the same God and his work, and thereby effortlessly achieve the most perfect saintliness.

Outstanding gifts and privileges are only so called because so few souls have sufficient faith to be worthy of them.[9]

Too often we who are Christians fear the world too much to enjoy it. One of the trickiest aspects of being in the world but not of it (John 17:14,18) is that we are afraid to let ourselves enjoy the fullness of this life. How unwise! This secular world holds many joys, and while they are not necessarily Christian, they can add to a fullness of life. Jean-Pierre de Caussade makes this point very clear:

> When God exists in all things, our enjoyment of his word is not of this earth, it is a delight in his gifts which are transmitted through many different channels. They do not in themselves sanctify us, but are instruments of the divine action which is able to communicate God's grace to the simple, and often does, in ways which seem contradictory.[10]

It is no oxymoron to say that we are to be joyfully serious as we live through our present existence.

Some years ago, I came to a life position that I like to call self-sacrificing hedonism. Hedonism is the pursuit of pleasure, and to pursue Union with Christ ends in the richest kind of pleasure. But we cannot enjoy his life in us until we first deal with cheaper temporal definitions of life. We are called to reckon ourselves dead (Rom. 6:11) as St. Francis said so long ago:

> Take a corpse and put it where you will. You will see that it does not resist being moved, nor murmur about its position, nor protest when it is cast aside. If it is placed on a throne, it will not raise up its eyes. . . . If it is clothed in purple, it will look twice as pale. This is a truly obedient man. He does not judge why he is moved: He does not care where he is placed. . . . If he is raised to an office, he retains his

customary humility: the more he is honored, the more unworthy he considers himself.[11]

We who are owned by Jesus are to be his living sacrifices (Gal. 2:20). But our sacrifice is to link hands with joy. We are to exult in our Lord's great love. We are not to fear this world; we are to enjoy it. Christian hedonism, rich in the pleasure it affords, is sacrament . . . the sacrament of the present moment:

> Everything turns to bread to nourish me, soap to wash me, fire to purify me, and a chisel to fashion me in the image of God. Grace supplies all my needs. Should I look for it elsewhere it will always find me and be manifest in all creation.[12]

So we are sacrificial hedonists. We sacrifice ourselves to know a richer pleasure. Filled with Christ, it is our joy to make the world better just by living in it. In him we sanctify the secular age just by passing through it. But we not only make the world more holy by being in it, we borrow from its beauty and steal from its joy. Saints may live in a pigsty and glorify the fullness of their circumstances. Paul seems to celebrate this spiritual pleasure till every sensation of poverty is made wealth. In prison he wrote:

> I know how to be abased, and I know how to abound. Everywhere and in all things I have learned both to be full and to be hungry, both to abound and to suffer need.
> (Phil 4:12)

Paul had learned to sanctify the present moment. Jean-Pierre de Caussade says there are at least four ways we sanctify the world. Let us consider each of them.

Four Ways to Sanctify the Secular

The First Way: Be Content Being Only What God Intended You to Be

I must admit that much of my misery, even in this world of hostile philosophies, is the result of feeling as though I must change everything that's wrong. I often see a great deal of neurosis among evangelicals who have to wrestle the devil and pin him three times before they can feel like they are really the friends of God.

Misery comes in the notion that we are called to set all wrongs right. In 1993 a very zealous Christian shot and killed a doctor who had performed hundreds of abortions. The killer was otherwise a gentle person who was very troubled about the wrong of abortion. My heart reached out to understand this lunacy. Christians are not to accept the evil of abortion without question. But when we become agitated and peaceless and cannot enjoy God's world, or when we have no peace, we sin against God. Playing God is a game we are ill-equipped to play.

When we try to take the enforcement of New Testament morality into our own hands, we discover our utter frailty. Alan Watts long ago wanted to call Christianity and Hinduism into synthesis. He loved the idea of Christian submission, but he noticed that Hindus generally had more peace. Christians talk about peace a lot but they are so intense about it. They agonize over all that is wrong in the world. They scrape themselves with potsherds and throw dust on their heads (Job 2:8) so that all will see they are sincere about the state of this fallen world. They accept some burdens they should let God carry. But they stumble along under gargantuan concerns that God would find much lighter.

Some of our peacelessness comes from our inherent heart of conversionism. None of us want the lost to die and perish forever. So we agonize until the lost are saved. We "care" ourselves into psychosis. We appear godly but not rested. Further, our need to convert others doesn't just stop when people are saved. After they are saved, we want them to be our kind of saved. We want them "Baptist-saved" or "Presbyterian-saved" or whichever is our favorite kind of "saved." Some years ago Missouri Synod Lutherans proved that even within denominations, Lutherans could quarrel over viewpoints that estranged them within the denomination. In our need to have others be "just like us," we lose all vestige of peace.

God called us to be a people of moral integrity. He also called us to take a stand against immorality. But he has not put us in charge of correcting all that's wrong. If we try to do that, we will have much unhappiness because we are trying to be something that God never intended. Jean-Pierre de Caussade illustrated this peace that comes from yieldedness by using the illustration of a silk worm:

> Be everything to all men and remain submissive and
> indifferent yourself. Exist little worm, in the dark confines of
> your narrow cocoon, until the warmth of grace hatches you
> out. Then devour the leaves offered you, and, forgetting the
> quietude you have abandoned, surrender yourself to this
> activity, until divine nature stops you. Alternatively active
> and passive, by incomprehensible transformations, lose your
> former self, manner and habits, and through death and
> resurrection, assume those which divine nature will herself
> choose for you. Then spin your silk in secret, unconscious of
> what you are doing, inwardly dissatisfied with yourself,
> envying your companions who are dead and at peace,
> admiring them even though they never reached your degree
> of perfection. By surrendering yourself you will be inspired

to spin silk that princes of the Church and of the state, and fine ladies, will be proud to wear. And then what will become of you? Where will you go? O miracle of grace! Whereby souls discover so many different forms! Who knows where grace may lead them? Who could ever have guessed what nature makes of a silk worm unless they had seen it! Only give it leaves, nature does the rest.

And so, dear sisters, you will never know either from whence you come or where you are going, from what purpose of God divine wisdom has taken you and to where it is leading you. All that remains for you to do is passively to surrender yourselves.[13]

Early in my ministry I found myself a church planter. I was out constantly knocking on doors, to tell people they were lost and in desperate need of Christ. Many people did come to know Christ and I was most excited about their coming to faith. But one of my new converts was not making the spiritual progress I thought he should be. He was a used car salesman, and his growth in Christ came slow. Even as a Christian he was having a hard time telling the whole truth to his customers. At first I grieved that he had been a Christian for some months but was still drinking himself into a stupor and leaving his family without the necessary funds to make life work. His language was vulgar and abusive to the ear, and, as I have said, he used truths much too sparingly in selling his cars. When someone bought one of his misrepresented vehicles and then called me (as his pastor) to complain about this morality, I decided to visit him and rebuke him for his un-Christian behavior. I did. After I had dressed him down "in the sweet love of Christ," he turned to me and said, "Cal, loosen up. When are you going to learn to enjoy life? Do you realize that you are always so worried about the sin you have just sinned or the one you're about to sin that you never have a happy day?!"

I couldn't shrug off his words.

The "rebukee" had become the "rebuker."

I took his confrontation home with me. I slept with his remark. It followed me. It was my meat and my drink as God intended it to be. Because of his well-placed rebuke, I learned that God had not made me a watchdog to keep my parishioners from sinning. Just letting God be responsible for the sins of humanity took an immense load off me. Trying to save the world all by ourselves is not only too much for us, it seeks to circumvent the saving work of Christ.

The Second Way: Confine Your Interests to the Present Moment

When Jesus taught us the way of peace, he taught us a life of acceptance. "Which of you by worrying can add one cubit to his stature?... Therefore do not worry about tomorrow.... Sufficient for the day is its own trouble" (Matt. 6:27, 34). Implicit in the idea of peace is an ability to make peace with the world as it is. Again the paradox arises. Aren't Christians out to change their world? Doesn't the world need changing? Isn't God's agenda for the individual or the world an agenda of change? Yes, yes, yes! But when we become so focused on changing the world that our joy is swallowed up in neurosis, we have lost the God-view of discipleship.

Jean-Pierre de Caussade must have realized that when we focus on how things *ought* to be, the *oughtness* can be so consuming it steals our peace. Evangelicals have been most uneasy with this double burden. We want to project ourselves to our culture as a people of peace, but I think we are usually seen only as the busy people. Even when our busyness is for the sake of saving a lost world, our "programming" turmoil makes us look nervous. To cover our absentee peace, we prefer to say we are *burdened* rather than *worried*. But our word games do not conceal the truth. We are uncomfortable with the moment. We live well for how things ought to be but not so well with how things are. The whole key to living in happiness is our ability to disentangle ourselves from *oughtness* until we have peace with *isness*:

It is necessary to be disengaged from all we feel and do in
order to walk with God in the duty of the present moment.
All other avenues are closed. We must confine ourselves to
the present moment without taking thought for the one
before or the one to come. . . . Each moment imposes a
virtuous obligation on us which committed souls faithfully
obey. For God inspires them with a desire to learn one
moment what, in the next, will uphold them in the practice
of virtue. They are drawn to read this or that, to observe and
reflect upon the smallest happening. In this way everything
that they learn and hear is fresh in their mind and no
dedicated novice will carry out her duty better than they
do.[14]

While we are often made peaceless by our overconcern for the
future, the same may be said with overconcern for the past. One
psychological game that destroys our peace is called: What shall
we ever do? Our unhealthy preoccupation with this question is destructive. That may be true even when we are asking, "What shall
we ever do about the fallen condition of the world?" For too much
cathexis with that sort of question leads to spiritual neurosis, so that
in the very name of Jesus we destroy our quiet walk with him.

But there is a second question that can prompt an equally
desperate game: Why did I ever do what I did? This game is a
game of unrelinquished guilt. It is hard to let go of our mistakes,
and yet when we insist on holding onto them, we suffer so much
pain for yesterday that we are prevented from living fully in the
moment. Thus, we make of our past a pointless shackle.

So many psychologists these days have described terrible prob-
lems of codependency, which feed on bad self-forgiveness syn-
dromes. Codependency poses as very other-centered. In actuality,
it is the opposite. The suffering wife of an alcoholic often prefers
her misery to freedom. The codependent is somewhat humorously
defined as that person, who, when dying, sees someone else's life
flash before their eyes. Still it is only self-centeredness dressed as
concern.

A casual acquaintance of mine has written a best-selling book on making peace with your past. If there is a fault in this idea, it is that Christians are not to work at forgiving their past. Jean-Pierre de Caussade seems to indicate that we are never to fondle yesterday in an attempt to make peace with it. We are merely to walk away from it. We must abandon that past which dogs us with an incriminating sense of failure. It is futile to try and dredge up what God has dealt with, once and for all, at Calvary. It is not merely futile, it is sin. When we are saved, all our sins are covered in the deepest part of the sea (Mic. 7:19), and God posts a sign that says, "No Fishing!" We must forget our past for two reasons: First, God has forgiven our past, and we must not hold to what God has forgiven. To try and make peace with what is covered in the blood of Christ is a hopeless attempt to improve upon the finished work of Christ. Making peace with our past is a simple matter of abandoning what God has already healed. Opening old wounds, even with the scalpel of Christian psychology, may question the value of Jesus' scars.

But there is a second reason: We simply cannot change the past. Remember Jesus' counsel, "Which of you by worrying can add one cubit to his stature?" (Matt. 6:27). Our broken past is largely unfixable. The writer of the *Rubiyat* wrote:

> The Moving Finger writes, and having writ,
> Moves on.
> Nor all thy Piety or Wit shall lure it back to cancel
> half a Line,
> Nor all thy Tears wash out a Word of it.[15]

The past is prone to roar against our present peace. But since we cannot change it, we must dismiss it. We are to abandon it, leaving its roaring behind us. Jean-Pierre calls us to cancel yesterday's heaviness in the momentary celebration of grace:

> It requires heroic courage and self-surrender to hold firmly
> to a simple faith and to keep singing the same tune

confidently while grace itself seems to be singing a different one in another key, giving us the impression that we have been misled and are lost. But if only we have the courage to let the thunder, lightning and storm rage, and to walk unfaltering in the path of love and obedience to the duty and demands of the present moment, we are emulating Jesus himself.[16]

Only as we meet and walk with Christ in the present moment can we triumph over the secular and threatening past. This is true of the future too. What we cannot change is best left to our forgetting. What we have not met we must not seek ahead of time.

The Third Way: See God in Everything

The secular world is often called "the real" world by those outside the church. But we who walk with Christ know that the "real world" is the world of the spirit—the world where God reigns over his people in all his holiness. When we quote Romans 8:28, it is often in a condescending sort of way. We give ourselves the passage as a balm for our disconsolation. When we quote it, we are usually consoling our confused souls, "All things *may* be working together to those who love God . . . but we're going to have to get a lot farther down the road before we see how any good can ever come out of the current mess." This kind of disconsolate interpretation comes because deep down we are still holding to the notion that Christians are not supposed to have bad things happen to them. We can't give up on the idea that in Christ everything that comes our way should make sense. When it does not, we feel cheated in a major sort of way. The key issue in our naïveté is that we have never really reckoned with 1 Thessalonians 5:18: "In everything give thanks." We must learn to see God in all things (2 Thess. 5:17–18), not just the good things. If we could learn to see God in our pain, we would never lose sight of him at all. We must bless the *omnipresent* God who inhabits fully *all* our circumstances. He both feasts with us at Sinai's table and dies with us at each of our small crucifixions (Phil. 3:10).

Jesus came to earth in poverty. The glory of his life was that he could sanctify his whole world. He saw his Father not only in the lilies of the field but also in his dying. Life was tough for this incarnate Savior of ours. Still, says Jean-Pierre, life's worst hardness can be endured by taking the present as it comes:

> Ah! The poverty, the humility of God reduced to lying on straw in a manger, crying and trembling and breaking Mary's noble heart. Ask the inhabitants of Bethlehem what they think; if that child had been born in a palace in princely surroundings they would worship him. But ask Mary, Joseph, the Magi, the priests, and they will tell you that they see in this dire poverty something which makes God more glorious, more adorable. . . . To discover God in the smallest and most ordinary things, as well as in the greatest, is to possess a rare and sublime faith. To find contentment in the present moment is to relish and adore the divine will in the succession of all the things to be done and suffered which make up the duty to the present moment.[17]

When I was a child, like most children I endured a kind of terror during our fierce Oklahoma electrical storms. My mother taught me that thunder was only sound; it was the lightning which might hurt me. Further, she taught me that I could tell how far away the lightning was by counting "1,000, 2,000, 3,000" and that each time I said another thousand, I had ticked off another mile between the lightning and the thunder. In such a simple exercise I put miles between the real danger and the roar of thunder. Why should I fear something so far away?

But my greatest conundrum came in seeing how God could even inhabit my terror. Once I learned that my terror was only a matter of viewpoint, I was free. For thunder did not make God afraid, and when I had his perspective, I could be truly free of fear. It was easy to imagine God looking at all that could ever make me afraid and counting, "1,000, 2,000, 3,000." Thus I could see that this counting Jehovah set the distant thunder far away from all I feared. I could then see God—victorious in anything, triumphant over everything. Thunder cannot terrify us unless we brace against it. Our peace lies in yielding to, not bracing against, our circumstances. As Jean-Pierre said:

> **Thinking only of my duty to it, I submit to the work of this skillful master without caring to know what it is.**[18]

In one of those near-miss traffic disasters for which all of us have some tale, I find an illustration of the story at hand. One long-ago winter day, Barbara and I were driving on an ice-patched Nebraska highway. As we approached a concrete bridge, my car spun out of control. I was overcome by horror. The steering wheel would no longer steer the car. The brakes would no longer stop it. Every joint in my body locked taut as steel. To this day I will never know how we missed the bridge as the car spun round and round, end to end. In the middle of my helpless feeling, the car at last shot out over the shoulder of the road. As we plunged from the highway into the ditch, I caught sight of Barbara who was sitting erect with her eyes closed, gently relaxed. As we came to rest out in the center of a field of ice-sheathed weeds, I was struck by the contrast between her ease and my tension. She escaped injury, probably because she was able to relinquish her anxiety when her circumstances ordered tension. When we were at last through the crisis, there sitting in the field, I asked her how she could be at such peace. "Well," she said, "I could neither change my circumstances nor remove myself from them." Jesus was there. He always is. The best answer, of course, is always to trade trust for terror.

This fear-gorged, secular world is the only place we have to call home. The moment is the only place we can yield to God's purpose. The Buddists have a story of a man who, in fleeing from a lion, fell headlong into a deep well. He would have been killed in the fall except that on the way down, his tunic was snagged by a root sticking out from the wall. There he hung over the bottom of the pit where he might soon fall, be crushed, and destroyed. Above him was that small circle of light which framed the head of a roaring lion. Panic could not help. Worry would not deliver him. So he reached out to a leaf growing out from the side of the well and saw on the leaf a drop of honey. Caught between unavoidable terrors he could not change, he licked the honey from the leaf and blessed God. God may be blessed in every crisis, for he inhabits every crisis. Hebrews 13:5 says that he will never leave us, so when life spins out of control, look not for him in any sense of desperation, lick the honey from the leaf, and bless his name.

The Fourth Way: Be Willing to Be God's Sequel to the New Testament

The canon has been closed, yet God continues to write his glorious revelation in the center of our lives. I am not optimistic about the outlook for morality in the future. The moral degradation of our world makes it appear that culturally we are on that oft-repeated slide by which twenty-eight civilizations ahead of us have been lost. It could well be that the secular world looming large will snuff out all who are weak of faith. Standing for Christ will require all we are and all we have. But God will never abandon this world without a strong witness to himself. Since secularians rarely read the Bible, God is writing his latest gospel on the pages of our lives:

> And so the sequel to the New Testament is being written now, by action and suffering. Saintly souls are in the succession of the prophets and the Apostles, not by writing canonical books, but by continuing the history of divine purpose with their lives, whose moments are so many syllables and sentences through which it is vividly expressed. The books the Holy Spirit is writing are living, and every soul a volume in which the divine author makes a true revelation of his word, explaining it to every heart, unfolding it in every moment.[19]

But most of us know our own lives so well that we are dubious that God could ever use something so frail as our witness to write such a dramatic story.

I now teach at the seminary with a man named David. He has academic degrees that only weakly speak to his godly strength. He was a missionary hero of mine years before we ever met. He was serving in Cuba when the communist takeover came and was destined to spend the next four years in a Cuban prison. Mercifully, through many trials and near scrapes with death, he survived. Not only did he survive but we now serve on the same faculty. My admiration of him always leaves me somewhat in awe of him. Yet he is so utterly warm and unassuming that he decries all admiration and welcomes me into his circle of friends.

During his years in prison, he learned the yielded life. He had a small New Testament that became his confidence. He hid it and read it, and day by day, year by year, he was nourished. His prison shut him in with a great God and a small book. He thrived peacefully in a hostile world. But what he never seems to see (and indeed what he might protest) is that God was writing a glorious word on the pages of his own life. His was a fleshly Bible that Castro could read. A Jesus-Bible where all the print was red with his unassuming courage. The dictator's atheism made no place for other kinds of Bibles. Yet David made the print as clear as Resurrection morning. May God write as clearly on our lives. Make no mistake he will, says Jean-Pierre:

> We are in an age of faith, the Holy Spirit no longer writes gospels, except in our hearts; saintly souls are the pages, suffering and action the ink. The Holy Spirit is writing a living gospel with the pen of action, which we will only be able to read on the day of glory when, fresh from the presses of life, it will be published.

> O what a beautiful story! What a beautiful book the Holy Spirit is now writing! It is in the press, not a day passes when the type is not being set, the ink not applied, the pages

not being printed. But we remain in the night of faith, the paper is darker than the ink; we cannot make out the print, it is in the language of another world which we cannot understand; it is a gospel we will only be able to read in heaven.[20]

Your life and mine are where God is now doing his writing. If we do not conceive ourselves to be noble paper, let us consider that we are at least necessary paper. Paper must lie flat—yielded to take the ink; surrendered till it bears all the characters of God's message to this secular world that leaves us so afraid. May God write upon our relinquishment of tomorrow a strong word for the world where we must live today. May we be worthy of Jean-Pierre de Caussade's final counsel:

> Forgive me, divine Love, for speaking only of my shortcomings and not having yet understood what it means to let your will be done, not having allowed myself to be poured into that mould. I have been through all your galleries and admired all your paintings, but I have not yet surrendered myself sufficiently to be worthy to receive the strokes of your brush. . . . I will devote myself exclusively to the duty of the present moment to love you, to fulfil my obligations and to let your will be done.[21]

IMITATING
CHRIST

Thomas à
Kempis

My son, the more thou canst go out of thyself, so much the more wilt thou be able to enter into Me.

As to be void of all desire of external things, produceth inward peace, so the forsaking of ourselves inwardly, joineth us unto God.

I will have thee learn perfect renunciation of thyself to my will, without contradiction or complaint.

Follow thou Me: "I am the way, the Truth and the Life" (John 14:6). Without the Way, there is no going; without the Truth there is no knowing; without the Life there is no living. I am the Way which thou oughtest to follow; the Truth which thou oughtest to trust; the Life which thou oughtest to hope for.

I am the inviolable Way, the infallible Truth, the endless Life.

I am the straightest Way, the sovereign Truth, the true, the blessed, the uncreated Life.

If thou abide in my way, thou shalt know the Truth, and the Truth shall make thee free, and thou shalt attain eternal life.

If thou wilt enter into life, keep the commandments (Matt. 19:17).

If thou wilt know the truth, believe Me.

If thou wilt be perfect, sell all (Matt. 19:21).

If thou wilt be my disciple, deny thyself (Luke 9:23).

If thou wilt possess a blessed life, despise this present life.

If thou wilt be exalted in heaven, humble thyself in this world (John 12:25).

If thou wilt reign with me, bear the cross with Me (Luke 14:27).

For only the servants of the cross can find the way of blessedness and true light.

—From *The Imitation of Christ*

THE CALL TO yield our lives to the will of God must face a formidable foe: ambition. Ideally most of us want to do all that Christ commands us to do. But before long we begin to notice that the sort of things to which Christ calls us often does very little to advance our annual income or social station. We become torn. Shall we serve Jesus or get on in the world? How hard it is to decide between following Jesus and keeping up with the Joneses. Forced to choose between Jesus and the Joneses, we often choose the latter. Our personal hopes and dreams are tightly connected to our getting ahead in this world. It is hard to disconnect them. Career advancement consumes our days. We work to build a proper roster of friends. We trade our birthrights for thirty pieces of silver from the purse of our high-currency ambition.

In 1991, I believed that God was leading me to terminate my twenty-five-year pastorate, in order to begin using the remaining years of my life in teaching. In the spring of that year, opportunities came from several major private colleges and seminaries to explore the possibilities of joining their faculties. One of those opportunities came from a prestigious West Coast seminary. I very much admired this seminary for its academic excellence and national reputation. I twice went for interviews with their administrators, who were considering me for their faculty. The first visit was one of splendid rapport and immense satisfaction. The call I pursued was heady. I savored the status ahead of time. The first interview went so well I hung my egotistic portrait over the altar of ego in my little chapel of success. I was as happy as Samson in a field of dead Philistines. I flew back out for a final interview. We were to settle on salary, housing allowance, writing expectations, annuities, and all that I was going to mean to the school.

Enter the demons of rejection.

By the end of the second visit, it was quite clear that they were not as impressed with me as I had been with them. I began to feel ashamed as I sensed failure. As from a spiked tire, the hot air of ambition began to hiss out of my punctured ego. The dean of their School of Theology squared with me and told me that I had been rejected by their faculty. I felt that terrible "knife in the gut" feeling that comes when we experience rejection. I flew home destroyed. My wife had so wanted me to have the position. Now I had the double problem of telling her that I had been rejected. My children, who knew that I was being interviewed for the position, would also have to be told, "Daddy didn't make it!" A couple of soul-wrenching things passed through my mind on the flight home. First, I realized that my own competence was under question by a very strong group of scholars. But most hurtful was the bruised ego that one feels in rejection.

That spring I forgot the impeccable wisdom of Thomas a Kempis:

> Be not solicitous for the shadow of a great name, or for the familiar friendship of many, or for the private affection of individuals, for these things distract the heart.[1]

Rejection need never be terminal. How beautifully Christ began to pick up the pieces of my soul. How tenderly he reminded me, as he has so often, of the dangers of headstrong desire. This yielding of soul reminded me that only one kind of esteem is necessary. Self-seeking had caused me to forget to seek the Lord and what he wanted for my life. I had followed ambitions where submission would never have permitted. I would like to believe that those who rejected me understood that I was acting out of spiritual arrogance, "solicitous for the shadow of a great name." I would like to believe that they were so much in the center of God's will that they could see I wasn't. But, in truth, I suspect they were merely acting more to protect some positive institutional image they feared I might defile. We rarely have our spiritual needs counseled by those who are deeper of soul.

No, in all likelihood we both sinned, basically for the same reasons: I was trying to upgrade my image and they were trying to protect theirs. If my judgment of them is too harsh, I beg Christ to forgive me. This I do know: My judgment of myself is exactly what it should be. I have often sought what was good for me without any reference to Jesus. I am confident that such self-seeking is a universal sin.

In another few months a similar position came along from another great school. This time, I remembered to seek Christ and to walk in submission. This time I begged the Father to prevent me from even looking at this seminary from the vantage point of personal ambition or self-image. How things have changed for me! No school is "lucky to have me." Only two magnificent pieces of fortune have ever really come to my life. First, the Father has called me his child. Second, Jesus has called me his brother.

Now that I am on a faculty, I must confess that I have found a community of scholars and brothers. The academy I serve offers me nothing so elite that it displaces my need to bow my head before Christ. Now I rarely think of that rejection without giving thanks to him, remembering that arrogance has no place in the life of God-lovers. He who called us to follow him never had our own promotion uppermost in his mind. Who am I to presume that any career appointment is to be set above God's ultimate plan? How we forget that the prior credential is not our education or some professional circle of influence. The prior credential that certifies all greatness is the call of God. Seminaries may enhance understanding, but only God creates the "slots" where our individual lives are to be used. Education may enlighten and equip, but only God saves and calls. My prayer is that my students will not experience me as an academe greedy for recognition, but as a submitted servant, bound to the service of the King.

Ungodly ambition leads us to spiritual presumption. Most of the pain we experience in our journey comes when we presume that we are worthy because we walk by faith. Serving our own image causes us to dream our private dreams for our own private advancement. We go on claiming the walk of submission, even as we crown ambition the lord of our lives. While we walk in self-sufficiency, obedient only to our shallow dreams, our egos harden with a crust of insensitivity. This crisp, brittle husk of arrogance grown thick enough is inpenetrable by Christ. Still, it is as fragile as an eggshell, so delicate that it is broken by the slightest fall from the pedestal of ego.

The sins of arrogance are widespread. Ambition often sits at the top of "Christian" enterprises. Many Christians, all their lives, have only a walk of personal ambition, which they believe to be a walk of obedience. In our continual crying of "Lord, Lord" (Luke 6:46), we assure ourselves of our reputation in Christ. We establish our communion in Christ by droning, pietistic chatter. We are convinced by the sheer volume of our confessions. Our testimonies become pompous "braggimonies" that dress Christ in glitzy egoism.

"It is a great thing to live in obedience,"[2] said Thomas à Kempis, for "we are too much ruled by our own passions."[3] Ego always makes a show of altruism. It gets lots of strokes by pretending to have no interests in ambition. In fact, our egos quickly learn how to play the submission game, by which Christians gain approval with each other. Like Ananias and Sapphira (Acts 5:1ff.), we foster the impression of giving all while giving only part. The key to winning the submission game is to keep all the action in our testimony rather than in demonstration. We are satisfied with speaking ardently about Christ rather than putting on Christ.

I left seminary in the early sixties. I was full of Greek, Hebrew, and hard-earned theology. I arrived at a small town in eastern Nebraska, ready to try out my years of study on the Nebraskans. I moved into my new study and hung up my degrees. I had both a bachelors degree and a masters degree. I was institutionally certified. The degrees said to all, "This man has credentials." I was schooled in Karl Barth and Paul Tillich. I understood the Swiss theologians, and I had a pretty good grasp of some of the leading Catholic thinkers as well.

When I had been pastor there for a few months, I noticed that nobody stopped me on the streets to ask me to explain the Swiss theologians. I seemed to know a lot more theology than most people felt a need to know. My credentials hung on the wall, but nobody asked about them. The church didn't seem to be growing. I wondered why. I wanted to see people coming to church in great numbers, but it simply was not happening. An early trickle of new members came slowly to a stop. In fact, after about a year on the field, the church had "grown" from thirty-four members to twenty-three members. The seminary from which I was graduated had not trained me in prophecy, but I had learned to spot trends on my own. I realized that if we kept growing in the same way we had been, I would grow myself out of a church in a very short time. Being desperate, I decided to invite an evangelist to come to our church. The man I selected to come and help me stop this death-trend syndrome was formally uneducated. He didn't know the Swiss theologians and didn't even suspect that Catholics had theologians. And to make matters unbearable, he tended to refer to my alma mater as the theological "cemetery." And while I was nettled by his slurs, I was fascinated that my people were riveted to his "low-brow" sermons.

Around his host of homiletical sins, wonderful things began to happen. Many, who under my preaching had only come to know Barth, under his preaching came to know Christ. Never had such astounding theological ignorance yielded such product. There was a spirit of festival joy. *Well, biblical ineptitude has its limits,* I thought to myself. *He will, of course, go back to the Bible belt, and I will get back to my elitist elocution.* Meanwhile, the church was packed night after night. Many received the lordship of Christ. *Never,* I thought, *have so many been saved with such poor hermeneutics.*

He left after the final, rapturous Sunday evening service.

Monday morning, I went back to my study and entered it. I was not alone. God was there waiting for me.

"Is something on your mind, God?" I asked.

"Are these *all* the credentials you have?" he asked. He seemed to be pointing to my degrees.

"Well . . . yes," I said to God.

"Ah, but you are struck with the importance of your head," he said.

I was about to protest the divine rebuke.

"These are not your best credentials," he seemed to say. "It is no sin to be educated, but it is a sin to begin to think that your degrees authenticate your calling. It is quite the other way around. The call of God is your prior credential."

I walked to my degrees. I took them from the walls. I removed some books from my bookshelves and put the degrees in behind them. I replaced the books. For the next twenty years, the degrees remained out of sight. In fact, I have never exhibited my degrees in my office since that time.

Am I ashamed of being educated? Certainly not! No one believes in education more than I do. In our day seminaries are often panned as irrelevant. Do not believe it! Ministers must be professional. They must be well-schooled in the Scriptures, counseling, administration, and pastoral care. But our prior credential is what Peter Marshall called the "tap on the shoulder," the call of God that wakes us to his unseen forces of redemption and change. I had an education but was no longer fascinated by it. I had been urged by a poorly educated man to imitate Christ.

All too often I have been a poor demonstration, but I know what authenticates my life. Yes, following that weekend the church began to grow and continues to do so. But the growth is as unimportant as my degrees. I was not called to get degrees nor grow a church. Both of these wonderful results came from pursuing union with Christ. From submitting, all the best things came to be. But for the truly submitted, they are rarely seen because of brighter more consuming joys.

How well Thomas à Kempis illustrates the importance of submitting ourselves to the imitation of Christ. Our Lord was committed to living the dying life. "If anyone desires to come after Me, let him deny himself, and take up his cross daily, and follow Me. . . . Whoever loses his life for My sake will save it" (Luke 9:23–24). Once we take the step of full submission, we abandon every private agenda. In such a step we recognize the world for what it is. As St. Francis counseled, we learned to live by reckoning ourselves dead (Rom. 6:11). The world has lost its claim over the dead. Those of high ambition must run the world, for the spiritu-ally submitted have died to all interest in the rewards of ambitions.

On our knees we discover the low entrance to self-renunciation, then we see the door of heaven as it is. It has a low lintel. It may only be passed by those who kneel in acknowledg-ment of his Lordship. The submissive may pass. But pretenders, made tall by their own arrogance, cannot.

The needle's eye, some have said, was that small portal that stood next to the large city gates. These smaller constrictions were left open at night. They would admit a straggler into the gates after curfew. But no army could pass. Any latecomer could only enter by taking off his weapons and passing them through the confining gate first. The low lintel of the needle's eye forced all possible aggression to its knees. When a soldier was utterly void of all self-defense, he entered, totally at the mercy of the city. With his bowed head exposed to his host and his weapons gone, he was subject to the caprice of his captors.

Is not this the glory of our repentance? In repentance we who submit to the needle's eye are at the mercy of our great Savior. How glorious is our need; how dependent we are on his mercy. Thomas à Kempis wrote:

> Learn now to die to the world, that thou mayest then begin to live with Christ. Learn now to despise all earthly things, that thou mayest freely live with Christ.
>
> Chastise thy body now by repentance, that thou mayest then have assured confidence.[4]

But Thomas à Kempis would not have us assume that dying is a later step of our discipleship. On the contrary, dying is where we start.

The glory of our submission is that it yields in darkness. It is Bartimaeus crying in the darkness, "Jesus, Son of David, have mercy on me" (Mark 10:47). The blind see only darkness, but they do see that they are blind. They have a kind of vision that sees that they are blind and must therefore trust. Our trust begins when we confess our blindness. "All perfection in this life hath some imperfection mixed with it," Thomas à Kempis said. "No knowledge of ours is without some darkness."[5] When we act out of our dark reason and fail, it occurs to us that we should have set our personal ambition aside. We might then have made our dark decisions in better light. The neck is a kind of switch. The instant we bow our head, the light turns on. Then we can make good decisions in the clear light of God. Submission provides us with instant access to the light, "for God will have us perfectly subject unto him, that being inflamed with his love, we may transcend the narrow limits of human reason."[6] Submission is rooted in love that is unafraid. It does not see itself as praiseworthy or courageous. Real submission never sees its own heroism. Heroes live in other worlds wearing other crowns. The submitted see their yieldedness only as a natural response to the love of God.

In Gladys Aylward's *Inn of the Sixth Happiness,* she tells of leading the children of an orphanage over the mountains through enemy lines to safety. It is odd that she does not allow her fears to disturb others. In the movie version of her saving act, her submission to Christ will not allow her to project her fear unto the children. Rather, she has them singing as they play their role in borrowing from her courage. Often the martyrs sang psalms at the time of their death. Jesus certainly quotes Psalm 22:1 at the hour of his death. And Paul and Silas sang at midnight in a Philippian prison (Acts 16:25). Gloriously perfect love drives out fear (1 John 4:18).

Fear-killing love is a fringe benefit of submission, says Thomas à Kempis: "Thou camest to serve not to rule. Know that thou was called to suffer and to labor, not to be idle, or to spend thy time in talk. Here, therefore, men are proved as Gold in the furnace."[7] If we are to get on with imitating Christ, we must conform our lives (Rom. 12:2) to his servanthood. But how is this conformity to be brought about?

I have told several times that wonderful story about a hunchback Persian prince, whose destiny it was to be king one day. He was so tragically deformed, however, that many in the kingdom could barely stand to think of the day when the deformed prince would assume the throne. Then the prince made an odd decree: He ordered the royal sculptor to carve his statue out of white marble, exactly as he would look if he had no deformity. When the statue was finished, he had it brought to the center of the palace.

Then, when the glorious statue was in place, the oddest kind of ritual began. Each day, this bent, deformed prince came to the tall stately statue of himself and took off his shirt. He then turned his own ugly spine toward the straight and regal back of his alter ego. He would back up to this statue and do all he could to throw his own shoulders against the stone shoulders of the statue, attempting to make his own back as straight as that of the statue. Always he tried in vain.

Nothing deterred his spirit, however. Sun, wind, the days, and indeed the very years could not stop his unusual routine. The years ground on, and his spirit of discipline never flagged. Then one day, his soul was brought alive, for he overheard some palace gossip say that they had noticed that the prince's odd physical litany appeared to be working: The prince did not appear to be so bent as he once had been. His zeal caught new flame. Then, who could measure the joy of that glorious day when he at last removed his shirt, backed up to his stone look-alike, and felt the naked thrill of cold marble on his own warm shoulders. Discipline and desire had at last made him like the image.

How beautiful it is to be conformed to the image of Christ. We who are the morally and spiritually deformed may, by discipline and prayer, become like him. The renewing of the minds by our Savior is the key to being conformed to his image (Rom. 12:2), for indeed Christ is the image and glory of God (1 Cor. 11:7). He is the image of the invisible God as well (Col. 1:15). "For whom He foreknew, He also predestined to be conformed to the image of His Son" (Rom. 8:29).

The word for image in 2 Corinthians 4:4 is the Greek word *eikon*. The word *eikon* is, of course, where we get our word *icon*, but the Greek term is more than just a simple image. It is this word which is also used by the apostle in Colossians 1:15, where Christ is portrayed as the "image of the invisible God." Its meaning there and in the Cointhians passage is rather like an archetypal image. An artist may make many statues from a single mold. But the statue from which he makes that mold forms the essence of all. That archetype makes all other *eikons* or images possible. The best definition of this idea is found in Colossians 2:9: "In Him dwells all the fullness of the Godhead bodily." Jesus is the archetype image; as we imitate him, we imitate the most splendid example of God that has ever been visible to humankind.

But in "imitating the image" of God, there is a word I like even better. Hebrews 1:3 says that Christ is the *express image* of God's person. The Greek word employed here is *charakter,* the word used to describe the impression made by a seal or signet in wax or clay. Jesus is the *charakter* image of God, the Almighty stamped in human form, the signet of his omnipotence. This impression in clay caused Charles Wesley to write, "Veiled in flesh, the Godhead see, / Hail the Incarnate Deity." And it led Jesus to say, "He who has seen Me has seen the Father" (John 14:9). Wouldn't it be marvelous if we who follow could have it said of us, "He who has seen us has seen Jesus"?

Thomas à Kempis said that, as we serve, we move into the heart of the glorious mystery of godliness:

> Therefore thou oughtest to dispose thyself hereto by a constant, fresh renewing of thy mind, and to weigh with attentive consideration this great mystery of thy salvation. So great, so new, and so joyful ought it to seem to thee, when thou celebratest or partakest in these holy mysteries, as if on this day Christ first descending into the womb of the virgin, was made man or was hanging on the cross, did this day suffer and die for the salvation of mankind.[8]

If, in spiritual discipline, you would throw your shoulders against those of the Prince of Heaven, you must realize his servanthood was modeled in the Incarnation. His descent to the womb of a virgin is the "icon" of our own discipleship. So great was his desire to submit his life to his Father that he agreed to become the *charakter* imprint of God in human clay. We, too, must imitate Christ, and Thomas à Kempis suggests three ways we can do this.

Submission Versus Ambition in the Obedient Life

Imitating Christ Is Making Room for the Bridegroom

O faithful soul, make ready thy heart for this bridegroom, that he may promise to come unto thee, and dwell with thee.

For thus sayeth he, "If any love me, he will keep my words, and we will come unto him and make our abode with him." Give therefore admittance unto Christ, and deny entrance to all others.[9]

Christ is our indwelling, unchanging spouse. He is the church's blessed, spotless Bridegroom. Christ is the Spouse, the Bridegroom of the individual believer as well. How these days of troubled marriages cry out for such perfect mates in marriage. For, indeed, self-will in our me-first age has become a terrible curse on marriages. Husbands and wives each insist on having their own way. Tempers flare. Every hint of submission is scorned.

Every idea of servanthood within the home has been stripped away.

How the homes of our own hearts are ripped apart by self-will. We who have entered into Union with Christ grieve our divine Spouse when we insist on having our way above all else. Is it any wonder that Thomas à Kempis begs us to make room in our hearts for Christ?

> The kingdom of God is within you, saith the Lord. Turn thee with thy whole heart unto the Lord, and forsake this wretched world, and thy soul shall find rest. . . . Christ will come to thee and show thee his consolations, if thou prepare for him a worthy mansion within thee. All his glory and beauty is from within, and there is his delight.[10]

Jesus describes himself as the Bridegroom in the parable of the wise and foolish virgins (Matt. 25:1–13), implying that the virgins were wise because they were waiting for the Bridegroom. If they were anxious for the marriage, what is to be said of the bride herself?

We are never to be stingy in the preparation of the bridal chamber. We are to prepare within ourselves "a worthy chamber," says Thomas à Kempis. For it is in this inner chamber that Christ will come unto us and show us "his consolations."[11] Never has there been a satisfactory marriage without intimacy. So, of course, it must be if we are to know the glory of our Union with Christ. "The marriage [union] is inward. Thou hast here an abiding city, and wherever thou art, thou art a stranger and a pilgrim: neither shalt thou ever have rest, unless thou be inwardly united to Christ."[12]

How quickly we trade intimacy for a hassled togetherness with Christ. It is easy to make of an all-demanding Christianity an all-consuming churchianity. We run to the house of God, convinced that we were made for running rather than for him.

I remember a woman who was the wife of the chairman of our church board. If heaven's report card gave good marks for

Christians who were all legs and no heart, her grade would have been A +. She donated hour after hour in the church office to see that everything "ran right." She was, in many ways, the soul of the church's business efficiency. She organized every aspect of the church program that was disorganized. And while she was often frazzled by her *busy-ianity,* no one would ever have called her unkind. She was the very model of how good people ought to be "frazzled for Jesus." She was a glorious example of Christian mileage, if not inwardness.

Then boom! In a kind of spiritual "Shazam!" her nervous system began to fail her image. Her husband brought her to my office. In tears, she confessed, "I'm a fraud!" She became utterly honest about the state of her heart: "I need to quit living this hurried and busy lie. I must come to know the Christ I have long suffered vertigo to please." What was she really saying? "I need to prepare a worthy mansion within myself for the union I so desperately need." And so she bowed her head and opened her heart to make it large enough to hold her marriage to the Bridegroom. She never ran much after that. Serving her Spouse was enough. But her radiance was never rehearsed after that either. And even today she is a marvelous woman whose dwelling place for Christ has moved from her shallow exterior into the Bridegroom's chamber of the heart.

Our marriage with the Bridegroom feeds on the desire of separated lovers to be brought together. Thomas à Kempis phrases it this way:

> If thou canst not contemplate high and heavenly things, rest thyself in the passion of Christ, and dwell willingly in his sacred wounds. . . .

> Christ was willing to suffer and be despised; and dares thou complain of any man? Christ had adversaries and backbiters: and dost thou wish to have all men thy friends and benefactors?

When shall thy patience attain her crown, if no adversity befall thee?

If thou are willing to suffer no adversity, how wilt thou be the friend of Christ?[13]

Our union is of wounded lovers. In the stigmata of Christ lies all our hope. But our own woundedness teaches us need. Two people whom I most admire came to our church. He was a brilliant young man, but totally blind. She was a beautiful young woman, but a paraplegic. He had never seen her face. She had never walked with him or carried his books. He had never driven their hand-controlled car. She had never entered the laboratory where he worked. Their incapacitation led them first to understand the hardness of life, then to appreciate the other's struggles, and finally to be married. Their union was made strong by their wounds. What a great picture they make of the body of Christ.

God could only lead Israel to Canaan after she agreed to trust him for the trip to Sinai. Israel at first believed that salvation was being out of Egypt. But not to have to put up with slavery to Pharaoh was an incomplete salvation, a salvation that ended in the desert. But Canaan was where God wanted to give them the very soul of his love. Sinai salvation was only halfway salvation. Canaan was where his finished dream of union ended.

To desire to be saved from sin merely to escape hell is Sinai salvation. But to desire to be in final Union with Christ is the joyous heart of all that the Father wants for our relationship. He wants us to "enlarge the bridal chamber."[14]

What then is to be said of those terrible adversities that God seems to send our way?

Think not thyself wholly forsaken, although for a time
I have sent thee some tribulation, or withdrawn thy
desired comfort, for this is the way to the kingdom of
heaven. . . .

> If I send thee affliction, or any cross whatsoever, do not
> be saddened, nor let thy heart fail thee; I can quickly succor
> thee, and turn all thy heaviness to joy.[15]

Never are we to allow our woes to break up this divine marriage.

In those first two critical years of human marriage, every little problem seems terminal. The smallest petulance brings on spontaneous talk of divorce. But let a marriage season, and that sort of talk is less frequent. Let a couple struggle with a sick child or face a horrendous time of disease or economic struggle, and then those woes that once threatened to destroy will bring the rapport that only wounded lovers can know. These common wounds sponsor a new forbearance, a fastidious loyalty.

Likewise, when we are young in our walk with the Lord, we are quick to indict God for the sufferings which come upon us. But let us grow older and live in his unceasing love (Heb. 13:5), and in the passing years, we will easily see that he never causes our sufferings but rather gives us the strength to bear them (1 Cor. 10:13). Then we understand that he was there all the time. We sometimes survey our past so foolishly. Like that angry immature soul of "Footprints" fame, we look back, supposing that the single pair of footprints means that God, there, forced us to go it alone. But schooled in his mercy, we better see that these were the very times that we have been carried by our divine Lover. The trials of life ever strengthen our union and endorse our relationship with Christ!

How embarrassed I am now to admit that when the western seminary rejected me, I was broken. My ego was shattered. I complained to God about his unfairness. How adversity makes us pouting children. Our infantile egos threaten to eat worms. How true the cliche, "If you no longer feel close to God, guess who moved?" Coming home from our hurts to our union, we are inevitably welcomed back with these words:

> I will cause you to forget your former pains, and to enjoy
> thorough inward quietness. I will lay open before thee

pleasant fields of holy scripture that thou with an enlarged
heart mayest begin to run the way of my commandments.
And thou shalt say, "The sufferings of this present time are
not worthy to be compared with the future glory that
shall be."[16]

Let us enlarge the bridal chamber and come again to oneness.

The Familiarity of First Names

Love all for Jesus, but Jesus for himself. Jesus Christ alone is
especially to be beloved; who alone is found good and
faithful above all friends. For him, and in him, let friends as
well as foes be dear unto thee; and all these are to be prayed
for, that they all may know and love him. Never desire to be
especially commended or beloved, for that appertaineth only
to God, who hath none like unto himself. Neither do thou
desire that the heart of any should be set on thee, nor do
thou set thy heart on the love of any; but let Jesus be in thee,
and in every good man.[17]

Intimacy has its language. Intimacy has its familiar reference.
My wife and children do not call me Dr. Miller. There is a place
perhaps for such a title, but it wars against all that a family should
be. The same may be said for the bedroom. There, where husband
and wife seek to know and love each other, there will be warm
and familiar relationalisms. All formality is swallowed up in close
affection.

One gets the feeling in reading Thomas à Kempis that his
friendship with Jesus was the richest discovery of his life:

O Jesus, thou brightness of eternal glory, thou comfort of
the pilgrim-soul, with thee is my mouth without voice, and
my very silence speaketh unto thee.

How long doth my Lord delay to come? . . .

Come, oh, come; for without thee I shall have no joyful day nor hour; for thou art my joy and without thee is my table empty.[18]

One thing that all lovers do is eat together. Here is laid out a lover's cry against eating alone. Nothing tastes good when we eat alone.

I discussed early in this book that early time of separation from my young bride. One of the painful memories of that time alone was trying to make my food taste good at mealtime. The separation created a desire for reunion, for no matter what I ate, without her, indeed, "my table was empty." Thomas à Kempis cries out for that wonderful union to be restored: "Come thou down to me, come and replenish me early with thy comfort, lest my soul faint for weariness and dryness of mind."[19]

In the name of Jesus is the end of all loneliness. When I consider the name of Jesus, I can understand why Bill and Gloria Gaither taught all of evangelicalism to sing, "Jesus, Jesus, Jesus. There's just something about that name."[†] Thomas à Kempis must have found the name of Jesus in about the same way as Helen Parker did:

> Today a man discovered gold and fame;
> Another flew the stormy seas;
> Another saw an unnamed world aflame;
> One found the germ of a disease.
> But what high fates my paths attend:
> For I—today I found a friend.[20]

Loving His Cross

Jesus hath now many lovers of his heavenly kingdom, but few bearers of his cross.

[†]"There's Something About That Name." Words by William J. and Gloria Gaither. Music by William J. Gaither. © Copyright 1970 by William J. Gaither. All rights reserved. Used by permission.

He hath many desirous of comfort, but few of
tribulation.

He findeth many companions of his table, but few of
his abstinence.

All desire to rejoice with him, few are willing to endure
anything for him, or with him.

Many follow Jesus unto the breaking of the bread; but
few to the drinking of the chalice of his passion.

Many reverence his miracles but few follow the
ignominy of his cross.

Many love Jesus so long as adversities do not happen.

Many praise Jesus and bless him, so long as they receive
comforts from him.

But if Jesus hide himself, and leave them but a little while,
they fall either into complaining, or into too much dejection
of mind.[21]

Here, comes the call to every lover to celebrate the artistry of his
or her beloved. Can you imagine a spouse that would not celebrate
what is her husband's or his wife's greatest work? Victoria Nelson,
in *Writer's Block,* tells of two twenty-year-olds who married
quickly to accommodate a surprise pregnancy. They lived in the
kind of poverty that ate pasty food and afforded a cheap apartment.
After the baby came, he wanted the three of them to go to Europe
where he could further his dreams of becoming a writer. His
dreams were ill-defined but in most ways ardent. His new wife,
at the end of one exhausting day, grabbed up one of his manu-
scripts from a nearby desk and shoved it toward a friend who was
visiting in their home. "Look at it! Read it! It isn't any good, is
it?" She obviously did not share her husband's dreams. She shamed
him in front of his friend and showed no interest in what her
husband considered to be his most important work.[22]

Lovers never shame each other, especially as it regards their
beloved's most important work. Jesus was an artist at redemption.
The Cross was his creative gift of life. He is our most important
Lover. We must cherish the work that he considered to be the

triumph of his life. The Cross is to be the center of our communion and, therefore, of our worship. This great and finished work of Christ cannot be important to Jesus and a trivial matter for the believer. Worship without the Cross is frivolous. It is what Thomas à Kempis called the concupiscence of worship:

> Lament thou and grieve that thou art yet so carnal.
> So unwatchful over thy outward senses,
> So often entangled with so many vain fantasies:
> So much inclined to outward things,
> So negligent of the interior:
> So prone to laughter and immodesty:
> So indisposed to tears and compunction . . .
>
> So covetous of abundance, so sparing in giving. . . .
>
> So wakeful to hear gossiping tales,
> So drowsy at the sacred services:
> So hasty to arrive at the end thereof,
> So inclined to be wandering and inattentive.
> So negligent in the prayers,
> So lukewarm in celebrating the Holy Eucharist.
> So quickly distracted,
> So seldom wholly gathered into thyself.[23]

It would almost seem that Thomas à Kempis was familiar with worship in our day and age. How often we are bored in church. But any time we are bored in our adoration of God, what we really are afflicted with is a love problem. Like the church in Laodicea, our lukewarmness may come from our material abundance (Rev. 3:14ff.). Truly the church today is "rich and increased with goods" but largely powerless. We always become lukewarm when our desire for the adoration of Christ is supplemented by needs for image and reputation.

Thomas à Kempis issues an eternal invitation: All who would imitate Christ must drink from the chalice of his passion.

We are made rich. How God calls us to remember his wealth

through which he supplies all our need (Phil. 4:19). When I was in Costa Rica speaking at a missionary conference, I met a wonderful couple who had been serving the Lord in the outer villages of the country for years. I always feel badly when a missionary wants to take me out to dinner because I realize that most of them barely make enough money to stay afloat economically. But these missionaries were insistent at a restaurant that they be allowed to pay the tab for the wonderful meal we had just enjoyed. When I insisted that I be allowed to pay, this wonderful couple became threateningly insistent, "God wants us to bless you with this meal." They were so firm that I reluctantly agreed. How often my mind has gone back to that moment. When poverty touches Christ, it considers itself abundance and makes sacrifices it never sees!

I am convinced that those Christians are fortunate who have learned the dying life. In such believers, submission is so constant that ambition is afraid to show itself. And those made rich are joyous, irresponsibly giddy, like big-time winners on game shows. Their joy approaches madness. Closeness to Christ results in what Thomas à Kempis calls their "imitation of Christ."

Quasi Modo, Victor Hugo's monster, was conquered by Esmerelda, who saw a hunchback as a person. She reached to him with love. To be sure, the hunchback was simpleminded, but wise enough to seek the worth of love. Suddenly he who had been so scourged and mocked as the king of fools was transformed. His ugliness passed beneath a cloud of grace. He was made new. Love rather flew at him. He "flew the cables and bell ropes of the cathedral." Soaring above the fearsome depth, he was set free by love. His wild delirium made the towers of Notre Dame sing. Can it be? The broken freak of French mockery flies? See him there. Quasi Modo is nimble at his furious trapeze of grace. Watch how adoration gives wings to gargoyles. In the name of love, clappers hammer bronze. The music from great deep-throated bells make all Paris hear his transformation.

Well, what of us? Jesus comes! Our own monstrous natures change. We taste the splendor of our Lord. Who can stand the storm of raging grace? Joy flies and bells ring. We have been loved. The Christ of Thomas à Kempis has tended us. In joy he has called us to life with a capital L:

> I am He, the lover of purity, and the giver of all sanctity. I seek a pure heart, and there is my place of rest. Make ready for me a large upper room furnished, and I will keep the passover at thy house.[24]

> I am he that have called thee. I have commanded it to be done. I will supply what is wanting in thee: come thou and receive me.[25]

AFTERWORD
Discipline: The Easy Yoke

I HAVE WRITTEN *The Unchained Soul* in an attempt to lure you into your own inward journey. Why have I called this pilgrimage *The Unchained Soul?* Because liberty is a cherished state of being. To be free is the cry of all those who have known the stones and bars that cage the human spirit. When Jesus comes into our lives the chains are severed. The iron links of pointless living fall away and we are free—free to live forever—free to serve God, and therefore free to live meaningful lives.

Although we talked earlier in this book about the Emmaus Road, let us return to it a final time. On the Emmaus Road (Luke 24:13ff.), Christ walked with those who lamented his death while despairing his aching absence. This walking, talking experience ended with the breaking of bread. Then they confessed, "Did not our heart burn within us while He talked with us on the road?" (Luke 24:32). Luke gives us an insight as to the length of this wonderful, confessional hike: it was a seven-mile walk (Luke 24:13) that ended the imprisonment of two souls who had traded their freedom for enslaving despair.

My wife and I walk regularly as part of our daily exercise. It takes us something under two hours to walk seven miles, but we are always reluctant to hurry our walking. Our gentle, unhurried discipline knows the joy of discourse the entire time. We are never bored while we walk together nor does the exertion of this mild discipline leave us too out of breath to talk.

When we walk, we take charge of our "couch potato lethargy," opting for discipline. When our love for God is right, we find Christ's liberty is our glorious state of heart and we are free. Soul freedom belongs to those who walk the Emmaus Road. Such freedom is never hurried. And all the free of soul know others have walked this journey before them. They do not dread the time they give for the journey. There is no resentment; they love the liberty that is born in the journey.

Those who are so in love with the quick trip and everything instant might prefer to drive to Emmaus. Such hurried souls usually want their discipleship needs met with prepackaged holiness. They often desire push-button servanthood and user-friendly, megabyte feel-goodism. Sorry! There are no moving beltways that whisk us to the summit of Calvary. If you are going to live the dying life it's always a walking affair. It is a discipline as rigorous as the Via Dolorosa.

Paul often urges us to the life of discipline, to "endure hardship" (2 Tim. 2:3). Or, again, he says in Philippians 3:14, "I press toward the goal for the prize of the upward call of God in Christ Jesus." He confesses, "I therefore so run, not as uncertainly; so fight I, not as one that beats the air: But I keep under my body, and bring it into subjection: lest that by any means, when I have preached to others, I myself should be a castaway" (1 Cor. 9:26–27 KJV). Here Paul suggests all real liberty comes from conscious acts of discipline.

Discipline is the believer's part in the conversation of holy faith. When God speaks to us, he speaks grace. When we talk to God, we speak discipline. I'm forever telling my students that grace is God's gift to us, and discipline is our gift to God. God will never force you into the disciplines of Bible reading, ministry, or prayer. If these things come to define your walk, it will be because you offer back to him the effort of your discipleship. As you "press toward the goal," your own discipline is your offering of love. It is the way you walk with saints. It is by grace that he discloses himself to us, redeems us, and deigns in Christ to enter into life with us. However, it is discipline that causes us to talk to him. Remember, *discipline* and *disciple* both come from the same root word: "student."

Students study, and study is the most arduous of work. For the past few years I have taught in a graduate school. Most of the students know that their job is to study. Sometimes I experience students who come into class and seem to be saying, "Prof, I don't want you to teach me anything. I just want you to *feel with me*. I'm into the emotive." Emotionalizing is a whole lot easier than education. Feeling is emotionally fun; getting an education is hard work.

But this must be said: True liberty comes from utter discipline, and such discipline can never be burdensome. Jesus states one of the most rewarding paradoxes of the faith:

> "Come to me, all you who labor and are heavy laden and I will give you rest. Take My yoke upon you and learn of Me, for I am gentle and lowly in heart and you will find rest for your souls. For My yoke is easy and My burden is light" (Matt. 11:28–30).

The disciplines of our discipleship are the source of our freedom. As long as you dread those exercises that wake your stamina and make you strong, you will serve your regimen with a grudge. But once you learn to enjoy your discipline, you will build your body even as you bless that discipline that creates a strong physique. As Eric Liddell exults in the film *Chariots of Fire*, "When I run, I feel His pleasure!"; when we "walk" we feel his pleasure. This walk with Jesus builds our inner life with such joy we feel nothing unpleasantly strenuous in the exercise. Indeed, we look forward to it. His yoke is light.

It is so light that soon we are unaware that we are under the yoke. The Emmaus walk is a walk so pleasant that the miles fly sweetly by. Is this supposed to be effort? Well, it is not. Here at the end of this book, I do hope you have found the beginning of that walk where your own individuality will be absorbed in his. You will then lose your small identity in his immensity. Emmaus will become your glory. Jesus will become your passion. Light will be your yoke. Joy will be your discipline, your meat, your drink. And the world through which you pass will be inadvertently changed forever.

Can you beat this light yoke? Can you walk these few miles of glory? Try it! Look! Even now, the sun is beginning to color the eastern sky of your hassled Jerusalem. Would you like to leave the rat race? Then get started for Emmaus, that peaceful town just seven miles distant. But the town doesn't matter. It's the journey that's important. Why? Because you never know who you're going to meet on the road. Those who travel it frequently know the pleasure of heaven's company. Oh, look! There are other travelers! Can you see them? Quicken your pace and pull alongside. Somewhere up ahead the bread will be broken by nail-scarred hands. And you will be lost in adoration. You will because of your appetite for God. Journey not toward Emmaus, but the center of your soul. You will celebrate not Emmaus, but the company, the pleasure, and the joy of knowing that the significance of the journey is warmed by the thrill of living in utter freedom.

Reach for the wounded hand of your Savior. Touch him! See, the chains are gone—your soul is free!

NOTES

Foreword

1. Walter Wangerin, Jr., *Mourning into Dancing* (Grand Rapids, Michigan: Zondervan Publishing House, 1992) pp. 33–34.

The Confessional Walk of Faith

1. Wangerin, *Mourning into Dancing,* p. 34.

2. Julian of Norwich, *Showings* (New York: Paulist Press, 1978) p. 279.

3. Robert L. Lewelyn, *The Joy of the Saints* (Springfield, IL: Templegate Publishing, 1988) p. 45.

4. Ibid., p. 53.

5. Ibid., p. 31.

6. Carl Sandburg, *Selected Poems* (New York: Grammercy Books, 1992) p. 20.

7. Lewelyn, op. cit., p. 183.

8. Ibid., p. 19.

9. Ibid., p. 130.

10. Ibid., p. 348.

11. Ibid., p. 282.

12. Ibid., p. 310.

Chapter 1: Beginning the Journey

Epigraph, Saint Augustine, *The Confessions of Saint Augustine,* trans. Edward B. Pusery, D.D. (New York: Collier Books, Macmillan Publishing Company, 1961).

1. Ibid., p. 46.

2. Ibid., pp. 79–80.

3. Ibid., p. 27.

4. Ibid., p. 134.

5. Ibid., p. 13.

6. St. Ignatius of Loyola, *Spiritual Exercises of St. Ignatius* (New York: Catholic Book Publishing Company, 1948–1956) p. 20.

7. Augustine, op. cit., pp. 129–130.

8. Ibid., p. 125.

9. Ibid., p. 129.

10. Michael Cassidy, *Chasing the Wind* (Wilton, CT: Morehouse-Barlow, 1985) p. 11.

11. Augustine, op. cit., p. 133.

12. Ibid., pp. 146–147.

13. Ibid., p. 151.

Chapter 2: Arriving at Security

Epigraph, Madam Guyon, *Autobiography of Madame Guyon* (Chicago: Moody Press, undated) pp. 243–244.

1. Henri J. M. Nouwen, *In the Name of Christ* (New York: Crossroad, 1991) p. 25.

2. Guyon, op. cit., p. 20.

3. James Stephens, *The Home Book of Modern Verse* (New York: Holt, Rinehart, and Winston, 1953) p. 348.

4. Ray Stedman, *Jesus Teaches on Prayer* (Waco, TX: Word Books, 1977) p. 17.

5. John Blanchard, *Gathered Gold* (Durham, England: Evangelical Press, 1984) p. 229.

6. Ibid., p. 230.

7. Guyon, op. cit., p. 47.

8. Ibid., p. 281.

9. Henri J. M. Nouwen, *The Way of the Heart: Desert Spirituality and Contemporary Ministry* (San Francisco: HarperCollins, 1991) p. 94.

10. William Shakespeare, *Hamlet,* act II, scene ii, lines 648–653.

11. Guyon, op. cit., p. 14.

12. Ibid., pp. 77–78.

13. Viktor Frankl, *The Unconscious God: Psychotherapy and Theology* (New York: Simon and Schuster, 1978).

14. Guyon, op. cit., pp. 140–141.

15. Viktor Frankl, *Man's Search for Meaning* (New York: Washington Square Press, Publication of Pocket Books, a division of Simon and Schuster, Inc., 1959) p. 99.

16. Guyon, op. cit., p. 244.

17. Petter Shaffer, *Equus* (New York: Penguin Books, 1973) p. 80.

18. Guyon, op. cit., p. 161.

19. Blanchard, op. cit., p. 12.

20. Guyon, op. cit., p. 161.

21. St. Ignatius, op. cit., p. 18.

22. Guyon, op. cit., pp. 326–327.

Chapter 3: Finding Purpose in Life
Epigraph, Brother Lawrence, *The Practice of the Presence of God* (Springfield, IL: Templegate Publishers, 1974) pp. 64–65.

1. Ibid., p. 65.

2. Dallas Willard, *The Spirit of the Disciplines* (San Francisco: Harper & Row, 1988) p. 9.

3. C. H. Spurgeon, "Peace by Believing," in *Metropolitan Tabernacle Pulpit* (London: Passmore and Alabaster, 1864; reprint, Pasadena, TX: Pilgrim Publications, 1979) vol. 9, p. 283.

4. St. John of the Cross, *Ascent of Mt. Carmel, 1, 4, 5* (New York: Triumph Books, 1991) p. 10.

5. Francis Thompson, *The Hound of Heaven* (Harrisburg, PA: Morehouse Publishing, 1992) p. 166.

6. Lawrence, op. cit., p. 91.

7. Ibid., p. 105.

8. Ibid., pp. 112–113.

9. Ibid., p. 12.

10. Ibid., p. 31.

11. Ibid., p. 122.

12. Ibid., p. 121.

13. Ibid., pp. 122–123.

14. Ibid., pp. 122–123.

15. Ibid., p. 123.

16. Ibid.

17. Mary Gardener Brainard, *Masterpieces of Religious Verse,* ed. James Dalton Morrison, (Grand Rapids, MI: Baker Book House, 1948).

18. C. S. Lewis, *The Screwtape Letters* (New York: Macmillan Publishing Company, Inc., 1961) p. 42.

19. Lawrence, op. cit., pp. 123–124.

20. Ibid., p. 124.

21. Ibid., p. 18.

Chapter 4: Healing Depression
Epigraph, Teresa of Avila, *The Way of Perfection.* Trans./ed. E. Allison Peers (New York: Image Books, Doubleday and Company, Inc., 1964) pp. 225–226.

1. Paul Billheimer, *Don't Waste Your Sorrows* (Ft. Washington, PA: Christian Literature Crusade, 1977) p. 70.

2. Teresa of Avila, op. cit., p. 253.

3. Ibid., p. 264.

4. Ibid., p. 154.

5. Ibid., p. 43.

6. Ibid., pp. 102–103.

7. Ibid., p. 50.

8. Ibid., pp. 191–192.

9. Ibid, p. 175.

10. Ibid., pp. 160–161.

11. Ibid., p. 155.

12. Ibid., p. 184.

13. Ibid., p. 209.

Chapter 5: Winning by Oneing

Epigraph, Julian of Norwich, *Julian of Norwich Showings*. Translated from the critical text with an introduction by Oddment College, O. S. A. and James Walsh, S. J. (New York: Paulist Press, 1978) pp. 187–189.

1. Ibid., p. 17.

2. Ibid., pp. 127–129.

3. Gerald May, as quoted in *Coming to Life* by Polly Berrien Berends (New York: Harper & Row Publishers, 1990) p. 56.

4. Julian of Norwich, op. cit., pp. 179–181.

5. Ibid., p. 312.

6. Ibid., pp. 201–202.

7. Martin Luther, *Table Talk Vol. 54*. Trans./ed. Theodore G. Tappert (Philadelphia: Fortress Press, 1967) p. 28.

8. Julian of Norwich, op. cit., pp. 335–336.

9. Ibid., p. 216.

10. William Shakespeare, *King Lear,* act I, scene iv, lines 294–295.

11. Julian of Norwich, op. cit., p. 327.

12. Ibid., p. 221.

13. Ibid., p. 142.

14. Ibid., pp. 299–300.

15. Ibid., p. 289.

16. Ibid., pp. 306–307.

17. Ritamary Bradley, *Julian's Way* (London: HarperCollins Religious, 1992) p. 208.

Chapter 6: Pilgrim's Progress

Epigraph, John Bunyan, *Pilgrim's Progress* (Chicago: Moody Press, 1959) pp. 182–184.

1. Ibid., pp. 26–27.

2. Ibid., p. 38.

3. Ibid., pp. 40–41.

4. Ibid., p. 41.

5. Ibid., pp. 67–68.

6. Ibid., pp. 178–179.

7. Ibid., pp. 185–186.

8. Ibid., p. 186.

9. Ibid., pp. 188–189.

Chapter 7: The Peniel God

Epigraph, Author unknown, *The Cloud of Unknowing*. ed. William Johnston (New York: Bantam/Doubleday/Dell Publishing Group., Inc., 1973) pp. 72–73.

1. Harold Bloom, *The American Religion* (New York: Simon and Shuster, 1982) p. 17.

2. Ibid., p. 15.

3. Ibid., p. 167.

4. *The Cloud of Unknowing,* op. cit., p. 58.

5. Ibid., p. 56.

6. Tim Bascom, *The Comfort Trap* (Downers Grove, IL: InterVarsity Press, 1993) p. 39.

7. Ibid., p. 23.

8. *The Cloud of Unknowing,* op. cit., p. 25.

9. Ibid., p. 167.

10. Harold Kushner, *Who Needs God?* (New York: Summit Books, 1989) pp. 4–12.

11. Sandburg, op. cit., p. 23.

12. Søren Kierkegaard, *Parables of Kierkegaard*. ed. Thomas C. Oden (Princeton, NJ: Princeton University Press, 1978) p. 11.

13. *The Cloud of Unknowing,* op. cit., p. 50.

14. Ibid., p. 75.

15. Ibid., p. 74.

16. Hans Urs von Balthasar, CREDO (New York: Crossroad Publishing Company, 1990) pp. 70–71.

17. *The Cloud of Unknowing,* op. cit., p. 91.

18. Ibid., pp. 43–44.

19. Ibid., pp. 77–78.

20. Ibid., p. 79.

21. Ibid., p. 76.

Chapter 8: Conquering Pride
Epigraph, Bernard of Clairvaux, *Selected Works.* trans. G. R. Evans (Mahwah, NJ: Paulist Press, 1987) pp. 125–126.

1. Ibid., p. 113.

2. Ibid., p. 112.

3. Bascom, op. cit., pp. 22–23.

4. Richard Foster, *Celebration of Discipline* (San Francisco: Harper & Row, 1978) p. 80.

5. Bascom, op. cit., pp. 37–38.

6. *Standard Times* (Illinois: Saturday, February 19, 1994).

7. Charles Wesley hymn, "And Can It Be."

8. Bernard of Clairvaux, op. cit., p. 103.

9. Ibid., pp. 108–109.

10. Ibid., p. 104.

11. Cassidy, op. cit., p. 56.

12. Ibid., p. 55.

13. Ibid., p. 54.

14. Bernard of Clairvaux, op. cit., p. 105.

15. Thompson, op. cit., pp. 4, 6, 7, 20, 22.

16. Bernard of Clairvaux, op. cit., pp. 124–125.

17. Ibid., p. 131.

18. William Shakespeare, "Sonnet 29."

19. Ibid., p. 51.

20. Edwin Markham, "Outwitted" from *The Best Loved Poems of the American People,* ed. Hazel Felleman (New York: Doubleday, Garden City Books, 1936) p. 67.

21. Ibid., p. 132.

22. Ibid., pp. 132–133.

23. Ibid., p. 133.

24. Ibid., p. 134.

25. Ibid., p. 135.

26. Ibid., p. 135.

27. Ibid., p. 137.

28. Ibid., p. 138.

29. Ibid., pp. 138–139.

Chapter 9: Sanctifying the Secular

Epigraph, Jean-Pierre de Caussade, *The Sacrament of the Present Moment.* trans. Kitty Muggeridge, from the original text of *Self-Abandonment to Divine Providence* (New York: Harper & Row Publishers, 1982) p. 31.

1. Ibid., p. 53.

2. Bloom, op. cit., p. 56.

3. Ibid., p. 56.

4. de Caussade, op. cit., p. 189.

5. John Blanchard, *Whatever Happened to Hell?* (Durham, England: Evangelical Press, 1993) pp. 13–14.

6. C. S. Lewis, *The Problem of Pain* (New York: Macmillan Publishing Company, 1962) p. 127.

7. de Caussade, op. cit., p. 15.

8. John Mohr, "Find Us Faithful" (Birdwing Music/Jonathan Mark Music, 1987. Administered by The Sparrow Corporation).

9. de Caussade, op. cit., p. 31.

10. Ibid., p. 80.

11. St. Francis, *A Classic of Western Spirituality* (New Jersey: Bonaventure/Paulist Press, 1978) p. 232.

12. de Caussade, op. cit., pp. 71–72.

13. Ibid., pp. 40–41.

14. Ibid., p. 15.

15. Omar Khayyam, "Rubiyat" from *A Treasury of the World's Best Loved Poems* (New York: Crown Publishers, Avenel Books, 1961) p. 67.

16. de Caussade, op. cit., p. 53.

17. Ibid., p. 64.

18. Ibid., p. 56.

19. Ibid., p. 74.

20. Ibid., p. 101.

21. Ibid., pp. 75–76.

Chapter 10: Imitating Christ
Epigraph, Thomas à Kempis, *The Imitation of Christ* (Chicago: Moody Press, 1980) pp. 259–261.

1. Ibid., p. 184.

2. Ibid., p. 37.

3. Ibid., p. 40.

4. Ibid., p. 75.

5. Ibid., p. 29.

6. Ibid., p. 48.

7. Ibid., p. 53.

8. Ibid., p. 284.

9. Ibid., p. 89.

10. Ibid., p. 88.

11. Ibid., p. 88.

12. Ibid., p. 90.

13. Ibid., p. 88.

14. Ibid., pp. 90–91.

15. Ibid., p. 88.

16. Ibid., pp. 195–196.

17. Ibid., p. 246.

18. Ibid., p. 106.

19. Ibid., p. 175.

20. Helen Parker, "Discovery," from *100 Portraits of Christ* by Henry Gariepy (Wheaton, IL: Victor Books, 1987) p. 139.

21. Thomas à Kempis, op. cit., pp. 114–115.

22. Victoria Nelson, *Writer's Block* (New York: Houghton-Mifflin, 1993) pp. 125–126.

23. Thomas à Kempis, op. cit., pp. 295–296.

24. Ibid., p. 311.

25. Ibid., p. 312.